CISO

Defenders of the Cyber-Realm

Dirty Deeds, Hackers & Heroes

MIKE LOGINOV

Ascot Barclay
Publishing

CISO Defenders of the Cyber-Realm
Authored by Mike Loginov
ISBN-13: 978-1725039186
ISBN-10: 1725039184

The real voyage of discovery consists not in seeking out new landscapes but in having new eyes.

(Attrib. Marcel Proust, 1871 -1922)

Contents

Acknowledgments

I could not have completed this book without the supporting knowledge, insights, and experiences provided by those within the cybersecurity industry and quite a few outside of it.

My grateful thanks go to the many peers, influencers, and advisers who have contributed toward the creation of this book over the past three years. These include: Paul Heffernan, Matthias Muhlert, Kevin Gjerstad, Ulf Feger, Nina Loginov (Ascot Barclay Group), Iain Hunneybell, Bharat Thakrar, Rafael Narezzi, Henry, the contributing team at the IOTSA including but not limited to, Sue McCauley, Ernie Hayden, Alexander Loginov, Tim Grieveson, Charlie McMurdie, Lek Tisanthiah, Maxim Silin, Andrei Petrovski, Mike Keogh, Dr John McCarthy, Kevin Borley and Adrian Davies. I would also like to extend my heartfelt appreciation to Professor Raj Roy (Cranfield University), Dr Rupert Francis (Jamaica), Professor Richard Benham, Adeoluwa Akomolafe, Raj Samani (McAfee), Heather Payne, Andrew Rose, Illyas Kooliyankal, and Amber Pedroncelli (EC-Council).

When it comes to chapter contributions my gratitude also goes to our associates outside of the industry. Nikolay Danev, who gave us more than a little insight into the real problems of data theft and some thoughts on how to remedy the issues. Mak, who provided us with a view from the 'other side,' and which greatly broadened our knowledge and understanding of the young hacker mindset. Bennett Arron who has been a victim of the crime of identity theft and now spends much of his time visiting companies to emphasize the real impact this has on innocent lives, and to Justin Coker (Skybox), who drew upon his many years of experience within the cybersecurity industry to provide readers with an enlightening additional perspective. To Karen Thompson for editing and Emily Cox for proofing and formatting, and someone I can only describe as an outstanding illustrator Marian Radu for designing the cover.

I'd also like to extend my special thanks to Adrian Davis (Visiting Professor, University of Sunderland), Tony Morbin (SC Magazine) for taking the time to read my draft manuscript, and to Vint Cerf, the 'Father of the Internet,' for not only reading it but also providing me with a foreword. Last, but certainly not least, I would like to express my heartfelt thanks to the man who has been involved in the CISO world of cybersecurity from its inception and is still contributing to our knowledge - Steve Katz.

Foreword
By Vint Cerf

If you are reading this preface, then you have already discovered that this book is worthy of your attention. If you are persuaded that digital systems around the world are vulnerable to wide-ranging threats, you will find confirmation in this book and practical advice from practicing CISO's. What struck me most about Loginov's work is the accessibility of his writing, the breadth of his thinking and the reinforcement that his interviews provide. There is nothing theoretical about the real-world experiences found in these pages.

If we could reboot the world, we might try to create software production environments that assist programmers to avoid the often stupid mistakes and wrong assumptions that lead to vulnerabilities that are exploited daily and often successfully. But this is an unlikely outcome. Moreover, some of the weaknesses in digital systems lie in the heads of users, not in the software they use. Phishing exploits and social engineering are proving to be effective tools in the toolkit of hackers intent on gaining unauthorized access to content and to systems.

If you think it is obvious that someone needs to step up to respond to the threats and vulnerabilities that headlines so blatantly confirm, think again. CISO after CISO confirms that there are many heads still stuck in the sand. The job is not merely technical. A CISO has to be a mix of technologist, evangelist, salesperson, bellringer, whistleblower and superb people manager to achieve the main objective: securing systems and content to assure access only by authorized parties. Success comes only with the cooperation of the trusted users of the system to be secured. No amount of technology will protect the system from willful or neglectful abuse. The threat of insider attack or neglect must not be discounted.

I hope you will find these pages as thought-provoking and pragmatic as I have.

- Vint Cerf

About Vint Cerf

In 1973, along with Bob Kahn, Vint (Vinton) G. Cerf invented the first Internet Protocol (IP) and Transmission Control Protocol (TCP) thus earning him the title of 'Father of the Internet.' Since then Vint has worked with many world leading organizations including Google, Rocketdyne on the Apollo mission, IBM, and MCI Digital Information Services. He is also, again alongside Bob Kahn, a founder of the Internet Society (ISOC). The awards, commendations, and honorary degrees Vint has received are too numerous to list, but they include: the U.S. Presidential Medal of Freedom, U.S. National Medal of Technology, Living Legend

Medal, Presidential Medal of Freedom, the Japan Prize, the Charles Stark Draper award, the ACM Turing Award, Officer of the Legion d'Honneur and 29 honorary degrees. In 2006 Vint Cerf was inducted into the National Inventors Hall of Fame.

Introduction

Never in the history of mankind have we had to deal with such swift developments underpinning the way in which we live our lives. Yet, for the most part, whether we are captains of industry or the man on the street, we remain resolutely human in seeing only what we want to see in respect of the benefits and conveniences that the new, and sometimes disruptive, technologies bring.

Through my work I came to appreciate and acknowledge the small number of people who not only understand the real dangers but who also confront the challenges set before us. Yet often those few stand alone, isolated and frequently frustrated by being the voice in the wilderness. It was then, with this in mind, that the idea of *CISO*: Defenders of the Cyber-Realm* evolved.

Marching forwards in the relentless pursuit of commercial success, enterprise and industry are at risk of becoming victims of their own strategies, policies, architectures and technologies, each of which in the wrong hands have the potential to bring any organization to its knees. But the flaws in the system also mean this pervasive and expanding problem now has the capacity to reach out and negatively affect each and every one of us where ever we may be on this tiny spec of space dust we call home.

Another significant breach hits the news, the months pass, the personal information belonging to millions and millions of people is compromised; by who and for what purpose? We hear much about the effect and the impact of hacker exploits but we hear little about the cause, the methods used to conduct such an attack, the people behind them and the impact on those innocent individuals affected. In this book we explore the threat landscape and interview those that are on both sides of the legal divide: those that would do us harm and those that aim to stop them - but who are all at the very heart of the issue.

Rarely though is the situation fully understood not only by individuals but even by those in control of the organizations concerned. Cybersecurity, for some leaders, is considered an irritant to be tolerated and occasionally scratched. For most companies it produces no direct income, the benefits cannot be easily mathematically calculated to sway either the board or shareholders, and its shifting nature demands consistent re-investment. Cybersecurity then lies outside of the boundaries normally considered by many traditional business models and this is often where the majority of problems begin. Yet do we really need to see multiple companies collapse before we realize the true extent of the dangers?

Having interviewed scores of CISOs in its making, as well as the hackers who seek to do us harm, this book provides insights into the challenging world of cybersecurity and the changes taking place across society that are affecting us all.

Written with executives and the general public in mind, it is not a book for CISOs but about them and seeks to champion the importance of the role and its place in securing our online futures. Amber Pedroncelli of the EC-Council's Certified CISO (CCISO) program, perhaps summed things up when she told me, "There has long been a push in the industry for information security to be taken seriously at C-suite level."

Yet this is not a book for the faint of heart or those who are convinced that technology, or indeed the Internet and social media, can only be used for good. It looks at the dark side of humanity, the potential for mass disruption to the way organizations, humans, and society function and seeks to clarify why we need to be cognizant of the rapid changes taking place around us.

But, as some might mistakenly presume, technology does not sit at the core of this book. And, unless you are a dyed in the wool cybersecurity coding expert with a focus on the inner workings of a cryptographic algorithm, you might be pleased to know that it is more of a human interest story which endeavors to provide insights into the mindset of both the attackers and the defenders.

If though through this book, you find just one piece of information or one action implemented helps make your organization, your company or your family, more resilient to becoming a victim of cyber-crime, then your investment will have been well made.

About Mike Loginov
Formerly a UK military secure communications engineer, over the past 30 years Mike has worked in senior interim

and advisory positions at Director and Executive level in U.K. Central Government Departments and on cyber and security within U.K. Law Enforcement. Across industry sectors he has covered energy, utilities, pharmaceuticals, high tech, media and telcos.

Mike was formerly Global Chief Cyber Strategist for Hewlett Packard and infoSec lead at a Big 5 audit firm. He is an experienced and Certified CISO, winner at the U.K. Industry Cyber Security Awards 2016, CISO of the Year 2017, Cybersecurity CEO of the Year 2018 and a finalist for Global Certified CISO of the Year on two occasions.

Mike is the founding partner and chairman of the IOTSA and CEO of the Ascot Barclay Group. His experience includes CSO at POWEL AS, Global CISO for AVON and Unipart. CISO and advisory roles at a global broadcaster, the Football Premier League and across the Banking and Financial Services sector.

A founder, deputy chair and lecturer for the U.K.s first University lead National MBA in Cyber Security. At the time of writing he is currently studying with Harvard University, and is an adviser to Cranfield University on the MSc in OT Cybersecurity.

Mike lives in the U.K. with his family and is a proud grandfather and husband. He is also a true lover of the Maserati.

CISO is normally pronounced SeeSo.

Interview With A 'Good Guy'
The Underworld and Compromised Data

*"53,308 security incidents, 2,216 data breaches, 65 countries, 76%
of breaches were financially motivated."*
- Verizon Data Breach Investigations Report 2018

Most people only have a fleeting understanding of the world of the hacker. In order to appreciate the undercurrents affecting our lives and businesses we first have to grasp the basics of what motivates those who hack. Whether they are nation-states, lone wolves, or highly coordinated and funded teams, listening to those who deal with the insider situation on a daily basis provides us with some insight into the basics of business that feeds on our corporate and individual identities - and which would die if we withdrew access and consent.

Mike Loginov: Nikolay, would you be kind enough to provide a quick overview of who you are and what you do?
Sure. My name is Nikolay Danev. I'm based in Sofia, Eastern Europe, and I'm CEO of a specialist company that identifies and tracks data breaches. After many years of dark web research and tracking stolen data, my honest take on the situation is that whoever wants access to compromised credentials, and all that sea of breached data, can quite easily get it. This includes governments, hackers, and numerous other actors all with their own agendas and justifications for using it.

Unfortunately, the only party that does not have easy access to the compromised data is actually the one who needs it the most. That is to say the one it protects, who can best use it and who has the most interest in it - the person whose private or sensitive information it is and who has been breached. Legislation makes it very difficult for people who have been breached to obtain their own information, whereas all the other parties are just taking it and, in many cases, for malicious reasons.

Mike Loginov: Who buys all of these compromised databases and from where?

Nikolay: Certain databases are bought by Russian and other crime gangs as opposed to the state. The state has the ability to collect its own data. A lot of the smaller criminal gangs and hackers are most interested in this information. It's sold by the many database traders.

Mike Loginov: Petty criminals are buying and hackers are supplying?

Nikolay: Mainly it's just hackers who want to crack accounts. Brute checkers mostly. They need these data sets to actually crack open other linked accounts where the same or a similar password is used. Then they are re-selling the hacked data to other cyber-criminals or just using the financial information to buy bitcoins or whatever else suits them.

Mike Loginov: What does the future look like for cybersecurity and what are the biggest challenges? What should company executives in particular be concerned about?

Nikolay: I could suggest something about protecting your data, but it has more to do with being realistic about how breached you already are and how secure your data is when looking ahead. So really the challenge today has more to do with how to respond after you finally discover your data is breached and also recognizing that it probably is already. That's the kind of mindset and mentality you should have. You should think ahead as well, not just trying to pretend your data will never be breached because it's going to be if it's not already. So, you've got to think "how can I check and what do I do if it's already breached?" And, "how can breached data be used against me or my company, if not immediately, but in the future?"

Mike Loginov: Your company is able to legitimately identify breached databases or compromised information available on the dark web and in the hacker forums. Is that how you approach things?

Nikolay: Yes. But you've got to realize that some of the information, well, when it's compromised, it's compromised forever. Your social security number, for example. But for other information, like passwords, you want to be aware of the problems and you want to make sure your employees don't use already breached passwords just so they don't perpetuate the whole breach. It often happens that one breached password can cause another breach as people very often use the same password. You want to make sure your I.T. guy, systems administrator or whatever the position, is not using a breached password because it is much easier for hackers to breach him and then your company as well. It's not a black and white situation, it's more of a gray area where you want to make sure you are as resilient as possible rather than protected or unprotected. It is not possible or even pragmatic to be 100% protected because there are always ways that hackers can damage you. The challenge is for you to make it as difficult as you can for them. Today it's too easy and the rewards can be high.

Mike Loginov: What more can companies do to protect themselves from this type of risk?

Nikolay: Based on the data we see the reality is that it would seem most companies don't really put very much effort into protection. So my advice would be that putting a small amount of effort, small steps in the right places, into protecting your company, are worth a lot more than you may think. Just tiny, tiny, little steps are all it takes to get to a more secure place. Critical small things make the difference.

Mike Loginov: So basic cyber-hygiene factors such as using unique passwords, making sure you are not using already compromised passwords. But how would somebody know if those passwords have already been compromised?

Nikolay: Well, I don't want to advertise our services in isolation, as there are plenty of places where you can check to see if a given set of credentials are compromised.

Mike Loginov: So you provide a personalized service to those who want to know if their data has been compromised?

Nikolay: Yes, we have a lab specializing in just that.

Mike Loginov: With Artificial Intelligence (A.I.) on the rise and some of the more advanced algorithms that we are now seeing, it would seem to be a pretty good position for a malicious actor to bring those kind of different components together for gain. What's your view on that?

Nikolay: In the underground A.I. currently doesn't play any significant role other than as an obstacle. It's utilized more by government organizations and big companies, although it makes the work for hackers a little harder because there are some aspects of Machine Learning (M.L.) that, let's say, are used by bigger industries to try to detect hacker activity. The way hackers dodge that as a security mechanism is that they just blend in as much as possible with regular customers. That means the machine has no way to learn this is actually a hacker. And the hackers just grow a technique of how to change, for example, user agents, just to dodge that whole system. The hackers though are still fine and extremely adaptive, which is their greatest strength. Hackers have the creativity to get around things.

Mike Loginov: When it comes to compromised passwords are you seeing evidence that large swathes of people are still using a single password across multiple accounts?

Nikolay: Again, this is not a black and white issue because there are more stages than just using the same password. If say, you have a password called 'password' and then update to become 'password1,' next it could become updated to capital letter P 'Password1' and so on. After that 'Password2' or whatever. Would you call that a different password with each update? It's essentially the same password or at least easy to guess. Really to make it stronger it should actually be something totally different. For Machine Learning, which I mentioned previously, it would be extremely easy for it to guess your password and even your future password - the one you are going to use next - because, in this case, it is obvious it would likely be 'Password3.' Also you will probably have some mechanism to personally remember your password, so it kind of makes sense that you are going to use the simplest one possible especially when you have multiple systems to access. It's a human thing and you cannot force a human to behave like a machine. So, from a security perspective, this approach doesn't really work well. Humans are the weakest link and we can be very predictable.

Mike Loginov: You mentioned earlier about tracking hackers on the dark web and how they constantly change their profiles. But, like we said with passwords, humans tend to have consistent behaviors. So while they might change their identity and profile there are presumably features within the way they behave which act like a 'signature' so you can tell it's them. Is that a realistic view?

Nikolay: I think so and that again is more of a governmental thing. Usually organizations such as the National Security Agency (NSA) are accused of doing such things, of keeping a particular profile about the way someone is writing, typing or behaving online. And it's not limited to just the machine aspect but the human one because, again, that defines us. I think that some hackers, especially the more proficient ones, have already learned how to mimic a different person by changing a lot of different things at once. Then, all of a sudden, they become a different online persona and they are very good at hiding in the shadows.

Mike Loginov: We hear a lot about, and indeed see a lot of compromised databases and some big ones - millions upon millions of people in some cases - how long before everybody's data is compromised? For example, I heard a statement that in the U.S. practically every citizen has likely had their data compromised at least once. Do you think that is a truism?

Nikolay: Well, it's impossible to compromise everyone, it would still only be 99.99%, but I think that a lot of people are compromised already, far too many. I rarely see people who are not compromised somewhere especially, shall we say, if they have a busy Internet life. And if they don't have that kind of life then there is some chance that they won't be compromised. But, then again, who cares about the people who don't have an Internet presence. So, yes, I do think that pretty much everyone is already compromised and certainly those who are very active on the Internet.

Mike Loginov: I asked you to check my details in the past and you were able to tell me what my level of exposure looked like on the dark web along with finding compromised personal details that could possibly be used for nefarious purposes. So, as you might expect, I immediately changed things. As I use the Internet a lot perhaps it shouldn't have come as a surprise to find that my details from certain recent large data breaches are there as well. It seems no one is immune, right?

Nikolay: If people know they have been compromised it's a good thing! It allows them to take action like you did. Then surely it's better to make this publicly available to help victims rather than shutting it down.

Mike Loginov: And that brings me back to your original point. I only know about my data being compromised as a result of coming to you and asking, but as you rightly point out the hackers, and some others. will have had that information well before I'm likely to find out about it.

Nikolay: Sometimes it can be many months or even years before you, as the victim, find out - if you ever do! Most people have no idea what level of compromised information there is available about either them, their organizations or their families.

Mike Loginov: So in your view, and to conclude, it's a case of assume you have been compromised and take action?

Nikolay: As I said even small steps can make a big difference. For example using multifactor authentication, better passwords, improving staff awareness and, at an individual and organizational level, knowing exactly what about them or their companies is compromised will all help reduce the damage from compromised credentials. Knowing means they can take back some control of their specific circumstances.

Mike Loginov: Okay, thanks Nikolay. Best I let you get back to the day job, keep up the good fight.
Nikolay: (Laughs), we do our best!

Nikolay Danev
Interviewed by Mike Loginov

Key Points

1. The dark web is awash with compromised data.
2. Professional hacking gangs use this to create and bridge to new data and compromise bigger databases.
3. Compromised data can be used for many purposes – including coercion, identity theft, financial gain, hacking organizations, but also for future yet undisclosed use.
4. It is still difficult for the average internet user or citizen to gain access or know exactly what has been compromised, and their exposure levels.
5. We need to be more proactive as a community in addressing the problem.
6. The industry should, and can help victims, by showing them what data has been compromised and what they need to change.
7. Good password hygiene remains important.

Chapter 1
The World Of The CISO: Who We Are And What We Do

"Here's to the crazy ones. The misfits. The rebels. The troublemakers. The round pegs in the square holes. The ones who see things differently. They're not fond of rules. And they have no respect for the status quo. You can quote them, disagree with them, glorify or vilify them. About the only thing you can't do is ignore them. Because they change things. They push the human race forward. And while some may see them as the crazy ones, we see genius. Because the people who are crazy enough to think they can change the world, are the ones that do."

Widely Attributed, including:
Apple Inc, Rob Siltanen, Jack Kerouac, John Chapman and others…

Compared to only twenty years ago, the modern world has changed from every conceivable angle. Technology now sits at the very hub of our society and, without it, we would not only be deprived of the convenience we have come to expect in our lives, but even the basics of existence would be beyond reach.

Without the Internet, tangible goods would become inaccessible, communication systems would break down, financial systems and access to cash disrupted, travel by modern methods would practically become impossible, and even pharmaceuticals and effective medical treatment would likely become a thing of the past. The point, if it should need any further reinforcing, is that we are now so dependent on the Internet that we have passed a tipping point where life would simply not be the same without it.

Yet, on a daily basis, our people, processes, and technological systems are not only under constant threat, but they are actively being attacked, and all too often breached. Although we might not yet have attained the heady heights of a national critical infrastructure meltdown, what we are seeing with increasing frequency are individual systems and infrastructure sectors coming under the influence of those who do not have our best interests at heart.

Despite our reliance on Internet technology, many people fail to appreciate that things have moved on from the days of clear divisions between personal and business breaches and their accompanying protection. Enterprise did whatever it needed to do and, we presumed, it was doing things the right way. Individuals, on the other hand, set up their own firewalls, virus protection or whatever personal choices they made. After all, what affects an organization on the other side of the world is nothing to do with us, right?

But, as the number of high profile cybersecurity breaches hitting the headlines continues to rise, what people are slowly coming to realize - whether they be the man on the street or captains of industry - is that once a single organization is hacked the knock-on effect has the capacity to touch the lives of many millions of people in myriad ways.

As the divide between individuals, enterprise, and even government continues to narrow, the ramifications of breaches on business also become increasingly dangerous, and not only for the big corporate guns but for any company linked to the Internet. This situation is no better exemplified than with recently released figures which indicate that 20% of small to medium enterprises (SMEs) hit by a ransomware attack had no chance of recovery and were forced to cease business immediately.[1]

But it's not only the little guys who bite the dust. Back in 2014, Nortel, one of the biggest telecommunications companies in the world at the time, uncovered a hack which they eventually discovered had been going on since 2004.[2] Later it was revealed that a Chinese competitor had compromised the organization at all levels and the information they acquired included executive emails and commercial documents together with research and development plans and commercial intellectual property (IP). After seeing around a decade of decreasing profits, the company finally declared bankruptcy in the same year that the hack was eventually discovered.

Although in reality it's more common for smaller companies to be hacked – even though most smaller companies are of the (mistaken) opinion that they are too insignificant to be of interest to hackers – what we also have to realize is that you can never be too big, or too powerful, to fail.

When it comes to headline hitting hacks, although the numbers involved might make for a good, brief talking point, they rarely send people reeling in the way they should. In 2017 the Equifax hackers got away with the personal information, including the financial history in some cases, of people not only from the U.S. but also those in the U.K. and Canada, which totaled around 143 million - half the population of America.[3]

Yahoo went one better when their 2013 breach was finally revealed to have touched the lives of around 3 billion people - nearly half the population of the planet at the time.[4]

These figures should not only send shock waves around the world, but should also prompt all concerned to ask many challenging questions and demand answers; we should be asking why our interconnectedness through Internet applications is reaching the stage where it has the power to negatively affect nearly all the people in the world if only one application or organization is compromised?

Yet most people aren't prompted into action simply because they believe it is merely 'data' which is being affected. But what does that mean in reality and how accurate is that belief?

Anything and Everyone
In the U.K., Tesco Bank, who are better recognized for owning a global supermarket chain, saw their customer accounts hacked directly over one weekend in 2016. Although they acted quickly by suspending all online banking, it wasn't before £2.5m had been siphoned from

around 9,000 individual clients leaving some people without any money to live on.[5]

Drug companies have also become a favorite of hackers and recently several have been targeted by a ring specializing in pharmaceutical attacks.[6] In 2017, production was brought to a halt by a ransomware attack at the Nissan car factory in Sunderland and, later that week, the National Health Service (NHS) in the U.K., was hit by the same WannaCry virus which resulted in thousands of consultations and operations being canceled.[7]

Physical damage is not beyond the scope of hackers and this has been evidenced on numerous occasions not least when, in 2015, a steel mill in Germany was hacked and control systems disrupted. The impact of that hack ensured that a blast furnace could not be shut down and it resulted in extensive destruction.[8]

More notably, sometime in 2007 or 2008, Iran's nuclear program was almost destroyed by a targeted state-sponsored computer worm known as Stuxnet. The worm, which was delivered on a USB thumb drive, affected specific Siemens Step 7 software and gained access to the industrial program logic controllers (PLC's) which disrupted production for an extended period. Over 15 Iranian facilities were attacked and infiltrated, one of those being the Natanz nuclear plant where, in 2010, a team of inspectors from the International Atomic Energy Agency (AEA) just happened to be visiting. They noticed that an unusual number of uranium-enriching centrifuges were breaking, and the cause was determined to be the Stuxnet worm. This case, just like many others, not only took a third party to ultimately identify the problem but also revealed that many cases of hacking could go on causing problems for years without being detected.[9]

If these examples are still not enough to convince you that every aspect of contemporary life can be affected by hacks and data breaches, maybe learning that 24% of all hacks take place on the food and beverage industry, might have more impact. This practice has now become so common it is referred to as 'Agroterrorism,' [10] and if nothing else it should clearly evidence that even food production could be affected or possibly contaminated.

There were a number of high-profile Agroterrorism attacks that took place in the U.S. during the 1990's, one of which was conducted by extremist environmental groups aided by disgruntled farm workers carrying out attacks which prompted a multimillion-dollar recall of dairy products after animal feed was found to be contaminated with the pesticide chlordane. The feed company targeted in the attack reportedly suffered a $250million loss as a result. A similar incident happened in 1997 when a fungicide was intentionally introduced to recycled poultry feed, it took investigators from U.S .17 states to track down the perpetrator, the owner of a rival feed company. Research work conducted for the RAND National Security Research Division entitled - *Hitting America's Soft Underbelly: The Potential Threat of Deliberate Biological Attacks Against the U.S. Agricultural and Food Industry,* by Peter Chalk, ISBN: 0-8330-3522-3 is a worthwhile read on this topic.

Maybe, just maybe, after all this you are still in denial and suffering from 'it'll never happen to me syndrome.' But you only have to look at some the individuals who have been directly affected to realize that no one is immune to the effects of hacking.

When the Panamanian law firm Mossack Fonseca revealed they had been hacked back in 2016, much of the confidential information accessed actually belonged to the rich and powerful. One of those affected by this breach was Iceland's Prime Minister, Sigmundur Gunnlaugsson, who was forced to step down from his position after it was revealed he hadn't declared assets when he entered parliament.

Another story doing the rounds was a CEO who fell foul of one of his employees and, as a result his computer was hacked and child pornography was placed on the system. Although the story ultimately has a happy ending in that he was acquitted of all wrong-doing, it took some nifty cyber-forensics to sort out the mess. In the meantime, he had been arrested, charged and held in custody. That is a part of his life he will never get back and must have been a living hell to experience - all the result of a vendetta by one disturbed individual.

Yet targeting those higher up the social scale is now becoming more commonplace; many celebrities have been lured into real life 'honeypot' situations, where a woman (or man) engages the victim in sexual encounters and only later do they discover they are the subject of porn videos or even blackmail and it would seem that those higher up the corporate ladder are not immune either because rumors are abounding that executives can also be subject to this kind of extortion. Unlike high-profile celebrities though, it is often a situation manufactured simply to blackmail the target into providing the information necessary to perform a hack. Here then we see the absolute extreme of social engineering where the real world clashes head-on with cyber and the two become irrevocably intertwined.

Another fine dividing line comes when we examine what constitutes a hack and misappropriation of data. Few on the planet haven't heard about the Facebook drama when Cambridge Analytica 'harvested' 87 million user profiles after a researcher apparently passed rights to information onto a third party.

Cambridge Analytica was a company offering services to businesses and political parties who desired to 'change audience behaviors.' In other words, they were a propaganda machine promoting specific political causes or points of view dependent on who's paying. By accessing the personal data, the Internet could then be further used to target individuals with campaigns which would lead them on a trail down a rabbit hole affecting their beliefs, behaviors, political stance, and ultimately how they vote. [11]

What this small number of examples should reveal to all of us is that anyone and any area of life, personal and professional, can be touched by industrial-scale cyber-hacking. Maybe our alarm bells should have started ringing some time ago when the news began to indicate that, as individuals in contemporary society, we are all vulnerable to cyber-crime.

That said, as the world becomes more interconnected, it is enterprise which is leaving these doors unlocked and resulting in individual susceptibility. Yet it is still enterprise that will likely bear the biggest impact in terms of lost revenue, legislative fines, and legal kick back as the world changes and becomes more technologically enlightened.

Because of the dangers you might then assume that, because the situation is potentially devastating, technological defenses would be the primary concern of all organizations. Yet, although research indicates that companies are becoming increasingly concerned about cyber-crime, only 49% currently employ a dedicated cybersecurity officer.[12] Conversely, many companies appear willing to invest in protection because spends on cybersecurity are now estimated to stand at anything between \$35bn and \$100bn. Surprisingly though, on a global basis, the number of breaches has actually gone up - from 21% in 2016 to 36% in 2018. If we take the U.S. in isolation the picture is even worse; their figures have risen from 20% to 46% during the same period. [13]

It would appear then that, no matter how much is being spent, whatever is being done with the money isn't the right thing and the adage attributed to Einstein seems quite apt when it comes to the subject of investment in cybersecurity: *"The definition of insanity is doing the same thing over and over and expecting different results."*

Who Are CISOs?

In a formal sense the role of the CISO (Chief Information Security Officer) is usually defined as someone who, 'establishes and maintains organizational programs and strategies ensuring information assets are protected.' Which all sounds very neat in theory, but what does this really mean in practice? Well, to start with it's usually the CISO who has to deal with most of the above scenarios we've already mentioned, and preferably in a preventative rather than fire-fighting capacity.

The image then is not of the usual corporate executive, and it's probably better to try and think of the CISO as being the guard dog of the corporate family - You might not necessarily want to pet it, but you still recognize that it performs a vital function in protecting the business assets - and so the CISO is absolutely essential to the survival of the business. Just how necessary becomes a lot clearer when you learn that a recent study revealed, of 1200 organizations polled, only one third had *never* been breached – or at least are unaware they have been – and 15% had not only been breached once but multiple times. [14] The odds are it's not a matter of *if* an individual enterprise will be hacked, but *when*.

Now the importance of not only employing a CISO but also employing the *right* one starts to take on a lot more significance. And this issue took on more urgency when, in May 2018, new legislation in the form of the General Data Protection Regulation (GDPR), also known in the U.K. as the Data Protection Act 2018, came into force which brought with it much higher financial penalties than industry has seen previously. Administrative fines for infringements of the act can be up to 4% of total annual turnover or 20 million euros, whichever is the higher amount.

Although less press coverage was given to the Network and Information Security (NIS) Directive which came in around the same time, this can have equal impact on some organizations. Where though the GDPR is designed to protect data, NIS legislation is meant to increase protection of national critical infrastructure sectors rather than 'just' data. For those companies affected the NIS Directive carries with it significant fines that can be in line with the GDPR, although in this case each member state is allowed to set its own penalties to a maximum of 20 million euros.

Ultimately though the end result of the new legislative protection means that it is no longer just hackers who have the potential to bring organizations to their knees. Now, if a company is breached because of security failures, they can expect to have the full weight of the authorities also land on their back with financial penalties capable of crippling many companies.

The first significant post-GDPR breach occurred at the U.K.-based Dixons Group and how the regulators deal with the situation might turn out to be a game changer. On the one hand it may set a precedent for new case law, but on the other, because the actual breach occurred before the new regulations came into force, the company may just escape unscathed from the new penalties.

What we see though is that both the changing face of technology and legislation is forcing a shift in organizational paradigms and this also affects the attributes required of cybersecurity officers at all levels. Not only do role functions need to be well understood and clearly defined, but skills and characteristics need to be established based on what the emerging evidence tells us is required rather than what we believe should be correct based on historical recruitment practices. The logic behind this principle is simple; the current recruitment strategies and application of the functions in the role are not, for many different reasons, working particularly well.

Recruiting a CISO is not the same as recruiting a Chief Technical Officer (CTO), for example. Non-specialist recruiters using automated technologies to scan CV's often fail to hit the mark because soft and intangible skills, that don't involve tick box certification routines, simply don't apply. There are, of course, one or two specialist recruiters who do seem to 'get it,' but they tend to be the exception rather than the rule.

Facing the Foe - What the CISO is Up Against

No matter which way we look at it the CISO enters the arena on an uneven playing field. Most of the foes they face are not only thinking outside of the box, but they are actively functioning outside of it. The enemy is unconstrained by small matters such as societal norms, organizational restrictions, legal boundaries or regional legislation.

Hackers live in a world where there is a continuous cycle of seeking out systems, processes, and human weaknesses waiting to be exploited. They are answerable to no one and have their own personal motives or those of the gang or group they represent. They take many forms such as crackers, hacktivists, carders, spies, extortionists, investigative journalists, and social engineers, and frequently they all have different motivations, but they are still united by one common aim – they would prefer not to get caught.

Is it realistic then to expect a CISO to be effective against these foes while working 'within the box' when it comes to being legally compliant and further restricted by individual organizational norms, models, and expectations? Can we really expect organizations, and ultimately individuals to be protected, when many companies are expecting the old paradigms to fit with a completely new and potentially devastating situation?

Many of the problems which industry now faces have arisen simply due to the speed at which technology and the threat landscape have advanced and few are aware of the real nature of the beast. Particularly in the last decade the developments have been so swift that those in positions of power within organizations have been left on the back-foot when it comes to understanding what needs to be done. In some cases, the catch-up has been so slow that those who head or manage companies still genuinely believe that basic software installations will protect them from all foes. More tellingly, they also believe that once installed, only an occasional upgrade or patch is required. This situation is most prevalent with Small to Medium Enterprises (SMEs) and is likely the main reason for these companies being the most frequently attacked - and it is also why they are the ones most likely to sink without a trace as a direct result.

But the situation is really not much better when it comes to large corporations, because the strategies being deployed often reveal that, even at C-suite and board level, few have more than a vague idea of the true role and functions of the CISO. Frequently executives and managers are still under the misapprehension that the position is one which primarily demands Internet or information technology skills and so they will actively recruit individuals with programmer or I.T. backgrounds to fill digital security officer positions.

Although there are times when technical skills are wholly appropriate, these need to be matched and balanced against the level of security maturity of the organization. At certain points, the need for individual CISOs with core skills such as strategy, operational or advisory are preferable but are actively demanded. The concept of flexing CISO skills to meet immediate needs, and to match these to the security footprint of the organization, are explored later in the book.

What we have come to recognize is that the emerging evidence and research suggest using standard managerial formats and applying them to the CISO role, but this will not provide organizations with an effective cybersecurity officer. In fact, indications are that greater weight should be placed on personal traits and characteristics when looking for a CISO rather than the usual technical skills and academic qualifications that are normally sought.

There are, however, several niche companies involved in developing tools which specify and 'fingerprint' the role of the CISO in individual organizations and which then go on to match those qualities to the specific needs of the company via a 'footprint' profile and these are starting to change the face of cybersecurity defense.

But companies hold the reins of change because, before anything else can be achieved, they must first re-engineer the role into something which is realistic and compatible with the true nature of the job. This means all factors need to be taken into consideration, particularly those of the extremely diverse threat landscape, the volatile dynamics of the technological environment, together with the myriad other associated problems. If organizations all around the world take notice of the simple statistics, such as U.K. businesses being subjected to 65,000 attacks in only the second quarter of 2017,[15] or that Microsoft's Cloud has to fend off 1.5 million attacks per day,[16] then the precarious nature of the situation becomes clear and we can begin to understand things have to change as a matter of urgency.

The main focus now should be placed not on the academic background of the CISO, or even the employment history, but on their personal traits and qualities because, like it or not, credential-focused thinking simply doesn't hack it in the world of cybersecurity.

Taking a step back from traditional recruitment practices, what we start to see when we look at an effective CISO is someone who needs to be strong, not only in displaying a high level of emotional intelligence but also in what are often termed 'soft' factors:

- Inquisitiveness
- Vision
- Persistence
- Tenacity
- Adaptiveness

Someone seeking to work in their comfort zone is not a suitable candidate for the role of CISO, and this becomes even more pertinent in environments where transformational change is needed to drive the organization from a lax or non-existent cybersecurity culture. Neither though are the character traits of a good CISO likely to result in the optimistic and rose-colored spectacle outlook normally desired of the company executive and a company seeking to employ a 'yes' man in the role, is highly unlikely to recruit an effective cybersecurity officer.

A saying currently doing the rounds might have been originally directed at software developers, but it is just as appropriate for those across the cybersecurity industry: "No one anticipates a catastrophic system failure by looking on the bright side." [17] Being permanently upbeat and toeing the company line are not particularly good traits to find in your CISO.

Bottom of the Heap?

The picture that is now beginning to build reveals CISOs as being a different breed to other executives within an organization simply because the environment they're dealing with demands it. Yet, surprisingly enough, currently the role of the CISO is often seen as being relatively junior to others in the corporate hierarchy.

Regularly CISOs report to the Chief Information Officer (CIO) or the Chief Technical Officer (CTO), but very few are members of the main board. If the Chief Financial Officer (CFO) responsible for managing the finances, is seen as a high-profile corporate leader fit for board level acceptance, shouldn't the person responsible for protecting the critical areas of the organization which keep it open for business be seen in the same light?

By definition then, the situation demands the organization deal with CISOs in a way which is often distinct from others at the same level, and they may well need to veer away from the recognized and accepted organizational protocols.

My argument is the CISO is essential in keeping the business 'live,' to help steer it through and contain the inevitable attack. So much so that the role must report directly to the CEO or at least have an unencumbered 'dotted' line allowing the communication of risk to be directly shared.

Dirty Deeds, Hackers, and Heroes

In a formal sense the ultimate role of the CISO is to protect the asset information and data of the organization. Yet, what we see in reality, is that the picture is much broader than this and the hacker has the capacity not only to steal data but to cause actual physical damage to the institution. Although there may well have only been a handful of known cases up to this point in time, there can be little doubt that the capacity certainly exists.

Asset information can also, albeit indirectly, cause physical damage to the individual person as the example with the National Health Service (NHS) in the U.K. revealed when appointments for thousands of patients, including operations, had to be canceled after the WannaCry attack. Although death may not have been the outcome in any one case, it's safe to presume that the people affected needed healthcare which was denied or at least delayed by the malware attack and as a result this caused some measure of personal suffering and trauma.

Enterprise asset information doesn't always refer to personal data – although this is most frequently the target – it can also include many other things, such as production or processes methods, commercial data, intellectual property (IP), and executive communications. Any and all of which, as exemplified by the Nortel hack, can bring individual companies to their knees if stolen or leaked.

Now we have reached a situation where the threat landscape has grown to such an extent there is an increased possibility of damage from which the organization may not recover. Yet nobody in particular is asking what the effects are on the individual souls who are touched by such breaches.

Neither, when it comes to the source of threats, are these limited to the dark, shadowy, and illusive hacker. In some cases, organizations might come under threat from 'insiders' or employees, ex or otherwise, who hold a grudge and intend to simply disrupt the organizational processes to exact revenge.

International competitors are also a threat because they might be seeking organizational information regarding products or production methods which would give them competitive advantage in the marketplace. They too, of course, would also benefit from disrupting the systems of their competitors if only to slow production or even to reduce customer trust by the revelation that their system is not secure.

When it comes to isolated professional hackers, although we might think these are people driven only by monetary gain, they rarely are and they also come in a variety of guises. For example, today we have come to distinguish between Black Hat, White Hat, and now even Gray Hat hackers. Although even here these terms are too simplistic to cover all the bases.

Black hats are the ones who hack for monetary gain, although it should be noted this is not always their only motivation. Quite often they will hack systems or organizations for the kudos they receive from their peers, and of course, for the sheer hell or challenge of doing so. The current worldview categorizes black hat hacking as being an illegal activity no matter what the motivation because entering systems without permission is the underpinning illegality of the offense. Yet, although we have the definition, it is here where the lines start to become somewhat blurred.

Some might think of hackers and some of the high-profile whistleblowers such as Julian Assange, Edward Snowden, and Bradley Manning (originally trusted insiders) as being motivated by the greater good. However, the law as it currently stands, does not. They are still considered to be carrying out illegal activities in the vein of the black hat because they extracted or shared restricted and classified data and accessed systems without permission to achieve this end. Here though, for the black hat, there is no obvious personal gain, but rather one might argue much pain in terms of the loss of liberty involved.

Conversely, though, association with the 'Dark Side' is rarely applied to those working at state level intervention in respect of deep surveillance, personal and industrial privacy, and restrictions to liberty. It would seem that black hats, although legally defined as those entering systems without permission, are not all prosecuted accordingly.

Another group which comes under the auspice of black hat are those normally considered terrorists. The ISIS Hacker Group, known as The Cyber Caliphate, would fit this category at least from a prevailing Western perspective. Again, they enter systems illegally to collect intelligence, disrupt or destroy the system for a diverse range of reasons. Yet, from our narrow perspective, they are still a foe of the CISO.

White hat hackers are often referred to as 'ethical hackers.' These are people who have the same skill capacity as the black hats, but who are employed or contracted by companies to test their systems out for vulnerabilities and are not, therefore, entering systems illegally. This practice is becoming increasingly common and is the industrial equivalent of fighting fire with fire. Where once these people would have been considered black hats, they are now being engaged by the corporate community and their skills are being put to positive use. Bounty or Bug Hunters such as these are becoming increasingly common, and even companies such as Microsoft and Apple offer bounty programs to white hat hackers in this capacity.

Despite the legalities of differentiating between black and white hat hackers, one other major distinguishing feature being increasingly referred to is the notion of a 'moral compass.' Black hats tend to have fewer morals and little remorse or empathy for the victims of their nefarious activities. White hats, at least in this perspective, are the arch enemies of the black hats – although for some a little nudge is all it takes for a former good guy to tip over to the other side. A disgruntled Systems Administrator (SysAdmin) for example, can make for a formidable enemy.

The category of gray hat hacker is one which has only recently emerged. In truth, these should really fall under the black hat auspice because it is only after they have performed the action of illegally penetrating a system that they may, or may not, become gray hats. How this is determined depends entirely on what they do next. However, for the majority of gray hats, the intention is to identify weaknesses in a system. If and when this has been achieved, the hacker informs the organization they have the potential to be hacked and a 'finder's fee' is requested before they part with details. The options for the organization in such instances are pretty limited.

Geopolitical hacking is another area which CISOs have to consider. Geopolitical hacking, where one country attempts to gain knowledge about another, should come under the banner of black hat because systems are entered illegally – although it's doubtful many countries would view it in such a base way. Any loopholes in the systems are then exploited and used as little less than spying or espionage tools.

Despite all the categories and definition of hackers, these are not the greatest threat the individual organization faces… the biggest problem a CISO has to deal with comes from inside the organization itself and not from a declared enemy.

The Insider Risk

Human error is the biggest underpinning cause of cybersecurity compromise. It's not deliberate, it's not malicious, it's not for any kind of gain. It happens because *staff make mistakes*. They might put in a generic password, they might leave a password exposed, they might not follow policies or procedures when accessing external websites or letting unauthorized people into buildings. They might not pass on important messages, or they might click on links in an email when it is unwise to do so. All of these, and many, many more, are mistakes that staff make every single day and which can often result in the organization ultimately being hacked.

The avenues where staff might make a simple, yet ultimately devastating error allowing hacker entry are endless. Staff and cybersecurity are the organizational equivalent of fitting a superlative burglar alarm in your home and then leaving the front door wide open. If you work in a company where Internet technology is used, then realize this one thing... the biggest threat to the company, is you.

No matter where you look, whether companies are large or small, staff error is reported as being the most frequent cause of cybersecurity breaches. If we take the Equifax hack as a case in point it appears there was a major, yet simple contributing factor – a member of staff did not pass on an email that stated the security system needed a patch to prevent a breach.

When it comes to the attack on the NHS in 2017, this was also widely reported as being preventable because the Trusts (regional departments) involved had been informed of potential vulnerabilities in their systems as far back as 2014. In addition to being warned of the problem they were also provided with guidance on how to patch the system. Yet, amazingly, nothing was done. In fact, the NHS admitted that, prior to 2017, they had no mechanism in place to even assess whether individual trusts had complied with previously issued guidance.

In this case, the human error factor was huge and undeniable. They were notified with a warning that their systems were vulnerable and no action was taken. Then no one followed through to ensure that the warning guidance had been complied with. If nothing else, the U.K. NHS breach was a beautiful example of human error at every step and is indicative of the complacency of the human animal when it comes to cybersecurity.

Yet neither the Equifax nor NHS cases are anything new and they are hardly likely to surprise most in the cybersecurity industry. This is because around 75 percent of large companies breached report that the hacks occurred due to human error.[18] It is human error within the organization which is most often responsible for leaving the system open to vulnerabilities and attack and it is also the biggest challenge the CISO faces.

So, What Exactly Does a CISO Do?

Taking all the above into consideration, defining exactly what a CISO does is not always an easy thing. Their enemies are a diverse range of characters and with many motivations and devices at their disposal. In the case of insider risk, there is no motivation at all, but strategies and systems still need to be put in place to prevent mistakes being made.

Although it is sometimes difficult to define what a CISO is, now we can at least begin to see what they are not. They are not merely an information technology technician or someone who has previous leadership experience. They are not data managers, nor are they there simply to put firewalls and anti-virus systems in place. The CISO has to face a diverse range of potential problems at any one time including, but not limited to:

- Quantifying internal and external risk
- Understanding vulnerabilities specific to the business and in the wider ecosystem and supply chain
- Having up-to-date knowledge of security technology and architectures
- Understanding privacy legislation and customer security concerns
- Having insight into the mind and motivation of a wide range of adversaries
- Identifying potential weaknesses and vulnerabilities
- Selecting and implementing security solutions
- Implementing mechanisms to monitor efficacy of security solutions

- Assessing and negotiating budgets for the department and smooth running of the CISO Office
- Negotiating, presenting and reporting to executives in non-technical language and to technical teams in theirs
- Continually assessing the environment and reinforcing security
- Minimizing the potential for human error
- Covering Human Resource, legal and compliance, commercial, marketing and technical issues
- Training, educating and communicating the need for security
- Transforming insecure organizational cultures

Security should be a viewed as a business enabler, not an unwelcome overhead. Yet, where there is conflict between security and convenience, security is usually the loser. And this is a point that CISOs are all too aware of. When we look at even these few aspects of the position, it becomes increasingly clear that the personal characteristics and traits of the CISO are at least equally important as their background skills and education. They at once have to be a confident negotiator, a psychologist, an accountant, a diplomat, and a specialist in the field of the business within which they are employed.

As part of our research for this book, and following interviews with scores of CISOs, we identified nine key competency pillars and 200 sub-categories that the CISO community is expected to look after in their day to day activities:

The Nine Key Competency Pillars
1) Governance Risk and Compliance

2) Security Architectures and Operating Models
3) Change and Transformation Project Delivery and Leadership
4) Business Enablement
5) Audits and Assessments
6) Budgets
7) Security Operations
8) Selling (Internally) and Reporting
9) Legal and Human Relations

Enterprise needs to appreciate that times have changed. The threats are bigger, they arise from an increasingly diverse range of sources, and they have the potential to be devastating not only to the company concerned, but to the population at large. Industry urgently needs to understand the role the cybersecurity officer plays and how to support them in keeping all concerned safe.

The CISO Perspective
Paul Heffernan - Group CISO
(Manufacturing and Logistics)

There can be no substitute for speaking to those dedicated souls working at the coal face of cybersecurity. For my first in a series of interviews for this book I begin with Paul Heffernan.

Paul is one of the youngest group CISO's in the industry and he sets the bar for a new breed of security leaders. He is responsible for looking after a significantly sized organization and one of the largest private companies in its sector. With its roots in manufacturing within the automotive industry, more recently it has developed a wide range of manufacturing, logistics, and consultancy offerings that are deployed across a range of industries including Financial Services, Retail, Logistics, and Transportation. The task of keeping this diverse organization secure is one that would present an exciting and challenging prospect for even the most experienced of security leaders. Here is what Paul has to say about life as a CISO.

"I've been in information security for around 10 years now but never started off with the idea in mind that I would end up in a CISO role as a career. It's just the way things turned out because I happened to be in the right place at the right time. Like a lot of CISOs my background was actually as an ethical hacker and from there I moved on to building my own cybersecurity business. We were pretty successful and worked for some big names and, one day, a client company who are a global supply chain organization, said that they were looking to employ their first dedicated CISO

and thought I was just what their company needed. I jumped at the chance, although the role back then turned out to not be what I expected because I walked into a 'team' of me and an analyst, although the company had previously had an information security manager role. So, you start 'Day One' keen to go and then you realize you are a general without an army. In the past couple of years I've now expanded that team up to about sixteen or so people, but that is all through internal selling, influencing and not because they have hard-core technical skills.

Although most people think the job is about technology, nothing could really be further from the truth because it is a highly varied and complex role. I'm a techie at heart and I also thought the role was going to be more technical and that I would get to use a lot of the technical skills from my ethical hacking background, but what I've found since is that it is actually a minor aspect of my role. It's more about stakeholder management, even salesmanship and the softer skills because as an industry we have traded off our technical knowledge and that has got us so far. Now though, board members are looking for that individual who can talk language of business and who are going to go on their journey with them in improving their business outcomes - using that technical language doesn't really pass muster anymore.

I still do research and talks outside of work to the technical community but you have to be able to change those communication channels depending on the stakeholders, that technical language would not work with the board. Doing this, you might capture their attention for a few moments at best, but then they are going to ask 'but what does this actually mean to me?' So, for me it's being able to flick in between all those different stakeholders, being able to communicate with them and also by being consistent.

I think the critical factor to be successful for this role is that you have got to be a good influencer. By that, I don't just mean to the board but that you have to bring technical teams on the journey with you, you have to be able to encourage talent into the industry, you have to be able to influence vendors. You have to be able to influence all those stakeholders to achieve what you are trying to achieve.

I have always felt well supported in any security leadership role I have been in and if a breach had happened, I wouldn't feel like I am out there on my own. We've all had our fair share of incidents, as most large organizations have whether they admit it or not, and in every case I've felt well supported by the board and by the organization. Clearly though, if mistakes are made they want to know they are not going to happen again, particularly if there are human elements to it and, let's face it, nearly all breaches are caused by human error. I avoid excessively worrying about the personal implications to the CISO role of a cybersecurity incident because I am motivated by helping my organization understand the threats. They in turn, understand the pressure CISOs are under. Of course this attitude can vary widely between organizations, and it's my responsibility to manage and address this in the CISO role."

Chapter 2
Who Took A Bullet?

"It's difficult to get a man to understand something when his salary depends on his not understanding it."
- Upton Sinclair

Few today would doubt that, no matter what the business or public department, it's often difficult to find where the buck stops when any kind of problem arises. The name of the game is absolution of responsibility because being seen to be squeaky-clean matters - and often to the detriment of the real long-term business.

"Lessons have been learned," has become a stock in trade quote which, the evidence suggests, rarely means they have. Specifics are avoided, reasoned responses are rarely provided, and if at the end of the day all else fails, someone simply takes a bullet in the name of organizational sacrifice. It would seem the only lesson to be learned is how to placate both onlookers and investors. Yet when it comes to cybersecurity the situation is further compounded by many factors and top of that list is the subject of secrecy.

Hitting the Headlines

No organization wants to see their reputation take a hit by broadcasting to the world their cyber-systems aren't secure and experience suggests that the best way to advertise a breach is not simply to fire the executive in charge but to do so in a blaze of publicity. Often then the opposite becomes true and, when it comes to CISOs getting the bullet, frequently the only cases that make the news are the ones where it simply cannot be avoided. This is perhaps the main reason why, although the CISO community is awash with fears relating to job losses, most know that firings are kept out of the public eye - at least until it is absolutely unavoidable.

The subject of employment termination secrecy is then common knowledge in the world of the CISO. And few, at least when they have been in the business a short while, fail to realize they will be lucky to escape without their career progression suffering the indignity of being fired or moved sideways at some point. Yes, when it comes to the CISO role there can be little doubt that getting the elbow is the real elephant in the room and, to quote Raj Samani from McAfee, CISO should actually stand for "Career Is So Over."

This problem is best exemplified by looking at the few cases which do hit the headlines because, even then, it's often just as difficult to establish exactly 'why' someone has been given the bullet even if you do manage to discover 'who.'

The Incorruptible Mr Stamos

One of the big names to recently bite the dust, at least within the confines of the Facebook industry, is Alex Stamos, although it must be noted that he has 'departed' the social media site rather than being fired. Could it though turn out that semantics are the Devil's plaything as so many issues with the social media site often are? Although most might assume that his departure is in some way connected to the recent Cambridge Analytica drama this was initially denied and, as it turns out, Mr Stamos had actually been crossing swords with the higher echelons of Facebook for some time. Getting to the root of the problem in this case, like so many others, is not easy, but it would seem that his troubles first became noticeable when he started to make everyone feel a little uncomfortable by mentioning that popular buzzword 'transparency.'

At the time the thing most concerning to Mr Stamos was the spread of misinformation via the site – a fact rumored to have come to light back in 2016 when he discovered Russia might be abusing the system during the U.S. election. Mr Stamos apparently considered that by applying the 'transparency' which so many companies insist exists in the first place, the problem would be mitigated, and he told them so.

The suggestion regarding transparency was, however, not taken well and it seemed the social media company were not particularly concerned about the situation. Instead, they preferred to direct their attention toward the stance of Mr Stamos because it would appear he was doing what CISOs often have to do; tell their boss something they simply don't want to hear.

This situation is reflective of what CISOs face every single day in organizations across the world, doing what they are supposedly employed to do and advising when they believe the company is putting itself in a position of risk, giving them the opportunity to both manage and mitigate it. Yet, in this case, although it would seem Mr Stamos clearly felt he was simply doing his job, Facebook couldn't, or didn't want to see, so far into the future.

As it turned out, Facebook misjudged the landscape quite dramatically. Despite part of their business model revolving around the monetization of personal data, they did not increase organizational transparency and as a result didn't foresee problems would arise in the form of the Cambridge Analytica drama. Yet, a few days after the media broke with that news, Mr Stamos' departure day was suddenly set. However, Facebook really should have known from the start that, when it came to their CISO, the writing was on the wall - because his employment history certainly suggested this was a man of real integrity.

Previously Stamos had been employed by Yahoo, again as their CISO, but this time it was a position which he occupied for only a year. Mr Stamos resigned, of his own volition, because he discovered the company had built a program which allowed for all emails to be scanned on behalf of the FBI or NSA.[1]

When it comes to Facebook though, and whether he was pushed or he jumped, Mr Stamos is certainly the one holding fast on the moral high-ground ... even if he isn't holding on to his position in the company.[2]

Uber Breach
Another big headline maker came in 2017 after the CISO of Uber, Joe Sullivan together with a company lawyer, were fired when it was revealed they had paid off hackers to the tune of $100,000. This was, apparently, in an effort to

prevent the hackers from disclosing personal and private information relating to over 600,000 drivers and 57 million customers which was acquired through a hack that took place in 2016. Again, detailed information about the incident is scant, although it is reasonable to assume it wasn't just Mr Sullivan and the lawyer who knew about the breach, although they were the ones to take the fall.[3]

Now, what we start to see now is a recurring pattern. Organizations discovering breaches, or even the potential for breaches, long in advance of the actual event. Then, when the inevitable ax finally drops, it is usually the CISO neck which gets in the way whether it was justified or not. In cases such as the Mr Stamos incident, the 'departure' semantics might play a bigger role than initially suspected because, at the end of the day, all he was doing was what he was employed to do in the first place, and it's pretty difficult to terminate someone's contract for that.

The Invisible CISO

Many organizations, however, do not have a formal CISO in place and therefore, when trouble brews, the buck keeps moving. That's when things get a lot more dangerous for members of the board, particularly when the company is expected to be seen to do something constructive to placate onlookers. In this case, it is often the CEO who suddenly finds himself the 'owner' of the cybersecurity risk because, without a CISO, when the buck does eventually stop it stops on a high card.

In some cases, the individual in question might find themselves feeling the urge to move on to pastures new with, of course, impeccable references and a Golden Handshake to help them on their journey. This is what happened to Richard Smith, the ex-CEO of Equifax, who collected $90 million before leaving and which must have gone a good way to lessening his pain.[4]

Dido Harding though fared a little worse as CEO of TalkTalk when they were hacked in October 2015.[5] Despite her frequent attempts to communicate with affected parties through the media, in many cases she only made matters worse. On one occasion she even told all four million customers to click on links in emails being sent out to them. In an interview, when asked by City A.M., a free London based and business-focused newspaper, if the stolen data had been encrypted, she replied, "The awful truth is that I don't know."

Listening to Baroness Harding speak at an Information Security conference in London mid-2018 about her earlier experience at TalkTalk, it was clear she had learned much about dealing with the aftermath of such a significant and high-profile breach. She mentioned the pressure of having to make decisive and fast executive decisions based on conflicting advice from the authorities and gave the police as one example. Their focus was on catching the perpetrators of the hack so they requested silence, but this conflicted with the industry and customer perspective where notification is of paramount importance. In addition to this, the Baroness, as CEO, mentioned one of her biggest lessons was the realization that cybersecurity is a board level issue and that it should not be merely confined to the technical or security sectors.

Amy Pascal, the co-chair in charge when the notorious Sony hack took place in 2014, was also fired as a direct result of a breach that was, by any standards, considered to be something pretty spectacular. Not only did the hackers manage to infect 3,262 of the company's 6,797 computers and 838 of the 1,555 servers – erasing all the information in the process – but they also used an algorithm to overwrite the data in seven different ways shortly before the code went on to corrupt the start-up software, basically killing all the machines infected.

What later transpired, as it so often does in many of these cases, was that the system was hacked many months in advance of the malware actually being released.[6] In Sony's case though, this little matter came to light because the hackers had used the intervening time to copy all the data from the computers before instigating the end attack. We know this because information from the company, ranging from unfinished scripts through to private email messages, were dumped on the Internet for the world to see. At the time only limited information about the status of Ms Pascal was available, it was only some time after that event that she finally admitted to being fired from the organization.

So, when a CISO isn't in place to take the fall, the heads that roll are often the ones at the top and the CEO is frequently the next available sacrifice even when, as the case with Dido Harding appeared to reveal, they hadn't really acquired much knowledge about cybersecurity. What this goes to prove is that someone, somewhere, does actually own the problem of cybersecurity breaches and, if all else fails, the buck will eventually stop on an ace.

Reputation is Everything!

Although the reputation of a company has long since been its biggest strength, today it expands far beyond pleasing customers, enticing new ones, and keeping the bank happy. Everything a company is rests on the image it projects to an often global and highly competitive audience. Where companies are not selling a tangible product but a service – Facebook and Equifax being prime examples – there are no goods to tempt customers and investors back; no solid product which can be used to remind those external onlookers what enticed them in the first place – from where the loyalty originally emerged – and which a company might reliably fall back on.

The reputation an enterprise projects to the outside world is undeniably its strongest ally but, when things go wrong, can be its most feared enemy. It is so valuable that protecting the reputation of an organization, particularly when its position sits close to indefensible, is almost a knee-jerk reaction even when that reaction actually makes very little sense.

Warren Buffett was certainly correct when he said, "It takes 20 years to build a reputation and five minutes to ruin it," and historically he has been proven correct time and time again. A dent in the corporate armor affects company confidence in everyone from customers through to suppliers and the stock market.

Yet maybe Warren Buffett's statement has been, at least to some measure, misinterpreted. If we apply a little common sense to the advice provided by the great entrepreneur himself, what he appeared to be saying, in a pre-internet era, was that it is necessary to think first and be proactive in protecting the reputation of an organization. In short, not to do anything which might ultimately damage image and subsequently confidence. If we take that stance and apply it to cybersecurity, the correct (and sensible) way to protect an organization's reputation, is to do anything and everything necessary to protect information data and act in a preventative capacity.

It would then appear that the type of situation Mr Buffett suggests preventing is one similar to the gaff offered up by Gerald Ratner back in 1991. This was when the orator described the products his company sold as 'crap' at a business ceremony. The words were, of course, spoken in jest, but no sooner were they out of his mouth did they hit the headlines. The company bombed as a result with its reputation in tatters.[7]

Prevention is clearly preferable to cure, and this is likely the light in which Mr Buffett's dose of advice should be taken. Yet, in the day of the Internet, many companies try to apply the cure even when they have failed to reveal that the personal data of thousands, or maybe millions of people, has been leaked. Trying to protect the company reputation simply by issuing an apology doesn't meet prevention criteria. Protecting reputation in this scenario means not only acting appropriately when the breach is discovered, but it also means doing anything and everything to prevent it from happening in the first place.

Most might well say that this delayed reaction strays into the realms of damage limitation. But how effective that is, particularly when the primary goal is to restore reputation rather than solving a problem which is likely to recur, is not really a solution to anything in the long-term.

If we apply the same reactionary responses which happen in many cybersecurity situations to that of product recalls the impractical nature of that particular stance becomes a lot clearer. For example, over the years we have seen recalls affecting everything from car tires through to baby slings. But imagine what would happen if the companies concerned did not issue recalls but simply ignored the problem or tried to cover it up? Imagine if, when the problem was eventually brought out into the open, the company merely apologized, fired the head of quality control, and then said, "lessons have been learned," in an attempt to restore reputation and confidence. Such a response would not turn out to be damage limitation but damage *enhancement*. The reputation of the organization would probably be irreparable. The lawsuits would not be smaller, but bigger, and it is even more likely that legal action would be taken by the authorities.

In the world of tangible products, apologizing and firing one or two individuals is rarely enough to mitigate problems, yet in the world of information security, many seem to think it is. In fact, as you will shortly learn, despite numerous organizations being breached not once but repeatedly, they continue to apply the same knee-jerk reaction as they aim to protect the organization's reputation for perhaps the second, third or even fourth time around.

When it comes to cybersecurity then, protecting the organization's reputation rather than the organization's information, automatically becomes the immediate objective. If the problem can't be hidden, when it is exposed, apologies are issued and someone's head rolls - even if that same someone has been trying to warn of the risk for some time before the breach. Then, we are assured, lessons have been learned. It's all tantamount to shutting the stable door after the horse has bolted. And, if you leave it open again when you get your new horse as many companies do, then it is certainly a practice which is going to be repeated because, once hackers realize an organization is more concerned about image than security, they may as well stick a target on their doors.

The hope then is that the breach is never revealed, hence the shrouding of such problems in secrecy wherever possible, so not even a public knee-jerk response is required. This we see happen time and time again even with the small number of cases which actually make it as far as the press. Yet most of this could be avoided completely if those in the seats of power really understood the nature of the beast and that cybertechnology is not only changing the way they work but actually necessitates a shift in the very foundation of the way organizations are structured and business conducted.

There really is no nice way of putting it, but the real truth of the matter is, simply feeding the company CISO or even CEO to the lions before bringing in a nice, shiny, new one, is not the way to go if the company is to be secure into the future.

Of course, the prime example of an organization failing to learn from previous problems before reacting with the knee-jerk is that of Equifax, which is an irony when you consider they are data brokers. When they were breached in 2017, outside of the vast number of people who were affected, both mainstream and niche media immediately fell upon another issue… because they had discovered the terrible truth.

Although the fact was advertised rather than hidden because the lady in question put her CV on LinkedIn, the news was out that the company CISO, Susan Mauldin, had an academic background founded in music.[8] The media erupted and those with an opinion, and few didn't have one, guffawed, belittled, and then slated the unfortunate Ms Mauldin for her lack of technical expertise and therefore apparent unsuitability for the job.

The articles echoed across the Internet and anyone reading the click-bait content would almost certainly have got the impression that the company CISO was rosy-cheeked and fresh out of university. And they had to be right, didn't they? After all, Equifax *had* been breached. Yet hooking on to one aspect of Ms Mauldin's CV, the musical education, proved that most were simply being selective and extraordinarily so. This is because the lady did indeed have a solid background in cybersecurity, working for companies such as First Data Corp and Hewlett Packard, and common sense should have told anyone taking the time to actually read the document that it was for this reason the position with Equifax was accessible to her in the first place.

Alas, no. What most focused on were the perceived inappropriate qualifications and, even then, ones which were decades old. Yet what the media response revealed was that the focus on her lack of technological qualifications exposed that most really have no idea of what the position of CISO actually involves and the skills and traits needed to perform the job effectively.

What we also see when we examine the high-profile Equifax leak in a little more detail is more in line with the standard knee-jerk situation. This is because the company was not breached once or even twice, but in several incidents stretching back over a period of years.[9] Although there were two major breaches prior to the big one hitting in 2017, Equifax actually has a much longer history of cybersecurity problems. Not only has it been noted that their site contained numerous vulnerabilities but, back in 2013 to 2014, a leak occurred, although it was said to only affect a small number of people. Again in 2016, another problem arose when the Equifax W-2 Express website was hacked which resulted in the personal information of 430,000 people being leaked. In 2017, although again only involving a 'small number' of customers, their partner site at Lifelock was breached and data leaked.

The bigger picture at Equifax does then reveal that the stable door was closed many times after the horses have gone, yet nothing really changed when it comes to organizational paradigms. However, even today, the focus still remains on Ms Mauldin's music education and the opinion that a CISO needs to be a technical whizz is voiced so frequently it's enough to make your head spin. In truth, for those that really know, music has nothing to do with it, and such commentators merely reveal that their knowledge regarding cybersecurity belongs in the dark ages.

One reason that academic achievements in information technology are more or less irrelevant is due to the rapidly changing environment. Technology moves on so swiftly that, even since cybersecurity certificates have come into being, they are outdated within a short period of time. The best technical education anyone thinking of entering the field of cybersecurity could hope for is to acquire a computer science qualification. Yet, even then, it has to be accepted this is a static academic achievement soon to be outdated. Neither does it take into consideration the traits a CISO requires to confront the diverse range of foes they have to face nor, as a standalone qualification, will it provide an organization with anything close to an effective cybersecurity professional.

When it comes to both hiring and firing the corporate security officer, it bodes well to take into consideration the same factors as their foes. Social engineering plays a major role in accessing systems and holding a technological qualification will not help you assess the threats from that single perspective alone. Where once upon a time cybersecurity meant little more than prevention of Worm viruses accessing a system, this avenue of thought is now assigned to history, or at least it should be.

Today the situation has developed into one where the CISO officer is faced with fighting organized gangs of heavily funded experts who infiltrate not only the technical environment but also the physical organization in an effort to achieve their end goals. Because of this, technical expertise plays only a minor role in effectively guarding the enterprise and, as most of those actually working in cybersecurity would agree, it is rarely a prerequisite to doing the job.

As it turns out, Susan Maudlin and her music qualifications were simply fodder for the overenthusiastic amateur, or perhaps even Equifax themselves, in the ongoing saga. But if qualifications weren't the problem, and she was in charge, why did the organization fail not only badly, but frequently?

When it comes to failures arising due to cybersecurity breaches the problems are countless, but the real truth of the matter is one of the major issues is few in the organization truly understand the situation. This is often the reason that the CISO, even when they try to impart critical information, is left stonewalled and unsupported in the position and is forced to sit back and wait for the inevitable to happen. And it will happen. Providing that is, that it hasn't already. Every single company in the world will be hit by hackers or data leaks at some point, at least once, and most more than once.

Hacking is now an integral, unwanted, intrusion into the business. It is just as likely to happen as your production line breaking down or a new entrant to the market squaring up to you as competition. No matter who or where you are... a... hack... will... happen. Ignoring it will not prevent it, putting poor defenses in place will not prevent it, and handling the situation badly when you are hacked by immediately offering up the usual apologies and head on a stick will not make it go away. In fact, that kind of response is far more likely to make your company attractive to hackers in future because they know if you are doing the wrong thing, they have a good chance of successfully hitting your company again in the future.

The CISO Perspective
Iain Hunneybell - Global CISO
(Financial Services)

"I suppose I've got a fairly long history in IT, starting in the good old days. From there I went into technology sales and from that to high technology marketing. First I was running an operations marketing group, and then a corporate marketing function for a large software house. All this was even before Netscape was out so it's the very early days of the visual web. My interest in that was in how it might transform a business, and in fact all the challenges it gave, because in those days pretty much what anyone would hear was very much constrained to what was in their own market.

Then came the thinking about how we might use it for support. Back then support was a major revenue stream, so that was my level of interest. I couldn't find anybody to do it, so I ended up writing the website myself. I still build sites and maintain them today. Then I was offered a tech position with a new online banking service, and after that I started to get work in security architecture. From there it was cybersecurity work, countering phishing, and the "in the last fiscal year the transaction has been worked out that you are due £426.17 refund, please give us your credit card and wait nine days," type of thing.

The degree of regulation is higher now, but the traditional approach of a business can be very compliance-led. We are transitioning to a risk-led approach, but it can be very hard to escape the checklist mindset. My interest is understanding the threat and do something to mitigate it. Hopefully mitigating will tick the compliance boxes, but I want to mitigate the threat and tick the compliance boxes, not tick the compliance boxes and coincidentally make things more secure along the way. You do get into silly situations with people and, in my humble opinion at least, they simply don't think through the problem. They just read the words and it says "it shall be black." But black in this instance is actually bad. "But it says black," they say, and I say, "I know it says black but it won't work." I have a few challenges like that.

The tasks and duties of the CISOs are growing massively. On the one hand we like to drive security and raise awareness, but can never be as the threats continue to evolve and so you are constantly chasing shadows. On the other hand, we also have to provide the support so we are drowning in requests because threats come from anywhere.

In my previous role for example, a big topic was supply chain security. Your information might be secure but your devices get compromised in a warehouse. If you take a mobile phone, it's designed in Delaware, U.S., and produced in China, and contains hundreds of components. Finally you have a highly complex product that gets produced in the cheapest place possible. I recommend a very tight and close cooperation with the vendor of those products. They need the proper insight and evidence so they understand the risk from their perspective and the risk from the customer.

Compromised devices are a huge problem. I know of one case were two big routers should have been identical. One stayed longer in a warehouse. Later I.T. found out that one of the routers was basically mirroring the traffic to an unknown destination. When they examined both they found the second one was not identical to the first and, after analysis, found one was tampered with in the warehouse.

CISOs now are absurdly busy and particularly because there's just so much change going on in the organization. You're just generally trying to overhaul and enhance the cyber-position and you've got a whole new digital start-up culture which can be somewhat at odds with the traditional compliance-led approach.

You also have a business which is trying to go very fast in digital so you've got a lot of velocity.

I would say, in my team of 13, we try pragmatic security, so less blindly follow business control standards. We try to understand what the risk is, and do something appropriate to it. One of the challenges I have is the inner compliance mindset, because people want to see progress, and they want to boil progress down to a very simple thing. Sometimes though, when it comes to statistics and reporting to the execs, it is reporting for the sake of it. For example, how many SQL injection attempts have been tried? Well, I can tell you that, but more importantly the ones I can tell you about are the ones we observed. But, if we observed them, we've stopped them. So actually the number we're really interested in is how many didn't we see. For me a lot of stuff doesn't really pass the 'so what?' test. I can give you the stat, but it's meaningless. How many spam messages do we stop? So what? How many didn't we stop? Now that might be interesting.

If we were breached then I would feel responsible because that's what I'm there to stop. Hopefully though I'm not one breach from the sack, although it depends very much on the circumstances. One of the challenges we have is just coping with the amount of change and that's not just change from the cyber program, that's change from the fact that the organization is changing. The whole digital area is new. What we're doing in digital is new, how we manage it and secure it is new, a lot of the tooling is new, the team is new, so everything is in flux, and that's part of the challenge. It's actually, when we talk about recruiting people, one of the things we've learned: Attitude and aptitude over technical capability.

When it comes to cybersecurity there are lots of analogies of it being like a war, and in some respects it is, but it's the same as the war against people trying to steal money from the bank or doing anything else they're trying to do.

I guess the challenge there is that the weakest link is the person. Hacks are not done against systems, hacks are done against people. We've proven that with red team testing. Attackers don't typically break in through, through firewalls and WAFs and similar control points they just need to send somebody a convincing email. I just had a phish test sent to me this morning. I can read SMTP so that's quite an advantage, but not many people can. That is the difficult bit.

I would though still take on the job even knowing what we now face. I could have a much more boring job. In my current role I'm working, to a certain extent, continuously. So I'm in charge of a team, I'm in charge of a budget, I'm a people manager, and yes, that's all fine and nice and positive, that's what I wanted to develop. On the other hand - 24/7 - and can you really have what we call work/life balance or nowadays work/life integration? How much do you want to achieve and willing to sacrifice for the goal of keeping the bad guys out?

Yes, there's a price to be paid for being a CISO."

Chapter 3
The Threat Landscape - Then and Now

"As we've come to realize, the idea that security starts and ends with the purchase of a pre-packaged firewall is simply misguided."
- Art Wittmann

Today it's difficult to get a balanced perspective when it comes to cybersecurity, the threat landscape, and the enormity of the problems we face because computer technology now sits at the very core of our society and affects every single thing we do.

Yet things haven't always been this way. In truth, few, even as late as the mid-1990s, could have predicted the direction technology would take us and how extensively it would affect the way we live our lives. Now we tend to use many words interchangeably such as 'computers', the 'Internet' and the 'World Wide Web', but these were once all individual components of a technology which would eventually come together and meet in the middle.

The Threat Landscape - Then

When War Games™ the movie was released back in 1983, our vision for the future of technology only involved those in power utilizing computers as another aspect of weaponry when it came to international warfare. It was a technology that few understood, and that most seemed to believe belonged to the sci-fi genre despite the real-time existence of genuine programs and systems similar to those which the film portrayed.

When it came to the real world, the masses had the majority of their early computer interactions through gaming, although the technology moved very slowly to start. Despite the video game Pong (Atari) being introduced in 1973, at first it was only available in commercial venues such as arcades. Then, even when it did make it into private homes, there were still no personal computers available as we know them today and it came as a single piece of kit. Developments being made in the early years of the video game were few and far between and, right up until 1993, most were still for single players only.

Computer development moved at an even slower pace with the first generation of digital computers by Atanasoff-Berry appearing in 1937 and MS-Dos turning up hot on its heels in 1980 – a mere 43 years later. Shortly after, in 1981, the first personal computer was released by IBM, but the Internet itself – which is simply a set of protocols allowing computers to communicate between each other – didn't really make its first public appearance until 1983 when military and civilian networks were split.

In 1984, Apple introduced the Macintosh, but Windows wasn't released until the following year and, in between times, there were other models of personal computers being unleashed on the world. Most of these were often marketed to companies as technological advancements which would assist with administrative tasks rather than having any meaningful purpose in the home. Back then, the personal computer was a tool designed to improve the efficiency of office environments far outclassing the old manual typewriters and even quickly superseding the new electronic versions and word-processors. In fact, many people today may well remember being sold the concept of the 'paperless office'.[1]

Feeling Your Age?

But the World Wide Web (WWW or the Web) was to be the invention that triggered the big changes, and that only came along in 1991 after being developed by Tim Berners-Lee. Few people were impressed at the time as it was a design which merely allowed a system of web pages or sites to be created, which in turn could use the Internet communication service. Initially, the experiment was both small and slow, and the first servers to be opened upheld only simple web pages describing the project, so it bore little resemblance to the Web we have come to know. Yet, if we try and put a little more perspective on the timeline, what this means is that people reading this book who are 27 or over, are older than the World Wide Web itself.

But the Web wasn't the overnight success you might think it was and it still struggled for another four years, until around the end of 1995 when the number of servers climbed to just over 500. From thereon in, the Web became a runaway success, or maybe worse depending on your perspective, because it took only another nine years, to 2014, for the estimated number of servers to rise to a staggering 75 million.

This sudden escalation was not only astronomical but now meant the Web was likely to be unstoppable. Yet the reason for the leap had little to do with the world of international warfare, recreational video games, or even speeding up office administrative processes. Commerce, as it turned out, was to be the real big player in the World Wide Web and, as soon as companies and investors realized it could play a major role in the advancement of enterprise, it turned into a marketing tool that suddenly everyone wanted to use and from every conceivable angle.

The Dot-Com Bubble

But it wasn't all plain sailing when it came to the wonders of the World Wide Web and especially for investors. Because e-commerce was a new technology and, by definition, few understood it, those with money to play with, and some who did not, were convinced that any company listed on the Web simply could not fail irrespective of whether they had a solid business model or not. As a result, by 1997 the dot-com bubble was in play and share prices were going through the roof.

Although everything originally appeared to be a screaming success and some of the early Internet companies, such as Amazon and eBay, are still around today, over two-thirds disappeared without trace. Thus, by the time 2001 came around the inevitable had happened and it is estimated that around $1.7 trillion was wiped off share prices.[2]

Focus on the Pros

What we can learn from the dot-com bubble and its subsequent burst is not only that greed often tramples common sense into the dirt but also that few truly understood either economics, business models or any of the real disadvantages of the new Internet technology. But this time when it comes to investment, the phrase 'lessons have been learned' might well apply. One thing is certain, no one really examined the cons of using cybertechnology within commerce, preferring instead to focus only on the pros and where competitive advantage might be gained.

Yet the dot-com bubble did not dampen enthusiasm when it came to users and, since that time, the merging technologies of the Internet and the Web have been used to help with everything from advertising services, the flow of cash between businesses, financial users and all things in between. They have been used to assist with research and development, to run production lines whether in manufacture or assembly, are invaluable to store owners who now couldn't purchase from big wholesalers without them and whose customers couldn't purchase in turn. They run our communication facilities, our transportation networks, postal services, utilities, heating facilities, and even corporate air-conditioning systems. In fact, there is precious little in contemporary society which does not rely at some stage upon merged computer technology to provide us with our needs. At the same time, it has ceased to be a tool to ease our existence because simply put, we have given it total control.

From Tool to Torture

Historically, we have a bigger picture not only of how Internet technology developed but a hint at the speed with which it suddenly evolved and took over our world. We can also see how it expanded from being a tool that could provide many businesses with competitive advantage to shifting into the driver's seat at the wheel of our lives.

The problem is, as it was with the dot-com bubble, most people only examine the pros of cybertechnology and, when it comes to commerce in particular, the prosperity it might bring. Right from the start and ever since most have been blind to the potential vulnerabilities it could eventually subject their businesses and potentially their lives to.

Hackers too, at least those with negative intentions, have come a long way from the original individuals or groups of kids who were driven by intense curiosity intent on accessing government systems just to see if they could. The world was starting to face a new breed of hacker because there was money to be made and potentially lots of it. So, from the mid-1990s the world started to see an increase both in the number of hacks to commercial institutions and malicious viruses being developed even if most were just for the fun of it.

In 1986, two Pakistani brothers, Basit Farooq Alvi and Amjad Farooq Alvi, wrote a virus called Brain which was the first to attack MS-DOC. They were initially accused of setting the virus maliciously but managed to survive the event and are still in business today.

Main Motivators
One of the first big, financially motivated hacks on a banking system came as early as 1994 when Vladimir Levin accessed the Citibank system and made off with $10m. Then, in 1996, things took a more sinister turn in realizing the destructive potential of Internet technology.

When Tim Lloyd planted a software time bomb in the computer system of Omega Engineering, a small company working out of New Jersey, the total cost to the company was $12m and job losses totaled 80 people. Yet, Tim Lloyd wasn't a hacker seeking a challenge and neither was he after information or cash. Tim was just an ex-employee, their network administrator, and was holding a grudge against Omega. His motive was pure and simple and as old as man himself – revenge; that's what drove this hacker on rather than anything to do with the mighty dollar.

But Lloyd's actions also revealed a couple of other things to a world that should have been watching a lot more closely. Firstly, he proved that a simple hack had the potential to bring an enterprise to its knees if not drive them out of business altogether. This is something which is happening with alarming frequency today and although Omega Engineering might have ultimately survived, it was also clearly a problem that both the company and the 80 employees who lost their jobs could well have done without. Secondly, what Tim also revealed was that time-bombs could be set up by hackers, meaning that the virus would not become active until it was programmed to do so. In his case, this meant that Lloyd, who had left the company three weeks before the attack, was well out of the picture by the time it happened and so wasn't, at least for a while, considered as a suspect.[3]

Yet Tim Lloyd was only the first of very, very many because what the world also saw from the mid to late 1990s was a consistent increase in the number of virus threats being developed and a corresponding number of people finding themselves on the receiving end of seemingly illogical and unsolicited attacks on their personal computer systems.

In 1998 the CIH virus was released and resulted in many computers being unable to reboot. Then, in 1999, we saw the devastation wrought by the Melissa virus. Come the year 2000 and the new millennium saw the early pioneers in the Web, such as Yahoo, Amazon, eBay and even CNN, stalled by DoS attacks which were the invention of nothing more terrifying than a fourteen-year-old Canadian boy by the name of Michael Demon Calce.[4]

Calce's attacks were really the first shocking indicators of vulnerabilities in a technical system which many had believed could only be of benefit to their business, not least because of his age and his ability to stop the new Internet giants in their tracks. His actions seemed to prove, beyond a shadow of a doubt, that the words uttered by computer expert Winn Schwartau in 1991 were now coming true:

"Government and commercial computer systems are so poorly protected today they can essentially be considered defenseless - an electronic Pearl Harbor waiting to happen."[5]

For commercial cybersecurity officers of the era, however, life was still relatively simple and defenses often consisted of only installing the latest software protection. The CISO role, at this stage in the game, was not one with an individual identity but one more often considered to be an extension of the Information Technology department.

The Technological Boom

Outside of computing, the Internet, and the World Wide Web, microchip technology was also continuing to influence the world in general. Whether the changes came to cars, white goods or even watches, manufacturing was taking advantage of the microchip and using it to provide the market with even more convenience than it already had. Of course, some would argue, and perhaps rightly, that the biggest change of all came with the invention of the cellular mobile phone.

Although radio and analog mobile phones have a long history of development stretching throughout most of the 20th century, hand-held mobile phones for the masses were simply not possible because the technology wasn't available. Yet geographical phone hackers, more commonly referred to as phone phreaks, also existed long before cell phones made an appearance. Just like computer hackers, phone phreaks were often young men who were simply attracted to the complexity of the systems by insatiable curiosity. Although what they did was an inconvenience for most companies, their actions were rarely motivated by criminal intentions or malice. Yet hindsight reveals they were really the computer hackers of the future.

The first cell phone call was made over 45 years ago on April 3rd, 1973 when Martin Cooper, an employee of Motorola, placed a call to the Headquarters of Bell Labs in New Jersey, U.S.A. It wasn't until 1991, however, that digital cellular phones really hit the mass market with the introduction of the second generation (2G) network. Even then it took another five years, to 1996, before the phones themselves evolved from an aesthetics perspective to a more pleasing design. Thereafter, it took further technological advancements to allow the mobile phone to commence its seepage into common use.

Going back to that timeline again, if you're 25 years old now, you're older than the first mass-produced commercially available GSM digital phone. Of course, neither did cell phones have the same functions back then. In fact, their primary purpose was, believe it or not, making telephone calls. You did get a few added extras and most incorporated two or three standard games, a calculator, clock, and calendar. In some cases, if you were willing to splash out, you might even get one with a built-in torch. But in general, most of the differences between models came with either the color or design rather than the plethora of features which we have come to expect today.

Back then, the cell phone was considered a simple tool of convenience rather than something developed out of any critical necessity to communicate. Most homes had landlines anyway and there were also things called telephone boxes which littered the landscape in every country across the globe. Besides which, mobile phones were very expensive not only to buy but also to use.

To give you some idea of how few were around, even in 1996-97 only 15% of households owned a mobile phone in the U.K., compared to 95% in 2016/2017.[6] A figure which, incidentally, is exactly the same as American ownership and both have stayed static since around 2014. Apparently, 5% of people in the U.K. and the U.S., whether through stubbornness or simply feeling they are too old to learn, are steadfast in their refusal to join the technological revolution.

Although text messaging had come along a little earlier, in 2003 the Blackberry 5810 made an appearance and this gadget incorporated both email and a keyboard.[7] Now the mobile phone was moving toward a mass merge with the Internet and Web and it stood on the cusp of changing not only the world of commerce and private communications but also social interaction in general… and it was also to attract yet another breed of criminal and hacker.

2003 is only 15 years ago and now perhaps it is starting to become clear why, when we question the lack of cybersecurity qualifications and experience, we find that the answer is simple; the Internet and cybersecurity, most certainly in its current form, is a very, very, recent development. Even where we do find information relating to historical hacking the presumption, back then at least, was that installing software could prevent a company from being hacked in the same way it was believed it could prevent personal computers from being hacked or infected. The only problem was, it couldn't.

The Hackers Emerge

By the early 2000s, technology was becoming a runaway horse although precious few truly understood the developments or the full implications. What happened was company executives could only see the advantages to their business and those interested in the technology itself were simply animated by what it could achieve and also with what would come next.

Hackers, however, had always been curious about technology in general and then, as now, they did not have the same distractions as executives worried about the everyday running of a business or what the market might do next. Neither were they like the cybersecurity officers who, although job-focused, still had to deal with organizational procedures, budgets, etiquette, hierarchies, and generally making sure they kept their jobs by saying the right thing in the right way out of fear they might displease those in power.

The hackers were different because they could focus on one thing and one thing only – getting through the cyber-barriers. They were insatiably curious as to how these systems worked, what the flaws were and ultimately, where a criminal mindset co-existed with the technical and creative drive, extremely interested in how money could be made.

Often, as the earlier case with Michael Calce exemplified and later Jake Davis was to reinforce, the real experts turned out to be little more than kids as opposed to professional criminals. Although it has to be said that these particular kids had a lot of curiosity for puzzle solving and been left alone with the computer for far too long, but they also lacked precious few life skills to indicate they might be being less than sensible. Yet, no matter what their goals, one thing was for certain, the hackers were always one step ahead of those inside the arena and likely because they were not limited by the confines of it.

Now, though, everything was going in their favor because the world of commerce had also changed at a base level. No longer was the focus on production and manufacturing but, with the decline of industry, it had switched to something called 'the service sector'. The companies which had once invested in factories and physical manpower were now businesses which provided peripheral services to the ever-decreasing numbers of companies who made the tangible products. Where once the majority of people got up to go to work in a factory or do other forms of manual labor, now they went off to do white collar jobs in shops and offices where technology was quickly going to become an integral part.

Where manufacturing jobs did still exist, some of the biggest companies involved only creating the products which kept the technological revolution evolving. Yet in the end, no matter where you worked, technology was going to sit at the core of the business function. The high-tech revolution also brought advances in respect of administration equipment, whether in the office or home, and it too was being touched by the Internet. Where once we had separate printers, fax machines, telephones, and computers, now they were all being connected to the Internet. Convenient it might have been, but once the Internet became involved in other tools of the trade, this also offered the hackers yet another way in.

Our Social World

Although the first social networking site, Six Degrees, came to life in 1997 and existed until 2001, with Friends ReUnited emerging in 2000 and MySpace following hard on its heels, it was the introduction of Facebook, or rather back then, 'The Facebook' as it was known, in 2004 which thrust social media into the spotlight. Suddenly 'connecting with others' was being sold to people as something they needed to do and the sales tactic was not limited to individuals. Companies too, who did not have a 'social media presence' were made to feel they were likely to lose out if they did not at least make a regular appearance and keep up with competitors. Yet, as it turned out, the social media necessity was all but a ploy, the real money was to be made from the data that could be gathered when people were kind enough to place all their personal or business dealings out there for everyone to see.

A Hacker's Paradise!

Originally, computer criminality had been limited to the invasion of government-based systems and, even after the introduction of the World Wide Web, hackers might have been somewhat slow to see the potential, or maybe there were simply not enough sites to pique their interest. Yet the fault is ours because even the early hacks should have given us some insight into the shape of things to come.

Already attacks had taken place which were instigated by disgruntled employees. Malicious viruses had been introduced to both large corporations and individual users by those with simple destructive tendencies that we might see anywhere in the physical world from smashed bus shelters through to graffiti. Banks had started to see user accounts targeted and thefts taking place and the potential of data theft, whether personal or corporate, although somewhat limited, had already been experienced. All of this was on top of the geopolitical hacking between nations which had been going on for decades. By the middle of the 2000s, the writing was already on the wall; nothing was safe and nothing, it appears, would be again.

The Gold Rush

By this time, those with negative intentions, whatever they happened to be, could see the Internet as being an untapped gold mine and their vision as to how it could be used to their best advantage was perhaps much more far-reaching than that of the masses. What most in society did not realize was the diverse nature and potential of the threats and the impact they could make not only on individual lives but also on individual enterprises. All anyone could see were the benefits and the up-side with the disadvantages, for the most part, remaining unexamined in any great detail.

But now the nature of cybersecurity in industry was also changing. Where originally basic hacking and virus infiltration had been the problem, as the targets changed the nature of security also needed to change. No longer was it simply a matter of making sure virus protection software was installed because the dangers could come from those trying to infiltrate the physical organization in an effort to locate weaknesses in the cyber-world of a company. Now employees became the issue, and not because they were hacking the systems but because they were simply not security conscious. Then, as it turned out, or more likely as the hackers predicted, there were far more vulnerabilities in the physical human system than would ever be found in the technology.

This picture has never improved, in fact, in many cases it has worsened, allowing hackers to play on social engineering techniques and likely better than ever by exploiting employee vulnerability in various ways. To the hacker's delight, what they discovered was the human element might be all too willing to provide information to strangers or to ignore procedures and let unauthorized staff into buildings or even share passwords when asked. They would click on links sent to them or maybe take work home and allow access to corporate files through an unprotected network. They would still use the same passwords for multiple sites or, even when it came to developers, they would send out software with a pre-released standard password.

Developers too could not resist the urge, when they had designed systems, to leave a 'trap door' or 'backdoor' in a program so that they, and only they, would have open access should they require it. Yet hackers did know, they knew only too well, and at each and every step of the game they were ahead when it came to their understanding of the human psyche. This knowledge they utilized to their full advantage to get access to information which would ultimately allow them to achieve their goal – infiltration of the corporate system. The weak spot in all cybersystems remains now as it did then – the employee.

But the goals of the hacker were also shifting. Where once money had been the direct target, at least for those with specific criminal intentions, whether credit card details or bank accounts, now it was the personal information itself which held the value either as direct information for sale or, as criminals later came to learn, simply by being locked down and held to ransom. And hadn't those social media sites shown the way, told them that not only could data could be monetized but that people were actually willing to give it to them for free?

In many cases, organizations were perpetrators of their own problems by making it their business to collect this data and trade it in whatever way they could. Although the Facebook drama is an exemplary example of this particular problem and, despite the fact it wasn't officially considered to be a hack, at its most base level it reveals how data is being misappropriated without the owner of it being provided with specific details regarding exactly what, to who, and for how much.

Clearly, where any company collects data it has a value and it must be a given that unscrupulous actors will attempt to access or take control of that information at some point in time. Yet this problem isn't limited to authorities such as healthcare services which collect data out of necessity. Neither is it limited to social media companies such as Facebook who form most of their business model around the monetization of the information. The truth of the matter is that most companies and websites today are involved in collecting information about you at some level. News websites are able to track your movements across the Internet and collect information. Free forums are likely involved in gathering who you are, what you do, what you say, and even who your friends are. If you've bought from a company, either in the form of a product or service via the Internet or even in the physical world where some form of ID or technological interaction was required, your movements can still be tracked whether you have provided them with your email address or not.

But the data providers are not the only potential victims because every time a company allows access to, collects, buys, sells, or rents data, it widens its own threat landscape. Collecting data is the virtual equivalent of sticking a target on your back. Is it any wonder that data brokers such as Equifax are major prey for the hackers and should, even at the most basic level of responsibility, show the highest deference for cybersecurity?

Now we can begin to see that the organizational CISO not only has to deal with cybersecurity and employee security but also the actions of those who are third parties in the data business – the traders. And, as the situation with Facebook clearly evidences, the ethical actions of their trading partners can never be guaranteed.

Although most people might accept the simplest of explanations offered them, that data collection is about advertising, the Facebook saga should come as fair warning that this is only the superficial excuse provided. Most professionals would have held Alexander Nix, the former CEO of Cambridge Analytica, in the highest regard prior to the unearthing of his unethical activities with the data of millions of Facebook users, and advertising, at least as we recognize it, was not part of the equation.

Transparency it would seem should play a major role in the prevention of such problems, at least by making customers fully aware of who is dealing in what and with who. Because if companies are willing to trade our data then they should at least be prepared to tell us who with. Yet, as the case with Mr Stamos goes to show, transparency is not something that many companies are willing to participate in despite the expectation that their users be as transparent as possible. Data collection, whether we have come to fully recognize it yet or not, really means when it comes to the individual threat landscape most companies are holding a tiger by the tail.

Here we can see that ethics form a significant part of the CISO role and indeed part of the Human Resource aspect of any organization when it comes to assessing risk. Because, although we often assume that companies are acting ethically, this may not be the case. Many are, in fact, only being legally compliant which is a different beast entirely. Acting ethically means considering the potential impact of organizational activity outside of the current legal requirements and, as the Facebook drama clearly revealed, it will often be ethical, or rather unethical practices, which drive legislation to change. For now, though, all such practices mean is the hacker has a lot to be attracted to and to practically every single company in existence.

The Threat Landscape - Now

In general, what we face today by way of viruses and worms is little different to what we faced historically. Then though, as now, most thought they could be prevented simply by installing software and the message that this has never been possible still hasn't got through. That aside, although threats have become more sophisticated and the vectors and landscape have broadened, the basics of malware are pretty much the same as they always were:

Viruses are malicious code which attach to programs, replicates, and then infects other computers.

Worms are also malicious code which can replicate but they do not need a program to attach to because they seek out vulnerabilities in a system.

Ransomware is also malicious code but is certainly a more recent and inspired development. Access is prevented because data or systems are locked and they're not removed until a ransom fee is paid. Ransomware could be used to lock any data or to prevent any system from functioning, but in general, its development has grown on the back of the value and significance of personal information. This could easily spread to the locking of access to critical commercial intellectual property (IP) or company secrets such as formulas, algorithms, and safety information and, of course, shutting down of critical processes or production facilities until demands to remove the locks have been met.

Spyware and **Adware** monitor computer activity relying on users opening attachments and these devices have also become more sophisticated over time. However, both depend on the susceptibility of the targeted human element who have not, unfortunately, become more sophisticated.

Trojans are malware which enter the computer disguised as a legitimate and safe software, but which then releases other malware when they have gained access. Trojans use several vectors or methods of access to gain entry:

Social Engineering: Again, this requires the user to interact with the malware either by reacting to:

1. *Phishing:* Where the target of the attack is usually approached by email from an apparently legitimate source and encouraged to provide sensitive data directly or lured to a fake website which enables the bad actors to gain accesses to sources such as bank records.
2. *Pharming:* This relies on similar fake websites but does not rely on an individual responding to an email to take

them there. Instead, viruses or a Trojan are installed on the computer which redirect the system to the intended site or sites. A second option is for a DNS to be installed on the target's computer and then they are redirected to the site where either information is collected or a Trojan is installed.

3. *Drive-by Trojans* are picked up when the user simply visits an infected website which is either fake or a legitimate website which has been infected and requires no prompting by either phishing emails or DNS infection.

4. *Man-in-the-Middle* (MITM): This approach involves intercepting and perhaps altering the communications between two people. Although they may think they are communicating with each other they are actually communicating with a third party, the 'Man in the Middle,' who has infiltrated their system. This way, extremely sensitive data can be collected and often from top-ranking officials. When it comes to theft using MITM techniques, our chapter with Bennett Arron provides a beautiful and recent example. It is still, though, a form of social engineering.

Bots have been around for a long time and for the most part they serve a legitimate purpose on the web. They are designed to do repetitive tasks as a web crawler and act in an indexer capacity. For example, search engines are bots, as are Alexa and Siri, which are digital assistants. Shopping carts also use bots and you'll find them popping up and making recommendations as you make your online purchases.

However, bots can also be a form of Trojan and become malicious bots otherwise known as botnets. They might be used to collect information and then send out spam emails or they can be used to perform Distributed Denial of Service (DDoS) attacks for web scraping or to harvest email contacts.

Originally, malware (malicious software) originated long before the advent of the Web. The very first computer virus, the Elk Cloner, appeared in 1982, and, surprise, surprise, it was the brainchild of a boy. Rich Skrenta decided it would be fun to play a joke on his friends and he infected floppy discs which were supposed to load a game. When used, instead of a game, the screen of the computer turned blank before revealing a poem. This can hardly be considered the crime of the century, but who would have thought where it would lead.

As the 80s progressed, so too did the development of viruses, with Brain appearing in 1986, Jerusalem, Lehigh and Stoned in 1987. The now notorious Morris Worm didn't show up until 1988, but it became important for several reasons, not least because it was one of the first viruses to be spread not by individual floppy discs but via the Internet. Viruses, it would seem, had the potential to infect entire networks and the advent of the Morris worm meant that malware infiltration shifted from being a micro problem to one of the macro variety.[8]

Although malware was essentially designed to disrupt and even destroy, after the advent of the Web viruses were developed which were specifically designed to gain unauthorized access to computer systems and this began to escalate after 2007. More recently we have also seen the growth of impersonation attacks where email systems are infiltrated by messages from apparently trusted sources. These often invite the target to inadvertently provide confidential data or transfer funds to malicious sources. These Business Email Compromise (BEC) attacks are also often known as CEO Fraud because of the tendency to target those in an organization who would act on the instruction of a high-level executive without question. The average loss for an organization arising from a BEC attack is around £35,000 although the largest reported theft currently stands at £18 million.[9] Again, what this goes to prove is the employee is often the weakest link in the cybersecurity chain and so they remain a consistent physical entry point for the hacker to gain access to technological systems.

As technology advanced, so did the opportunities for hackers to gain entry. Androids were added to the hacker entry point list, as too were simple devices such as printers. Wherever technology expanded to embrace not only convenience or benefits but also the Internet, the opportunities for hackers to gain entry increased accordingly.

The CISO's job was now becoming untenable in its original concept. It no longer demanded simple technological expertise to barricade against incoming attacks, but on a psychological level it required officers to assess each and every link in an ever-growing chain of technology and vectors in an attempt to establish where the next risk might arise. This, in a world which was not only arming itself with myriad devices but which was also stockpiling the data hackers were after, began to make for a mission impossible.

Who, for example, would have considered that the next move the hackers might make would not be to steal from systems or even to destroy them but to actually use specific malware to hold organizations to ransom by keeping the data hostage? Yet the effects of ransomware have, just like physical hostage situations, been effective because the principles are still the same. Firstly, organizations are not guaranteed to get the data released even if the ransom is paid. And, even when paid and released, the very act of conceding to a hacker's demands means that your organization has been marked as a potential future target.

Target lists are an attractive proposition in the hacker world. Knowing you are a 'payer' is manna from heaven making you a qualified prospect for further exploitation. Unlike the physical hostage situation though, one of the biggest threats lies in the potential to publicly shame the target organization with the knowledge that their system is vulnerable, which brings us back around to the secrecy issue and the relevance of reputation.

Often, when we look at the threat landscape, our main focus, and likely distraction, lies in the technology. After all, it is a technological attack and it would seem logical to examine our technological weaknesses. Yet hackers do not limit themselves to understanding the technology. For them, the devices they use are simply tools manufactured after they have identified where the real weaknesses, and potential profits, exist.

On the other hand, our organizations are often structured to be both deferential and defensive but rarely in respect of cybersecurity. The organizational structure is the antithesis of the hacker mentality. It is rigid, confined, compliant, and reputation-focused. It is rarely openly transparent. Communication structures are all too frequently slow, work from the top down, and by default demand a 'can do' perspective as opposed to the skeptical, or perhaps critical and challenging posture which must be adopted by the CISO.

Where hackers see spending as an investment, organizational budgets are more likely to be directed toward marketing than cybersecurity which is often seen as a cost rather than insurance. Boards like to be presented with solutions to problems and evidence of how money can be made and are not predisposed to hearing that the app they have just invested in, which is designed to improve organizational functionality and ultimately profits, has the potential to indirectly bring their organization to its knees. What they don't want to hear, for sure, is that technology is simply not designed with security in mind and that often problems only come to light after it has been incorporated into service.

As time has progressed, what we have seen is an increase in devices and techniques being designed to access cybersystems and a corresponding increase in successful hacks and breaches. The losses are growing incrementally too but, as yet, they are not enough as a percentage of GDP to make many authorities officially sit up and take notice. Yet the capacity for devastation from many angles is most certainly clear and, the more commerce embraces new technology, the greater the threat becomes.

As we open our arms and welcome in the advent of further advances such as Artificial Intelligence (A.I.) and machine learning (M.L.) we cannot hope to find things get better anytime soon. But the warnings to look at the cons just as closely as we look at the pros are already being voiced by those with the capacity to examine things objectively. For now, though, they are often being drowned out by those who are blinded by their admiration for cybertechnology or those hoping to make money from it. Which, unfortunately, is highly reflective of the dot-com bubble we saw at the advent of the World Wide Web.

The Industry Perspective
Ernie Hayden - VP IOTSA
(Critical Infrastructures)

Ernie Hayden can only be described as a legend in the world of Operational Technology (OT) Security; a much sought-after adviser, speaker, and trainer. When it comes to understanding cybersecurity risk to critical infrastructures, industrial control systems (ICS), and the supporting infrastructures he is at the top of the list for many organizations as the go-to person. In his capacity as Vice President of Education for the International Operational Technology Security Association (IOTSA), I asked Ernie if he feels that the threats in cyberspace are well understood and if industry is on top of the risk.

Ernie Hayden, CICSP (Gold), CISSP, CEH, PSP:
"The vernacular I would use is 'people don't get it.' Even in the CISO suite there is too much focus on privacy and data. I was recently at a meeting and there were some people there from a winery and another guy from a gas utility and they were really worried about the I.T. protection. Yet when I started asking questions like, what are you doing about your industrial controls? The response was either,
a) It's the same thing we do for I.T.
Which I know right away is a problem, or,
b) Waddaya mean?

These are very classic answers. If I get to a point where somebody says, "Well, tell me more. What do you think?" Then I would start asking questions about how they are segregated and make sure that they're updated. Stuff on the O.T. side can be old and probably not only out of date, but likely can't be updated. For example, I've been in factories where there is an active Windows 2000 machine on the floor and the only reason I found out was because it kept on getting infected with Conficker. So, the message is that the whole world runs on O.T. The real factories, the dairies, the trains, everything. So we need to get a better emphasis and perspective and to realize that,

a) there is a difference,

and,

b) you still have to pay attention on the O.T. side and maybe even catch up to where you are on the I.T. side.

Using Emerson as an example, I'll show you what often happens. They had this big focus on I.o.T. and essentially getting sensors into the plants and bragging about how they were upgrading a refinery in Eastern Europe. They were going from essentially 70 sensors to run the whole plant to 700 sensors, and there was to be no hard-wire, just wirelessly connected. I thought it was crazy. I used to run power plants for a living. If I was in the control room and had 700 alarms coming in because someone turned off the Wifi, that's not going to do me any good. From an engineering perspective you get better data because you can figure out temperatures and pressures and look at flows and optimization, but it doesn't belong in the control room because it is too much and it also increases the profile for denial of services attacks or injects. Someone could figure out a way to get into a system by doing a hack on one of the end devices.

What you've done is widen your threat profile 10 times. Management, though, sees this as sexy because they've been sold the bill of goods about making the plant more efficient. But it should be a case of "What have I done to my security posture?" CISOs understand this, but most executives, even engineering executives don't.

A lot of the people doing the plant work are getting ready to retire. Generally, they're not really interested in the new gadgets, hand-held devices and all that. So, I think there's an opportunity here to do training and orientation for the younger up-and-coming engineers. The problem is, if you try and talk to a manufacturing engineer student they're interested in games, working in the software industry, Cloud, and I.T. stuff. It's very hard to find manufacturing engineers trained and oriented in O.T. security. For instance, I was at a manufacturing plant about 6 months ago and had a meeting with 7 or 8 young manufacturing engineers about 30 years old. I drew a sketch of the Purdue Model and they'd never heard of it. So, there's an opportunity to do training and get people up to speed.

Although the industry has improved substantially, often the enemy knows what the game book says. "Here's what the architecture will look like." So, they could take care of that approach. Then you get a combined utility like electric and gas, or electric and water, and the water side or the gas side doesn't have the same form of security as the electric side since it generally needs to comply with the U.S. NERC CIP standards.

If you look at Ukraine they got through the attacks by sending trucks, technicians and field staff to the different substations. But on the other hand, think about the senior operator in the control room. The guy was probably some crusty old bastard like me, 65 years old, knows the grid from the seat of his pants and remembers every idiosyncrasy. The kind that could say, "Okay, I want you to go over to substation whatever, get in there and close the third circuit breaker from the left." Now, that guy's going to retire and take that innate knowledge, of how to restore the system when automated systems fail, with him.

In Southern California, a huge utility, 61,000 square miles of property and zillions of substations and I don't know how many lines of distribution, went through a huge lay-off and downsizing, offering early retirement. Now the average seniority or level of experience in the grid control rooms is about five years. If I were a *bad guy, I know who I'm going to target. But I'll target the slow nasty stuff, do an inject similar to the Ukraine or phishing attacks.*

There was a physical attack on a substation in the States -- Metcalf -- where guys went into a communications vault and cut a bunch of phone lines. Then they shot the transformers resulting in draining of the oil housing. This meant they had created an environmental problem and closed the transformers which were overheating. It took a long time to replace those transformers because of the damage. Although it was moderately sophisticated attack, the grid was never impacted because, when the operators saw there were hiccups, they just did some switching and essentially bypassed the substation. So, there is a resilience. But that was an attack on only one sub. What if ten 500kv substations had been attacked with a kinetic or cyber-attack simultaneously? That might cause a bit of a problem and it would also psychologically scare people. But an attack like that would have to be very coordinated.

All these Wifi routers add more opportunities for the attackers and that's through the I.o.T. environment. What happens if they find something that turns off the water to a city? What about petrol, food, if you could somehow attack that then it's getting pretty serious.

Today it is essentially a broke/fix mentality. Where a device is broken it just needs fixing. In a lot of cases with electronics now it's just monitor. You just take out the other box and you shove it into the rack and no one's paying attention to cause, let alone the root cause. So that's where it would be good to take the younger engineers and train them in more critical thinking. We know the PLC broke, but don't just pull it off the rack and hide it, do some analysis to figure out what it is. Schweitzer does that pretty well. When you have a failed relay or electronics device, they literally mail you a new one in a day, so you have one to put onto the rack. But they – Schweitzer - do an analysis on the old part to figure out why it failed so they can improve designs. But that's time and expense. I can send my black box (or really "blue" box) back to Schweitzer and then a year later they send me a letter that says, "We think you've been hacked."

There is also the concept that I call a wartime reserve, which means a nation-state could hide some potential injects in different systems - whether done through supply chain, or drive-by's or whatever - and there is no obvious impact initially. But somewhere in the bowels of the code is a little tiny switch. So, when the nation-state is deciding which country to invade they flip that switch and then, all of a sudden, smart meters in Washington DC, don't work anymore."

Chapter 4
Interview with a Hacker: A View From the Darkside

"Always the wrong person gives you the right lesson in life."
-   William Shakespeare

'Mak' is the pseudonym of a hacker who kindly gave us anonymous insight into the world of illicit database trading specifically to be used as content in this book. The interview was conducted remotely over Skype, and Mak insisted he use a device to disguise his real voice. While he was happy to have his story told, he was equally concerned about not being identified.

ML: Hi. Is it okay if I call you Mak?
Mak: Yes, sure.

ML: So, I don't know who you really are or where you come from or even which country you are located in, and I don't need to know. Please do not tell me anything that would identify you or give information that you are not comfortable telling me. I'm really just interested in what and why you trade databases. Is that all okay?
Mak: Yes. Okay.

ML: Can you give me a little background on what attracted you to becoming a hacker?
Mak: As a child I was just checking out YouTube and other Internet sites and I came across a few groups such as the Lizard Squad.* Other people had started to do a few hacks and there was quite a lot of drama going on. To be honest, I thought it was cool with all the power they had over the computers and how someone can fuck with people and stuff like that. I really just thought it was funny. So, I tried to understand how it all worked and when I did I came across the databases with tons of information. I was just sat looking at my computer and seeing all these passwords and I started to feel that I had control over people just by having these documents on my computer. After that well, then I started to collect all these databases and other information and trying to learn how to hack and all about the social engineering side of things. Only after a couple of months, I had tons of info and I didn't really know what to do with it because, by that time, there was nothing more to collect. So, what I decided to do was to join a couple of big forums for database trading. You may have heard of them, Dumpbase.ga and CriminalCat?

ML: Were these sites openly available sites or on the dark web?

Mak: They were public sites, not hidden, because at the time I didn't so much care about the risks. In fact I didn't even know the risks of database trading. But the sites were popular anyway and lots of people joined.

ML: Can you explain what you mean by database trading?
Mak: Well, I know it's a bad thing, but databases just store information about other people on computers. To me, at the time, it all seemed like pretty stupid stuff. General information, maybe private things like stupid letters.

ML: So, it's collecting people's private information for sale?
Mak: Yeah, exactly.

ML: And it's a form of Doxing, where you search the web for information about another person and then use what exposed documents you find to further your quest?

Mak: Yes. The database information I first capture means that I can do more doxing and even better, more targeted, social engineering. What the data does is help me perform even better when it comes to hacking. I have more supportive intelligence to work with.

ML: So it's kind of surveillance and intelligence gathering to craft a social engineering attack. Is that right?
Mak: Yes. And the more you have the better you become at it.

ML: How long have you been doing this?

Mak: I've been doing it for around three or four years, but I got sick last summer so I haven't been doing it for a few months now.

ML: How old were you when you started?
Mak: I don't really want to comment on that.

ML: Are you older or younger than 20?
Mak: I'm younger.

ML: Is it your experience that most hackers are younger people?
Mak: Yeah. Most of the people are quite secretive and they don't really want to talk about this. So it's mostly shadding so I don't really know for sure.

ML: So, even within your community you don't really know each other that well, is that the way it is?
Mak: Yes.

ML: It's a closed community, right?
Mak: Yes.

ML: What kind of hacker would you say you are?
Mak: I don't know really because I wouldn't actually say I am a hacker. I don't see myself that way. From my perspective it's only gathering information about other people and then, well, it all depends on how you use it. But I don't like to call myself a hacker. The word these days ... well ... I don't like it from all the movies and stuff like that.

ML: You don't prescribe to the concept of Black Hats and White Hats? It's a movie term in your view?

Mak: Yes. Yes, exactly. So I gather information and then use it. People call me a hacker, but I wouldn't call myself a hacker.

ML: So if you are not a hacker what are you ... a service provider?
Mak: I'm just a normal guy. I'm trying to gather information and look through it, just shadding ... I don't know what I'd call myself.

ML: But that information you are gathering is not publicly available. It's not information posted on Facebook, Twitter, LinkedIn, or the like. It's private information that you are obtaining by gaining access to closed databases?
Mak: Yes. That's right

ML: But, if it's hacking private databases, that's illegal?
Mak: Yes. Some people collect databases by themselves and some people do the trading parts. I mostly do the trading because one of my friends got me into all the databases and he had a private one - I played Grand Theft Auto at the time - and there was a kind of big, private database and I really wanted it but it was private so he gave it to me. And with that database I traded my myself up. You know, I got more and more private ones.

ML: Okay. To be clear. What you will do next is sell that database online for a sum of money, for a profit, right?
Mak: Yes. Sometimes. But it doesn't happen all the time.

ML: Why do you do this then if, as you say, it's not always for money?

Mak: It's just because I can. And sometimes it's helpful to research the databases and you can use it for good or bad.

ML: And so would you take an order. For example, if someone wanted a database with private data of all the executives from a certain company who are signed up to one of the social media sites, would you attempt to get that?
Mak: If I had it. If I have a database already. But if somebody wants something I won't go and try to hack it or get it.

ML: It's like having a shop, you only sell what's already available in the store?
Mak: Yes, that's right.

ML: What type of people are buying these databases from you?
Mak: People come to us to find if their database is hacked and they want to get it back. Other people as well, Russians mainly, those who launch big attacks using some kind of program. Then they use all this email and password information trying to get accounts and then they sell them. We use the information from one database to try and access the Spotify login page, Instagram, Netflix, PayPal, and bigger databases to see what we can access and sell for even more money.

ML: So it's compromised accounts with passwords and usernames, that's what you are after and what you sell?
Mak: Yes.

ML: And they are using the information you provide to perform exploits against PayPal and the like?

Mak: Yes. Spotify, Netflix, accounts like that.

ML: Is it mainly for money that they find ways to compromise these accounts?
Mak: Yes, and also some people also just give them away. Just for fun.

ML: They just give databases away?
Mak: Yeah.

ML: You mention Russians, which makes sense because those guys are hot on the financial side and trying to make money out of this, are there any particular groups that you are aware of?
Mak: It's random. People just contact me and they are mainly Russian. They are leechers or spammers who come to the forums and they are mostly Russians because, to get access to a certain forum you need hundreds of posts, so they just spam the posts until they get in there.

ML: So they are spamming their way in to hit a level that allows them to get on to the hacker sites. You've got to build a level of credibility and trust to get in there? You have to prove you are a hacker not a cop?
Mak: Yes. That's right.

ML: If I wanted to buy one of your databases how much would I need to pay?
Mak: It depends, because sometimes I just need fast money. I just want to go out and do something with my friends. If I do I might just sell out a database for something for like $30.00

ML: Can you give me an example of what you have sold for $30?

Mak: Oh yeah, I have one right now. It's a gym membership database with around 42,000 members, full of private information and stuff like that. What you get with that is all the information they give out when they started to go to the gym. You get phone numbers, everything, all the information you give when you sign up to a gym.

ML: So you hacked the gym's private database?

Mak: Yes, that's right.

ML: And it's all stuff that would be useful for social engineering attacks?

Mak: Yeah, right.

ML: How hard is it to hack a database?

Mak: How I do it?

ML: No. How easy is it to compromise a private database?

Mak: Well, it depends on what you are trying to hack. That's a hard question, so I can't really answer that.

ML: If we take the example of the gym member database you mentioned, was that quick to compromise and attack?

Mak: Yeah. Pretty fast. It was actually on a forum that I first saw it mentioned. People were talking about this gym and I was like, shading it out. I just saw there was the chance for a blind SQL (structured query language) injection and I went for it.

ML: Is that typically how you would find an exposure? Are you also password cracking – how hard is it to do?

Mak: Oh, I can't answer that because it depends. Different situations mean different attacks. It all depends. It's a hard question.

ML: What's the most challenging hack or the one you are most proud of to date?
Mak: That would be a forum called the ********** (removed for privacy reasons), that was a really big one. The forum itself is very big, you can check it out for yourself. It's difficult though because it's full of the type of people who want to do physical harm to others.

ML: That sounds like pretty nasty stuff!
Mak: Yeah. And so we took all the members and played with them. Then we doxed the owner, the moderator, and the other members of staff.

ML: So, you found a really antisocial, putting it lightly, website. It was promoting nasty stuff and you publicly exposed the member's and owner's details? So, at least in your view, you used your skills here for good in this case to bring a bad site down?

Mak: Yeah, kind of. I shared all the data and doxed them. It's for good, but at the same time it's bad for them, of course. The owners and members. If I was in their situation I wouldn't want all my shit on the net, you know.

ML: What was the result of this, is the site now down or are they still doing it?
Mak: Yes, they are still doing it. It's still open. But it was good. I guess the site owner got pretty scared and the members got pretty scared too, but I don't think all the

members know about it. But yes, their data is out, and we took the owner's Skype, too.

ML: If you exposed the information on these people and this site you would expect law enforcement and the Feds to pick this up and deal with it right?

Mak: Er, yes. You know when you are in the hacking and doing these things you always have competitors, and we were in the group called Criminal Cat. And this forum, it was getting kind of big and we were doing all this stuff and then the domain got suspended. I asked why and they said they'd been contacted by the police. But, if they were, then we would have been caught, so it was probably just a social engineering attack against the domain holder by a rival hacker.

ML: I don't know who you are or which country you come from, on that point however, how concerned are you about being caught?

Mak: I think the possibility is high because we have done big hacks, you know. We did a the rock 'n' roll band. Well, we hacked their official forum. That was a pretty big one. I'm not scared because I have been doing this for a long time. It's just like a routine, normal for me now. At first I was scared about all the hacks, but now I get relaxed.

ML: For you then it's just part of your normal day now. Is this a full-time occupation for you, do you make a living from this?

Mak: I would say it's more like a hobby because I don't make enough money off this to actually live. The money I get, I just go shopping, buying new clothes or eating, stuff like that. So it's just more money.

ML: Do you work on your own or as a team?
Mak: Erm … it depends, but all the big hacks have been with the team.

ML: What's your aspiration, if you could hack any database where would you go?
Mak: I mean, of course, it would be something really big, but it's hard to say. The biggest would be Google, but I haven't really thought about it because I don't generally think like that.

ML: Tell me a bit about how you do think? I'm interested in understanding the reasons why you do hack databases like the gym member database which is just ordinary everyday people, right?
Mak: Yep.

ML: Do you go after celebs or VIPS, for example?
Mak: No.

ML: Just normal people?
Mak: Yep.

ML: So how do you think, and indeed feel, when you hack a database with the information of ordinary people and that gets sold to someone else who might use that private information to do harm to that person or those people. Does that bother you in any way?
Mak: No. No. My job is to get the database, put it online on the forum, get the team to download it and then we get something to happen. It's the Internet, you know. I can't see you, you can't see me, and it's different. It's like, as we say, a

kind of war or gangsters. If you say, "It's real life," I would feel bad for you if I do something bad to you. But it's not.

ML: To confirm, you see it as remote, distant, and completely anonymous?
Mak: Yes, exactly. So I don't have any feelings about it. Well, I do feel bad if I really know what's going on, but I don't know when I'm just shadding the database. What others do with the information, well, it can be anything.

ML: Do you use hacker tools such as Kali Linux, Burp Suite, Parrot Security OS?
Mak: No. I mean I wouldn't because I don't need to use those tools for what I do. I do database stuff and for that you don't really need those types of things. For example, to do doxing, you don't really need any of those, you just need to know how to use Google and search engines.

ML: So, it's more straightforward, right?
Mak: Yeah.

ML: To learn how to do what you do and to get the right skills, how quickly can someone learn what's needed?
Mak: If you're really interested then it is easy to learn quickly. But there is basic stuff and you have to learn by your mistakes. I mean, I've made tons of mistakes, but that's how you learn.

ML: If you were mentoring a young hacker that was inspired to follow in your footsteps, what advice would you have to get them started?
Mak: To get on a forum. Get to know some people. It's hard because everyone is striving to get to private databases and

that makes it difficult to do on your own so you need friends. Go get some friends, people who do the same thing. Get into the shadding, get into the community, just speak to them and get together a small collection. Then you can do some trading and try to dox someone off the data you have. See how much information you can gather about them and, depending on what you do, apply different skills and tools for different things. So on the forum we had not so many hardcore hackers because maybe they do different stuff. They may be using some forum or another, but they aren't like really active on the hack forums and places like that. But we are really good at the database and the information gathering. Which is a whole other thing.

ML: I fully understand, there are different skills deployed at different parts in the cyber-kill or exploit chain. In essence you operate at the front end, intelligence gathering, which is required further along the chain to execute an exploit. Have you been tempted to use the data or information you gather to conduct your own exploits?
Mak: Well, yes. When I do some hacking I use the data I already have to get to the stuff I want, of course.

ML: So, if I understand correctly, to get you deeper and to drill down to get more useful information, you use the data you collect to get you more of what you want?
Mak: Oh, yes.

ML: Okay, on that, another mindset question – how far would you go with that? If you identified a high net-worth individual with a lot of money or high-profile person and you felt you could get away with it, how far would you push it?

Mak: I think you can push it pretty far.

ML: You are saying that if the prize was big enough you would push it pretty far?
Mak: Yes. But it's not so much about the money, it's about the attention. That's why I looked up so much to, and admired, the Lizard Squad and people like that.

ML: So it's not so much about the money, but the kudos?
Mak: Yes. That's why if you've ever been with black hats and stuff like that, it's good. On our forum people were posting like real booties with our website name and our administrators' names and their friend's names and stuff like that. So, it's like being famous. Like being a superstar.

ML: It's all about being a famous community 'rock star'? You would like to be famous maybe as the guy who hacked one of the big social media sites as that brings a lot of fame within the hacker community?
Mak: Yes. Like everyone knows you and you are on this big forum and there is an organized team on it and, well, you are making fucking big hacks.

ML: It's a buzz, right?
Mak: Yeah!

ML: What advice would you give to a company owner or director of a company that is trying to secure and protect their data from guys like you? If you were speaking to the gym owner for example, what would you advise? How concerned should they be about you guys?
Mak: Be really careful! If they have live chats and stuff like that, the hacker can try to get tons of information about their

staff and, when you have their staff information, you can use it for exploitation. For example, in a chat they should use fake names and aliases. Also, use mostly fake information and no common passwords, nothing like normal words and not normal email addresses either. They should use a custom email. I have a custom email for almost everything I use.

ML: They should use alias emails?
Mak: Right. And they shouldn't store more information than they really need because it's better for the hacker.

ML: We have this new regulation called GDPR. Have you heard about this?
Mak: The new European Union Data Protection, yes.

ML: This means big implications if you hack their data. They have to disclose to the authorities in 72 hours and big fines involved – many companies don't even know they have been hacked – what's your view on this?
Mak: Well, I would say it's up to them actually. They should have at least a security guy who knows his stuff or they should contact a team who can inform them when their data is getting leaked. What companies and teams like that are doing is great. That's a really good thing. I think every company that is serious and wants their shit together, they should have a company like that or something similar that can help better protect things.

ML: What's your view on some of the new technologies that are coming along like Blockchain? Do you see them making your job any easier or more difficult?

Mak: Bitcoin and stuff? I mean, there's nothing that stops me. And, if I want to sell something, I don't need blockchain. If I want money, I can tell him to send me some money through a post office or something.

ML: You would just use Moneygram or Western Union?
Mak: Yes. If something like that has to be done, we'll do it. We'll figure it out. Nothing like that can stop us, we find a way to transfer money.

ML: So are you for hire – if someone wanted to hire you to breach a database you are available, right?
Mak: No. I don't go after stuff like that. If there is something that I know I can go after, and just take it right away, I do it. But otherwise, no.

ML: How do you identify and know what it is you do want to go after?
Mak: It's usually that we find someone who can get their hands-on exploits or something like that. In one group we were in for example, we used a particular exploit to hack a lot of forums, I think we got about 100 in total. With that one we just dumped all the biggest ones like that, fast.

ML: Anything else you would like to talk about or share in the book that might be useful?
Mak: Basically, if you want to stay updated or people want to secure their stuff, they should hire someone or at least be on these forums which are trading the databases. I mean, talk to the administrators or something like that. Get in touch with them. Because, if someone comes to me, I can help. I mean, I just do my job, but if someone comes to me and tells me to look out for something, if they ask to keep an

eye out for their database on the forum I'm in and wants to be contacted, I can do that. So, people shouldn't be afraid to ask.

ML: So you are saying that the business community should work with the hacker community to find out what data has been compromised?

Mak: Oh, yes. The hacker community will help. They will also explain about target selection, optimization, give you some idea of tools and how to protect your private data. And it hasn't got to be the big places. A lot of these forums which trade private databases are usually short-lived. They come up, then they die, so...

ML: I heard a story the other day about a hacker who uses a version of SIRI that is set to trigger an instant shut down and wipe off his systems when it hears the word 'POLICE.' What do you do to protect yourself if you are raided?

Mak: Yes, I've heard of that one. It's this tool you have on your keyboard. I think it's called something like Swatted or something? I just reset my computer. Then I encrypt this with Bcrypt, if you are familiar with that? After that I set up my computer so if it gets restored there's no files left. That's important because usually when you reset, say your Windows computer, you still have files left. So, basically, I disable all that stuff and that's pretty much it.

ML: How do you know who you are talking to on your forums?

Mak: A lot of the time you don't, because basically everyone in the community is changing their usernames, maybe once a month, so that's why people come and go. So, they say they are someone, but they aren't, and you always have to be on your watch. That makes it's tough. For example, if someone comes to our forum spamming this is what happens to them. We dox them and put their profile public and expose their IP address to the community, stuff like that. But it is quite funny, some of the threats and some of the social engineering that goes on like the Dominoes Pizzas method. That's where you basically call Dominoes and you say that you need emergency help and get Dominoes to call the police. Just messing people around. And then there are Bulletin Board Systems where you can go and find markets and stuff like that there. But it's also risky when you go on these markets because you can't really trust anyone. That makes it hard.

ML: Are you concerned about the Police or Feds monitoring your activity online?
Mak: You know some people are good people and some are bad. Many people have come to the forum and they are really friendly, and they share all their private stuff and social engineering things and then it's hard to gain their trust because they are so nice and want to be your friend. And, of course, you are scared that the police are watching.

ML: So what does the future look like for you?
Mak: I've been thinking of making something good of all the bad and starting something like one of these cybersecurity labs but for my specific country. I sometimes feel now that, because I feel bad for the people who got harmed, it's time to do some good. I know it's bad when I share databases and things, but it's not like I'm, "Oh, why did I do that?" Not like if I were to stab someone. Still, there are other things I think I would like to do.

ML: But, like you say, a lot of it isn't to do with money, it's to do with attention?

Mak: Yeah, like with the booties, just for the attention. Ho's, money, it's like being a famous rapper on the Internet. You know all these hackers use rappers profile pictures like with AK 47s you know. It's really funny actually.

ML: Well, many thanks for taking the time to answer my questions and for helping provide some insights into the hacker world, I'm sure you will be disappearing back into the shadows now.

Mak: Yes, All the best. See ya.

* Lizard Squad - a Black Hat hacking group
* Shadding - the act of someone moving in the shadows without being noticed (or at least that's one interpretation, it's not clear to those outside the community as to what exactly some of the terms mean)

The CISO Perspective
Rafael Narezzi - CIO/CISO
(Financial Services)

I met Rafael at the Rela8 Group Elite CISO Summit in Portugal where we were both speaking on the subject of cyber-crime. It was clear he has that much-needed skill that most of the top CISO's possess; the ability to see the world from the perspective of the adversary. A native of Brazil and now living in London, Rafael started life and indeed learned his craft on the dark side. Intrigued, I asked Rafael to provide some additional insights into his world and the role he holds today.

Rafael Narezzi: CIO/CISO

"I've been in internet security for over 20 years now and it started when I was 16 years old and living with my mother. We were not very well off and, through economic necessity, I hacked into my ISP provider to get free access because my mom was going crazy at the bills. So I guess part of the reason I got into hacking was also my way of getting back at the provider for all the pain I was getting. Thing is, with great power also comes great responsibility and, at that age, we don't have the capability of thinking "What are you doing? Hacking is wrong, it's illegal and I might get into trouble for doing this," I just did it.

I think it's very important to define hacking at that time and hacking as it is now because, as we speak, it is very different. At that time I was very proud of myself, I was showing off to my friends. You know, "I am capable of doing this," but now it is a completely different picture. Back then it was a pretty big thing to do, but bear in mind that we didn't have any reference about what or how to do this. Today we have blogs telling people how to hack, and YouTube videos which show people how to do it, and other such helpful learning tools like that. You can even buy out of the box hacks and pre-built exploits and then get support in using them, so it's a very different starting point. I was self-taught and learned through trial and error, I just kept trying until I got the results and outcome I needed.

At the moment I think the U.K. and Israel are developing very nice programs in order to raise the awareness in kids and their responsibility in the digital world until they get more mature and can assess both good traits and bad. This helps kids to have more perspective and I think it's a very good cyber-education program which can start as early as five years old. Part of our responsibility is making sure that the next generation can fill the gaps that we can no longer fulfill, and mentoring is going to be very important in the CISO role. But being a CISO is still a very stressful job. I see people who start on a CISO career and they drop out. They go open a bar or something because it's too much, because it's very hard to keep up and be at the top of your game all the time. Hacking did though open doors for me and it gave me the opportunity to work for the ISP provider that I hacked because, when I was caught (through a 'friend' informing the authorities on me) they offered me an internship.

I've been with my current employer in the U.K. now for around five years now and my passion is still finding vulnerabilities and gaps. The consequences of what I do are a different matter because the business, the company, the board, don't really understand what you do and what your role is, either in terms of being a technologist or being a CISO.

Many companies are spending more on marketing than they are on developing secure code. Sometimes you see them saying they spent $2m on cyber resilience or security, but when you compare the spend to sales and marketing, it's nothing really. So they are not in reality concentrating their efforts on security, although *some companies do have bounty schemes. In reality though these schemes actually pay peanuts, and you have to ask why a hacker would want to spend time and research to help them? Some do, and that's good, it's right, but only around 20% of hackers. The other 80% are selling things on the dark web or even on the normal web. But you just have to learn what they are doing. It's like a weapon, how you use it defines your character. So, if you use a gun to shoot people you are bad, if you use it to protect society then you are good. Hacking is like things in the physical world in that there is nothing different happening in the virtual world than the physical.*

As a CISO I spend many hours studying and being adaptive to risk and change. We have to read and learn many books, threads, news items, and the role itself is changing constantly. Our job is very hard. There is no technology around that is going to fix all the problems and your job is always at risk. You are always a target, you are always going to be vulnerable. We are humans, we are not perfect, we are a CISO not a hero, and it only takes one little incident that you did not foresee to result in a breach. If that happened… I know that it's not my company, I don't own it, but I have serious respect for it and don't want a breach to happen. It's my reputation, too. But the problem is you always feel short of time and counting to 'the day' - when is it going to be 'the day?' - that is how we live. There is pressure from the board, pressure from the hackers trying to get into the organization and threats can also come from insiders, from anywhere. Companies, when they hire a CISO, think they are hiring someone to handle all the problems and they don't see things the way the CISO does. You might have already asked for more money, told them about potential problems, but then it becomes a political game. Then, when the breach happens, they tell you that you had the autonomy to act even though you weren't given the money to do it. Sometimes you feel like you are a kid playing a game and fighting all the corners at once. A CISO today has to be pretty brave, in fact very brave, because it's not an easy job. And, even when you are brave, it's still going to happen."

Chapter 5
A Different Breed?

*"Challenges are what makes life interesting and overcoming them
is what makes life meaningful."*
- Joshua J. Marine

Although today we have come to understand the word
'hacker' to mean someone who illegally accesses computer
systems, that definition is something which has developed
through popular culture and the media. The word 'hacker'
originally defined anyone who was skilled at computer
programming and had more to do with legitimacy than
illegality. Now, though, it is commonly associated with
someone who is not legitimately employed to access
computer systems, although we have managed to break
down the definition into the broadly defined, White, Black
and Gray Hats.

So who are the people who 'hack' our systems, why do they really do it, and what makes them different from other people, such as our CISOs who are often just as skilled?

Born to Be a Hacker?

Semantics and job descriptions aside, what many of our CISO interviews reveal is that most hackers do not start off with the intention of performing any criminal activity. They do not wake up one morning with the brilliant idea that hacking is the thing to do when it comes to earning money. Neither are hackers a criminal fraternity who are shifting into hacking as an alternative to other crimes. Although it has to be said that criminal fraternities utilize the skills of the hacker to achieve their own goals and because the threat landscape is expanding, there are no guarantees things will not change in the near future.

The hackers themselves however usually start off pretty innocently, likely as young men with a strong interest in technology and do what others, such as Phone Phreaks, have done before them – simply follow their insatiable curiosity for technological problem-solving. This is little different to the earlier hackers who came before the Web who hacked Internet systems just to see if they could. The only dissimilarity is today the potential stakes can be very high if they choose to enter into a world of criminality.

The initial motivation might appear to be little more than talent driven curiosity, but for most hackers, things go a little deeper. Not only are they curious about how things work, but they are also driven to establish if there are any flaws in the system to see if they can be overcome. Then they look to exploit these vulnerabilities just to see if it can be done. This behavioral pattern is something we see repeated over and over particularly in early-teenage males. Yet it is often found to frequently co-exist with another, much discussed common factor; that of being 'troubled'. This is, of course, a very broad and non-specific definition, but it certainly arises regularly and most often when hacking cases hit the press.

These young men – because they are rarely females – when caught hacking are regaled as having problems at school, a tendency to shun social groups, and display general issues with communication at a personal level. When you combine these issues with their apparent obsessive proclivity toward technical investigations this regularly leads to conclusions being drawn that many suffer from higher functioning autism. It is a subject which has been discussed by medical researchers and also in courtrooms when provided as a defense. How much of a factor it might play in fostering the growth of the hacking community is perhaps worthy of broader discussion. Perhaps though, when these young hackers are caught our major takeaway should be that no matter what we think of their activities or the reasons for them, these young men are such technically talented teenagers that they have the capabilities to breach defenses that adults, often those highly qualified in their field, have been paid to put in place.

Another factor which rarely receives much attention is the lack of focus on the lower number of female hackers and how and why they enter the field. Although we know the world of hacking is primarily male-dominated, the same could be said for the world of commerce when it comes to comparing the number of male executives to the number of females who make it through the glass ceiling.

In fact, much the same thing could also be said when it comes to the male-dominated world of the CISO. Yet nobody suggests that the men reaching the top of their game in these fields are autistic or even socially disabled; often the positive spin provided is they are 'driven'. So perhaps this is the first indicator that the case with hackers is not as clear-cut as we might originally think. Yet neither does it mean that females lack the capabilities or the capacity but suggests more strongly that they are rather more disadvantaged by those already in positions of power – whether in the boardroom or the hacking forum.

But there are several renown female hackers who are at the top of their game. Their hacking activities do differ from the males as they often find themselves defined as being 'hacktivists' rather than hackers because they tend to participate in online campaigns against sites such as those trading in child pornography, rather than using their skills to cause destruction or trade data. The research, however, is surprisingly scant when it comes to female hackers, but a quick search of the Internet reveals the top hitting frequent headlines to be those of 'World's Sexiest Female Hackers' or 'Top 5 Most Beautiful Female Hackers,' which indicate that sexism is as much alive and kicking in the world of the hacker as it is in the corporate culture and elsewhere.[1]

The prevalence of male hackers compared to female, combined with the obsessive nature of their activities and their lack of social skills at least in the physical world, frequently strengthens the argument for hackers suffering from higher functioning autism. But again, when it comes to autism itself the research has issues in respect of who it investigates and, more importantly, who it elects to omit. Although studies in this field are in their infancy it has recently been revealed that when it comes to females suffering from higher functioning autism, they are less likely to display the most prominent symptom of avoiding social contact. In females, although social interaction might still cause them some distress, they are still capable of being sociable in the physical world for short periods of time and often extremely so. Since the avoidance of social interactions contributes significantly to the diagnostic criteria of higher functioning autism, then females, it would seem, are frequently excluded from studies simply by definition of their not displaying that particular trait.

Yet the facts still remain that there are no entry qualifications into the world of hacking and so, out of choice, it is the male of the species which predominantly opts to enter the field. It also stands true that the majority of boys do so in their early teenage years and often show skills far in excess than is normal for their age group, although over time this gap is perhaps narrowing. We also know that many are considered to be 'socially disabled' when it comes to physical interactions and are obsessive about what they do, and so are more likely to become professional hackers. Clearly, there are potential links between autism as a disorder and the almost obsessive nature in which they pursue and often find answers to technical puzzles in their passionate quest for knowledge.

However, this doesn't mean all young hackers suffer from higher functioning autism, and also by definition, those who have been diagnosed with the condition might be greatly skilled in some aspects but in equal measure they can also be naive and uncomprehending in others. This scenario is typical of those suffering from this type of disorder and it can often be seen when we take a look at cases which have hit the headlines and made the hacker a household name.

Jake Davis was only 18 when he was arrested at his remote home in the Shetland Islands which lie far off the northern tip of Scotland, U.K. His user ID was Topiary and he was charged with five offenses including attempting to carry out a distributed denial of service attack on the then-named Serious Organised Crime Agency's website. Although part of a team of hackers, Jake had started developing his skills during his school years when, like so many others, he started to come under the 'troubled teenager' banner. Of course, this banner also meant he was given plenty of time and opportunity to hone his talents simply because he was not attending school. Really this should also figure into the debate when we are discussing how technically developed the hacker's skills are.

After he was arrested, it was widely publicized that he was possibly suffering from higher functioning autism and simply due to his technical prowess, he was viewed as someone who, although socially disaffected, was highly intelligent simply because he was able to achieve what he did. Indeed, although they might actually swerve from the tags of both hacker and autistic, many hackers also frequently perceive themselves as being more intelligent than most. Rarely though it is acknowledged that these skills are usually confined to a specific field, such as a proficiency in performing calculations or creating artwork and, in the case of the hacker, solving systemic technical problems. In Jake's case, his level of naivety in respect of real-world issues and his disconnect to it can still be seen today even though he does now admit that immaturity played its part at the time of his arrest.

What happened after he got arrested gives us a little insight into his thought patterns. Initially, he expressed nothing less than surprise at his predicament and, as he himself now recognizes, this could be in part put down to his age and lack of worldly experience when it comes to actions and consequences. However, we might glean a little more when we learn that at the time one of his major concerns was his indignance at being tagged on release in a location he did not know, London. Even today he recites the story of how he simply could not find his way around and was panicked when it came to returning home in order to meet his curfew because, he explains, he had been denied access to his mobile phone and thus GPS. What Jake didn't appear to realize, either then or now, was that entering the nearest newsagents to purchase a street map would have seen an end to at least his curfew stresses. To most people this would seem to be the obvious solution, yet to Jake, with all his technical expertise, clearly it was not.[2]

If we also take into consideration the age at which people start hacking, this group go one step further than simply following their insatiable curiosity for technical problem-solving or even finding out how something works; they want to find vulnerabilities in the systems that others have designed. They want to discover the imperfections rather than the mere functionality.

This mindset is also often combined with several social factors including the noted behavioral pattern of hackers tending to shun interactions on a personal level. They prefer instead to interact through the virtual world and with those having the same interests even though, as our hacker interviewee explains, there still exists a level of mistrust and frequently they may never get to know the true identity of their 'friends'.

Once we have the broad, 'brushstroke' basics out of the way, what we then find is there are apparent and clear differences between hackers and everyone else. But how true is this and are we really asking the correct questions? Would we learn more if we stopped looking at the differences between 'them and us' but instead at where the similarities lie?

Our New Social World

One of the primary observations made when discussing the behavior of hackers is how they find it difficult to connect with others when it comes to social interaction on what we might consider to be a 'normal' level. As the case with Jake Davis revealed, frequently they prefer the solitude of their own private space and communicating with others about their main interest electronically, to stepping outside the door and interacting in the real world. Although this kind of behavior may have been very distinctive back in the day when Jake Davis was arrested, how true is that observation today? In other words, how different is the behavior of hackers from the majority of people in 'normal' society?

Few would doubt that issues are arising among the general population when it comes to the ways in which we interact socially, and the buck often stops not only with the Internet but with social media in particular. Although observations have been made for some years, it is only with the advent of the publicized Facebook drama that we are coming to accept that a reliance on social media has developed or even been cultivated. This is resulting in issues for many millions of people who are frequently being referred to as being socially disabled or suffering from a social disconnect. In short, our behavior when it comes to interacting socially is being negatively affected by Internet communications and to a degree where many people could be described as being addicted to virtual communications. We might then ask if, outside of their technical interest and expertise, hackers are displaying only slightly more extreme behavior when it comes to social habits and the current preference for interacting? After all, there are now many millions of people who would feel disadvantaged if they were to make the decision (and it is merely a choice) to give up social media. But this need for the majority to interact technically rather than physically would suggest that the hacker is only suffering from a more extreme version of social disability than the rest of us. Therefore, we might come to the conclusion that the gap between 'them and us' is not quite as wide as first believed.

Although the situation may initially appear to have little foundation, science has been gathering a mountain of evidence which suggests there might be more than a small amount of truth in the theory, and there are in fact sound biochemical and psychological reasons for our addiction to technological communications. Many might be uncomfortable simply reading the word 'addiction', but, whether we like it or not, addiction is addiction no matter what we are addicted to and recognizing that we are addicted is the first step in overcoming the problem.[3]

Looking at psychological or biochemical addiction rather than obsession would also answer, at least in part, the question as to why hackers do what they do. We know both from research undertaken and from our own interview with a hacker that often money is not the primary motivation for what they do. In fact, over and over again we are told, and our own hacker told us the same, the primary motivator is the kudos and admiration they receive from their peers. If we measure this behavior against that which we would consider to be more 'normal,' is it actually so very different from people on Facebook counting how many friends, likes, and interactions they have?

We can take this issue one step further when we look at the scientific forces behind the addiction to Internet interactions or even social disconnects in the physical world because science, when it comes to the biochemical issues, has been revealing to us for some years now how the Internet, information seeking, and dopamine loops are developed in the brain. Although most of the research has focused on the effects of everyday posters on sites such as Twitter or Facebook, we shouldn't forget that these same biochemical principles also apply to those who spend their time seeking out critical vulnerabilities in cybersystems. Yet frequently, when discussing hacker behavior this fact is omitted when clearly the same principles apply to them as to the rest of us.

Dopamine Disruption

Humans produce the chemical neurotransmitter dopamine as part and parcel of our basic survival mechanisms. As it turns out, though, it is a major player in reward-based behavior simply because it is essentially a survival motivator. Although for many years dopamine was believed to be responsible for making you feel happy when you find a solution to something, more recently it has been recognized as the motivating factor which gives you the thrill of going out to seek that solution.

The dopamine high you get is the anticipatory factor when you're looking for something prior to succeeding. Then, when you find what you are seeking, you get a hit of pleasure from opioids in your brain before the dopamine motivator sends you out again on another seek and search mission. If we were still living as early humans, the dopamine hit would be the chemical that gave us the thrill of the chase when we went out on the hunt, and the opioid hit would be the pleasure we experienced when we captured our prey. In the natural world the loop would not start again until it needed to, until perhaps we became hungry and concerned about where the next meal was coming from.

On the Internet, however, the seek and search mission becomes a continuous loop because there is no natural progression to moderate our behavior. The Internet actually fills this gap in our natural urges because it is constantly seeking, searching, anticipating, and finding. It is also why when you go on the Internet, even if it is just to look for a piece of information or to check messages, it is virtually impossible to stay there for a short period of time and then leave because you now have a self-inflicted addiction to dopamine and opioids. Yes, you are addicted to the chemicals being produced.

But unfortunately, the problem does not end there because what dopamine also likes is that tension of unpredictability, and this is exactly suited to reading that next text, email, social media message, getting a 'like' or hearing that someone new wants to connect with you. You anticipate that happening and although you don't know when or what it will be, the anticipation is part of the seeking action of dopamine and strengthens the addiction to it. When you get your new friend request or another like you are rewarded with another opioid pleasure hit and the whole cycle starts again.

If all this is starting to sound a little familiar, it should. If you were taught at school or in college about the behavior of Pavlov's dogs who were trained on 'cue' behavior, this is exactly the same thing and is also now recognized as being caused by the dopamine loop. So, if you take away nothing else from this chapter then remember that when you turn on your automatic notification for messages, you are reacting in exactly the same way as one of Pavlov's dogs.

That's not where things stop when it comes to dopamine because it also governs many other survival related functions. One which is certainly high up on the list in respect of relevance to Internet users is the function to keep you awake and alert. Again, if we relate it to the natural world of the human being, this makes perfect sense. For example, maybe you are going out to hunt for food and it is to your benefit and indeed survival that you are kept alert and on your guard. In this capacity dopamine is a life saver. However, it is not so beneficial for those same humans existing in the modern world who are looking to unwind before bed because they have to get up with the alarm clock. In this situation, dopamine is doing the exact opposite of what we need – when we need to sleep it's keeping us awake.

Our brain does trick us, as it does with all addictions, into believing that checking our emails, messages or social media account just when we should be relaxing is doing us no harm, when in actual fact it is. Sleeping when you are tired, or at least turning off all electrical communications, is far more likely to help you feel rested and to wake refreshed than taking a few dopamine and opioid hits before bedtime. In reality, using the Internet to 'unwind' before bed is biochemically achieving the exact opposite and is keeping you awake long after you would naturally be inclined to sleep.[4] If we look at the bigger picture and compare what should be our natural behavior and how it is governed and supported by our biochemical mechanisms, what you begin to see is an extremely efficient system assisting the ancient human striving to survive and see another day. When you apply that same system to the modern human who is, among other things, utilizing electrical technology, what you get is a completely unsuitable biochemical system that is building a very destructive addiction from our own internal cocktail of chemicals.

What we are examining here, though, is the behavior of the hacker measured against that of the so-called 'normal' person, but what we see when we look a little closer is actually a direct correlation between the hacker's behavior and our own. This should come as no surprise because clearly the dopamine loop affects them in exactly the same way that it affects us. It should be considered that it is likely, at least in part, to be a contributing factor to their behavior – which we often choose instead to describe as obsessive rather than addictive.

There is perhaps an irony in respect of who is really being exploited. Although hackers are noted and indeed proud of their capabilities in exploiting vulnerabilities not only in cybertechnology but also human psychology, could they themselves actually be being exploited by their own chemical responses to what they do?

Legitimate or Illegal?

Although this might explain at least some of the reasons as to why hackers choose the path they do, it does not explain why they continue on into a profession or even hobby which would be construed by most as criminally motivated. Our own CISO interviews clearly reveal that many people, despite having the ability to hack and make money from it, often elect to use those skills to benefit commerce rather than benefit from it themselves.

Certainly, the choice in some cases is made easier simply because luck plays a significant role early on in the game and when these young hackers are caught they are offered a job precisely because they are so proficient, and some employers at least are capable of seeing this potential. Here again though, perhaps our hacker interview can provide us with a little more insight into why some hackers go into legitimate employment and others into criminality and how their social behavior does not veer so dramatically from that which is quickly becoming the norm.

Perceived Realities

Our hacker interviewee revealed there is a disconnect in the hacker's mind between the reality of hurting people and the actions he performs when invading their privacy. This, he explained, is because he sees no direct, physical link between the perpetrator and the victim. In part, this can be due to denial but it might well be the way in which the Internet diminishes the ability to experience the physical reactions of others also contributes to the decrease in empathy and realization that there can be devastating personal consequences to actions.

We can see a similar response to criminality when it comes to crimes such as burglary where the perpetrator insists that the crime is not 'personal'; it is seen to be a crime against property rather than the individual. Of course, there are still many repercussions on the victim, but the disconnect allows the criminal to distance themselves from such issues. In the case of cyber-crimes, the disconnect is even greater because the hacker is committing the crime against content, often over many hundreds or thousands of miles, and there is no connection between the two individuals in any way.

This lack of empathy or disconnect can also be correlated with the behavior of the ordinary hacker and how he views his victims and those using social media. Today there is much discussion around how the Internet, social media in particular, is not only propagating an inability in people to interact on a human level but building a situation where the virtual self, the illusion, is essentially taking over.

Ex-Facebook executive Chamath Palihapitiya is speaking more and more on this issue and explains that an unexpected consequence of the social media website and others like it is they have become a breeding ground for unacceptable and atrocious behaviors, even among ordinary members.

In a Talk from the Top interview at Stanford Graduate School of Business, he specifically recalls an incident where a hoax rumor was spread via WhatsApp which claimed that children in India were about to be kidnapped by child traffickers and warned people to be wary of strangers. The hoax resulted in panic and vigilante groups were formed to seek out the non-existent perpetrators. As a result, several innocent people were lynched.

For many people, examples such as this might be too distant or extreme for them to connect to. However, closer to home we see more subtle criminality in the form of social media sites being used specifically for the purposes of cyberbullying and there is little doubt that this is widespread and that cases are on the increase. Most often the problems discuss the effects on the younger age categories, usually up to around 24 years, and here we see many reported cases of suicide as a direct result.

The picture is not too different when we look at the older age groups and find that at least 40% of adults who use social media websites have also reported they too have been victims of cyberbullying.[5] In the adult world, the perpetrators are often those who appear to have surface validity but they are also, just like hackers, skilled in social engineering and manipulation. Frequently, they will falsely accuse individuals of acts which are usually highly emotive and therefore guaranteed to stoke the feelings of others, and their victim will be targeted from many sources who, just like those in India, believe the misinformation and essentially form 'mobs' to attack innocent people. In this scenario, although it may not be physical, the mental assaults can be equally as damaging and many deaths from suicide are recorded in addition to problems associated with depression.

Again, there are connections between this type of behavior – which is no less criminal than that which the hacker performs in that it is an electronic attack which can ruin lives – because an apparent disconnect exists between virtual reality and physical reality. This not only allows the activities to take place, it also distances the perpetrators from physically experiencing the result of their actions or seeing any personal punishment. In short, most people, when they have been encouraged to participate in cyberbullying, will not feel that they have done anything wrong even when they are presented with the true facts that frequently reveal their 'victim' to be entirely innocent of blame.

What we are seeing is the same or a similar disconnect between hackers and their victims that we see in cases of cyberbullying and this is thought to be due to the virtual rather than physical reality, meaning the consequences of actions are rarely experienced. Both are crimes against other human beings and both are actioned without consideration for the damage being inflicted. In the case of data theft, for instance, the hacker places the blame on those who use the data after they have obtained it. In the case of cyberbullying, the abuser feels they are justified in taking action, maybe even seeing themselves as vigilantes, even though they have no solid evidence, only one side of the story, and rarely the legal authority to act in that manner.

The trend it would seem, whether we are talking about hackers or social media users, is at least a breakdown of the normal human instinct of compassion and often an increase in cruel and abusive behavior. And, when it comes to cyberbullying, although this type of behavior is more frequently associated with those of school age, it is by no means limited to them.

In 2014, Brenda Leyland committed suicide after being approached by a news reporter investigating the fact that she had sent hundreds of malicious tweets to the parents of the missing girl Maddie McCann who is believed to have been abducted when on holiday with her family in Portugal.[6] Whatever your opinions on the case, and Brenda Leyland certainly had her own views, after she was exposed as the troll behind the tweets the enormity of what she had done and perhaps the potential consequences apparently became too much for her to bear and she took her own life. If nothing else, this sad case should expose the fact that when the real world comes knocking at your door it might have been wise to check your behavior in the first place because that disconnect between our virtual and physical lives, whether you are a hacker or just an Internet user, is imaginary. What you do really does have an impact and can have serious consequences not only on the life of the victim but also on your own.

Not everyone though, even when they have the skills, curiosity, and drive to hack, actually follows through to join the road to criminality and some of our interviews with CISOs clearly reveal this. Despite many of today's foremost cybersecurity professionals starting off their career as hackers in youth and following an almost identical path to those who continue to hack, these individuals veered from illegality into legal occupations. Indeed, as some will admit, luck often plays a part, others made the conscious choice to use their skills legitimately and embarked on business ventures or further education, ultimately being offered permanent positions as a result.

Fate might well lend a hand, but what we also come to understand is that many cybersecurity experts have a strong appreciation of the need to communicate on a physical level. This evidences itself regularly throughout our interviews and it may well be the one factor which distinguishes between the hacker who actively avoids personal interaction and continues on his criminal career, and the one who appreciates the necessity of personal communication and takes the turning onto the road of legitimate employment.

Another factor which could swerve our ardent hackers from the path of legality is the organization itself, no matter how it's constructed, brings with it confines and limitations which in many cases are extremely restrictive. Whether these restrictions relate to communications or budgets they are issues which the hacker does not, in a sense, have to either deal with nor tolerate. Neither do they have to tolerate a management structure which is often less than engaged with the subject of cybersecurity. The world in which hackers live embraces cybertechnology and little else. It may be an insular world, but it is certainly focused, passionate, and intensive. Again, these may be factors which deter hackers from legitimizing their skills and making a career from their talents.

The facts of the matter are that, although we sometimes view hackers as being people who are entirely distinct from the remainder of Internet users, the way in which the technology triggers chemical secretion in the body, the way in which we respond and become addicted, the way in which it feeds our growing disconnect to the real world, might reveal to us that hackers are affected in ways which are very similar to everyone else, simply to a greater degree.

Maybe they do have tendencies toward social disconnection, maybe circumstances have given them the opportunity to hone their technical skills and, on top of that, the Internet propagates these tendencies and fosters the perfect home for a hacker to develop. Whatever the case though, the scientific findings which are emerging in respect of how the Internet affects the rest of us cannot simply be ignored when it comes to the hacker. We cannot tag them all with the same 'higher functioning autism' label and expect that to fit all situations. Looking at individual circumstances and at how the Internet affects all of us, both biochemically and socially, may assist in building a better and bigger picture of why hackers do what they do and perhaps might help us to prevent the predilection developing in future generations.

The CISO Perspective
Henry – Consulting CISO
(Banking Sector)

Henry is one of those larger than life characters with a constant smile and infectious laugh. He is the type of CISO that makes cybersecurity interesting not least for his enthusiasm and passion for the subject but from the range of international experience he holds and the situations he as a security leader has faced. Henry reminds us that not all CISO's work in the cozy and relatively safe confines of the developed world, so his full name is not disclosed here to protect the innocent.

Henry – Consulting CISO:
"Hello, I'm Henry and I have about 15 years' experience in information and cybersecurity starting back in the days when it was still referred to as I.T. Security. So I came in when it wasn't really a profession. My background was software testing before moving into networking, desktop support and things like that. But I got into security pretty early and quickly adopted an approach on how it can provide business value. I try and look at it from a business standpoint. Over the years I've worked in different capacities, over different industry verticals from finance, healthcare, telecoms, and mainly as an interim CISO and contractor on a variety of security projects with a lot of financial companies.

The driver for financial industry security is regulation, so that's why it's taken seriously. There are other industrial verticals, like educational institutions and private sector companies that have quite a lot of personal, sensitive data, but who don't really take it as seriously as the banks. So you have telecoms, financial companies, pharmaceuticals, but generally speaking, most companies would rather not spend too much time trying to implement security controls because they don't see the value and it's hard to see how it affects the bottom line. Financial companies take it seriously, but because of regulation. The data they possess is not more sensitive than others, but the value put on it is really dependent on the company itself or its customers.

The biggest challenge for a CISO, taking a broad view, is report positioning. Not being close enough to the real decision makers, to board level, or even close to it. A typical example would be, no matter how scaled, no matter how well-informed a CISO is, if he's too far down the food chain he can't make an impression. I've seen it so many times, where the CISO is basically compromised because he can't provide oversight to his own boss if he's reporting to I.T. or the CIO. He can't be objective, he can't buck the trend where I.T. is mainly delivery-focused, despite the fact that lip service is paid to improve security even at board level. That means it's not properly understood by the board.

Sometimes, because organizations understand physical security, the CISO gets shoehorned in under that type. It's another emerging trend. But structure is key and that's often overlooked, undermined, and then effectively communicating cyber-risk becomes a problem. Again and again you see CISOs talking about tech stuff and the company say, "Yes, but how does it affect the bottom line?" And that's not properly communicated. You need to hire someone who understands business, I.T. and risk. Someone who can lead from the front, rather than deploying a lot of tools but with no context. That type of CISO cannot demonstrate business value.

If there's a breach often the CISO will be blamed. Although he shouldn't be. It's almost as if you've been set up by the firm to be the fall guy. The CISO can be easy to blame because they don't have full autonomy or power. CISOs can refuse to accept risk, but *a lot get power drunk and take on more than they should accepting risk on behalf of the business, which means they face the bullet when the time comes.*

Some companies pride themselves on having no incidents, but it does not mean they've not been breached. It could be worse, they might not even know. I'd prefer to know if they've gone through an incident, how it's been handled or how shackled the CISO is.

With breaches a lot of the information doesn't come out, it's suppressed. Within the African banks there was a situation with a massive breach and it was written off as bad debt. This individual came in, said he was the branch manager from somewhere else and there to do some work. The branch manager took him into the comms room and gave him a console. The guy was a hacker. He had codes, usernames and credentials of two members of staff from another branch in a different part of the country who had the necessary access rights. Then he posted the equivalent of US$5,000,000 to different customer accounts. Those people had been prepped to expect the money drop and immediately withdrew it. Mule accounts, basically. It was obvious the guy knew where all the CCTV cameras were, so his face couldn't be seen. But it happens frequently and it's just written off as a bad debt. There are no lessons learned, which tells you that it's almost condoned.

The new generation banks though, they embrace technology a bit quicker and have better controls. Some have man trap style revolving doors just to come in. I mean, it still happens, only not to that degree. But access to the back end isn't as secure as it should be. Sometimes money is just credited or debited from an account and the bank doesn't take responsibility for it. Or accounts are just cleaned out and the guy's in Europe or something. So the controls are pretty poor, but some banks are still operating on the very regimented, bureaucratic setup. In a few banks cybersecurity is being recognized as an operational risk and viewed as a risk theme, so it's an enterprise-level risk that cuts across everything, whether operational, credible, affordable or whatever. It's the level of understanding. If that is appreciated and seen as a potential threat to the business, or something that could really reduce the bottom line, it's good. We're beginning to see more of that now, where it's affecting share prices or evaluations of companies, or the cost of a breach is quite substantial. The more people appreciate that this is a business issue and not an I.T. problem the better. Warren Buffett says it's the biggest risk that he sees on the horizon, and he's not called the Oracle of Omaha for nothing.

National threats are a new frontier, and some companies, including those in the private sector, are starting to recognize that they are part of the critical infrastructure of the country. That's going to bring it to the fore where it becomes a necessity for certain institutions to fortify their defenses because it can bring a country to its knees. It's not just water and power, the financial institutions need to take this seriously. The NHS issue that happened last year was a key one as well. So, where private and public sectors converge and see themselves as part of a whole, that's something organizations need to take seriously.

I would encourage younger people thinking of entering the business because there are lots of opportunities. Understanding how I.T. works, how it delivers value to the business, that helps implement security controls to ensure that business objectives are still being met but in a secure fashion. It takes time to understand how I.T. works, how it's aligned with business. So it's a journey that young people can embark on before gradually moving into a CISO function that needs an enterprise-level view. Technology people have a glass ceiling in terms of how far they can go in a business, but the challenge is that technology changes a lot and very quickly. Five years ago, ten years ago, we were talking cloud technology and cloud security. Now we're talking A.I., machine learning, so if you went to university you are now playing catch-up. For someone more mature, go for the professional certifications.

If you have the background in I.T. already, keep yourself fresh. Personally, I train quite a few security professionals who want a change from the I.T. world where things are just black and white. It's configure this, configure that, they don't know why or understand the risk. They just know you push this button and it's supposed to do that, and that's about it. But this is where the bulk of people who want to get into security come from.

With surveillance it boils down to the age-old phrase, who watches the watchers? Does it provide a false sense of security? Then, with A.I., if it's compromised it will be devastating. It's too much power being left to something. How secure is the integrity of those algorithms? Is there anybody certifying those algorithms?

I think this is where the conspiracy theorists have a field day because, somewhere, that power or that level of power will be concentrated ... and we don't know where."

Chapter 6
A Victim of the 'Victimless Crime'

"We must rapidly begin the shift from a 'thing-oriented society' to a 'person-oriented' society. When machines and computers, profit motives and property rights are considered more important than people, the giant triplets of racism, materialism and militarism are incapable of being conquered."
-    Martin Luther King

What is it like to have your identity stolen, to be the victim of a fraudster? Just how easy is it to regain control over your own identity after such a life shifting event? These are questions I put to Bennett Arron who experienced this precise scenario. Here, Bennett provides us with some valuable insights into the impact on his life along with those close to him.

Bennett Arron: My Story

One of the positive aspects of my experience is that, as it turns out, GDPR has been good for me and kept me very busy. For example, I've recently been to one of the large financial services companies visiting all their offices and speaking to staff. I was doing four talks a day, which was pretty full on. Four, one-hour talks, back to back; nine-till-ten and ten-till-eleven, then a break for half an hour, then another two. It was good, but it was proper full on. I'd love to do more and you just never know... I've done them for the Post Office in the past, going around all their Royal Mail offices. And the feedback, well, that's been fantastic, so... yes, all very nice.

Sorry, I haven't introduced myself yet, have I? I'm Bennett Arron. I'm a professional comedian and, back in the late 1990s, I had my identity stolen which is why I do the talks and stuff now. What happened back then, the end result of the identity theft was that both myself and my then pregnant wife were made homeless and penniless. Then, even when I tracked down the perpetrator of the crime, the police didn't do anything about it.

Identity theft is a 'victimless' crime, you see. Gosh, thank heavens someone told me that or I might well have started to think of myself as some kind of victim and wanting something done about it!

Instead, I ended up writing a book[1] and making a program about identity theft for Channel 4 in the U.K., and tried to prove my point about how easily it could be done by getting a driving license in the name of the then Home Secretary of the U.K. For that, I got arrested and thrown into a jail cell. I guess the 'then Home Secretary' must have thought of himself as a victim, so maybe he hadn't heard that it's a 'victimless crime.'

But, of course, when it happened to me it wasn't online, it was done the old-fashioned way. The difference now? I found that people won't believe you when it happens to you. When it happened to me nobody believed me. I had to convince people that 'I' was 'me', and not the person pretending to be me, and convincing them was not as easy as you might think. That was a nightmare because nobody had heard of identity theft back then and there was no infrastructure in place to help. There was no one at all to turn to because no one really knew anything about it so they didn't know how to help. Things like credit reference agencies didn't have anything in place to help, so they just gave you the data and said, "These are all the companies that you owe money to. Get it sorted." So that appears to have changed for the better.

At least today there is one good aspect in that because it happens so frequently, a lot more people believe it and they're there to help. The downside though is that it's a lot easier to become a victim because of the Internet. When it happened to me it was a physical hack in that my mail was stolen after a redirection went wrong when we moved house. Now everything is online so the stealing has been upgraded to email and the like and I would say it's a lot easier. I would also say that banks and credit companies don't understand how identity theft can affect you. When they go, "Oh, do you know this money's taken from your account? Don't worry, it's fine, we'll write it off." Or a credit card company will say, "If you're a victim of fraud, it's okay," They don't understand that affects your credit rating and, if your credit rating is affected, then you're screwed until you clear your name. They just don't seem to understand the importance of this.

When it comes to physical hacks, when the credit card companies send out marketing mail with your name and your address actually already pre-printed on the form in order to try and get more customers in... let's face it, if you can't fill in your own name and address on a form you probably shouldn't have a credit card, but it helps the fraudsters.

Yet still nobody seems to understand the implications of being a victim of identity theft. Nobody understands how it can affect you, how credit rating is so important for things. I can't believe that's still a thing, that companies still don't understand how important that is, let alone the stress and emotional trauma of it all. Now it's a lot easier for it to happen and we are also giving out too much information without even thinking about it. We give out too much personal data for other people to use. Nobody used to do that. There was never the online social media aspect where we say, "Here's everything you want to know about me without you even asking." We tell them where we are going on holiday and when, all those things. So we have to take some responsibility for making it easier for the criminals and it can turn your life into a nightmare.

It's the same with companies sending emails and asking for data they don't need; it's ridiculous and I'm hoping that's going to stop. But the thing is, these emails are coming from legitimate companies and they aren't the ones you have to worry about. You're not going to get scammers writing and saying "Hi, I'm a scammer. Is it okay if I keep you on my list?"

The good thing about GDPR is that organizations now have to report a breach within 72 hours. That, I think, is the main thing. The fact that people have your data, have your email address, fine - if it's secure. What difference it's going to make is the fact that companies like TalkTalk and many others have had a data breach and kept it quiet. Those are the things where I'm pleased that GDPR has come in to try and sort that out. But at TalkTalk that was over a year after it happened before it was reported. At least now it's 72 hours or you get penalized. And the fines are absolutely huge.

But now I don't think anyone can enjoy their own privacy, I think that's gone. Everything is out there. Again, a lot of it's out there because we're too quick to give information. I went to buy cinema tickets last week and the amount of information they wanted from me to get cinema tickets was just ridiculous. You don't need my date of birth for me to buy a cinema ticket. Ticking an 'are you over 18?' box is silly because, you know what, if I'm 16 and I'm applying for an over-18 movie, I'm not going to be honest.

So what's the point of that? It's just unnecessary, the hoops you have to jump through to try and do anything because they want the data. But, as you know, if you Google your name the amount of stuff that comes up now people are just shocked by.

If you're the managing director of a company, why have they got to make all that information public on the Company's House website? I don't get it. I don't get why they need to publicize your name, your address, your date of birth. Why? Who needs that? A lot of these organizations are collecting it, presumably as marketing data to sell onto somebody else. It's the old story – nothing's free online. If it's free, then you're the product, right?

And the 'right to be forgotten'? No. It's words, it's meaningless. What that means is you can say to a company, make sure you delete my data. Okay, that's one company.

Fine. That's not being forgotten, is it? That's one company going, okay, that person isn't on our mailing list anymore. It's a nice idea, but in reality, I don't think it's going to come to anything. Our information is so widely distributed it's almost an impossibility now.

When I try to explain to people what it's like to have your identity stolen, and they ask me why it's referred to as a victimless crime, I say, "You know, if somebody breaks into your house and steals your laptop or your DVD player, something tangible that's going to cause you hassle, it can still be replaced. Yet having your identity stolen, can't be replaced." But people don't see that. I certainly felt like I was the victim of a crime because some villain effectively stole me!

But that's intangible and so people don't see it as being a big deal because it's not something physical you can see. I try to explain the fact that having somebody using your name, pretending to be you, it's not just the weirdest feeling on a purely personal level, knowing there's somebody out there being you for whatever reason – in my case for nothing good – but there is also the fact that, until you clear your name, there's so little you can do.

I mean, when it happened to me I couldn't open bank accounts. I couldn't get credit cards. I couldn't do anything because I had this black mark against my name. So, when I'd try to do anything, no one knew it wasn't me that had run up the debts. No one considered that my identity had been used. They just look at you and see there is a black mark against that name.

It took me just under two years before my name was cleared and I had to do the majority of the work myself. That's such a devastating feeling and it's made worse by the fact that you just don't know what the next day is going to bring. Which company is going to accuse you of theft, or who's going to accuse you of this or that. It's soul-destroying and you feel powerless. In my case it had been going on for a year and a half and I knew nothing about it because no money was taken from my actual account. The thefts were all done through new accounts opened in my name.

There are so many ways in which an identity can be stolen. In my case it was a mail redirection that failed after I moved house. There were only a couple of things that floated through but it was enough to get the ball rolling. The guy who moved in after me just used the information in the mail because, as I say, companies doing mailshots pre-print all your details on the forms they send out, and it worked. There were mobile phone companies involved, credit cards, and I knew nothing about it until I applied for a mortgage.

The police weren't really interested so, in the end, I tracked him down myself. I got his name, his current address, and even a description because I went to the house. Then I gave it all to the police and they did nothing. Then again, it's only just coming up to 20 years since the crimes were committed so I'm expecting that any day now they'll get him. Only joking. I'll be filed somewhere in a forgotten and dusty place. But the point is that, despite the police knowing who this man was and having evidence put in front of them that he'd done it, he got away with it completely. And, to be honest, the clues that he was a less than honest individual were already there. He stayed in my former place for about six months and only paid one month's rent. The landlord couldn't get him out and he trashed the place. So the indications were there.

It also only takes someone with criminal intentions, not a habitual criminal as we might be led to believe, to fill in forms in your name or pretend to be you. In my case the guy knew exactly what he was doing because he was living there and I wasn't, yet he still pretended to be me. Even the CID admitted they had enough evidence for a case, but they just didn't go ahead with it. It's as simple as that. Something has gone wrong somewhere because the fact that there was no punishment, retribution or compensation for the victim means the guy will go on to do it to someone else. What happened to me, happened and I couldn't turn the clock back. But seeing this guy locked up so he couldn't do it to someone else... well, that meant a lot to me and I felt it was the main thing.

Today I know that identity theft affects one in ten people and that it's the fastest growing crime. The problem is that it will continue to grow because it's a relatively easy crime to commit and it's actually getting easier. Let's be honest, with things like phishing emails, GDPR isn't going to stop that. But the main reason that it's becoming easier and growing so fast as a crime is really because we are making ourselves targets. We go out there and play on the net and we click on these links and we are taken in by many things. Yet we keep on doing it and we keep on providing people with more and more information who don't need it and are not entitled to it. But conversely, I also think some companies, where things need to be more involved, shouldn't be too fast to take on new clients without doing the proper checks.

A short while ago a friend of mine had a horrible experience. He's a clever guy, a doctor, and he was buying a flat for his kids, investing it for them because he'd been left some money. The purchase was progressing normally, it was all going through without a hitch and he was communicating with his solicitor on a regular basis. On the day of exchange my friend got another email from the solicitor, there had been several all the way through the transaction, and he was told that all the paperwork had been completed satisfactorily and for my friend to transfer the money. Now, this is the same company that he'd been dealing with for many months. So, he sent the money, no problem. Then, an hour later, he gets another email from the solicitor saying more or less the same thing, that the paperwork had all gone through fine and to transfer the money. Of course, my friend phoned them and told them that he'd sent it an hour before after their first email. The solicitor said no, we've only just sent the email. What all this means is that somebody had been following the transaction, intercepting emails, and knew exactly when to send the fake email - which they could do because they'd hacked the solicitor's account - asking for the money to be transferred to a particular, fake account.

The money was all gone. Just like that. It had been spoofed from start to finish. It might have been a bit of work for the criminals, and it took a while to complete, but the rewards are so high and the risk of being caught is so low, all they had to do was wait and bide their time. Now, of course, my friend is devastated but no one takes responsibility. The bank is saying, what can we do? They acknowledge that it's very upsetting but say that my friend simply shouldn't have transferred to the wrong account. The money, when tracked, moved from three or four different banks and accounts and then it just disappeared.

For me, well, I have to wonder where all this is going to stop, at what point? I mean, whatever firewalls you put up, it's going to be very difficult to stop anybody from hacking into your emails and even more difficult to follow the trail to catch them. Yet, at some point, these criminals opened bank accounts and the first one was in the U.K. That means the proper checks weren't done by that particular bank. The money, from there, moved out of the country. But from my perspective the first bank should be held responsible and accountable because clearly they did not make sure the checks were done correctly. So I don't think they should be so fast to take on new clients and then move on to the next.

It's those checks, those basic checks that have to be done more thoroughly than they are being done now. We are talking about personal accounts here, though. I'm led to believe that, at the company level, the checks are more refined. Either way, when it comes to the personal account level, there doesn't appear to be enough scrutiny.

Because of my experience I try to raise the level of awareness not only as to how easily it can be done, but also in respect of how damaging it is for the victims. I tell my story and show how it can affect at an individual and human level, and I'm not just speaking to the public but to the organizations who are also involved. Often I talk to a lot of the people who deal directly with customers through phone calls and emails, customer service teams and people like that. I put a face to the voice on the other end of the phone and show them, if they don't do their job properly and are not careful with data, what can happen and that the repercussions can be huge.

It's easy to forget about mistakes when, at the end of the day, you put your phone down and go home. It's forgotten about. But staff have to realize that these mistakes can have terrible consequences for customers and often for years. They have to understand that if a mistake is made it can affect someone's life really badly.

So that seems to help and gets across a stronger message rather than simply giving staff a training talk. If you show them what can happen to somebody if mistakes are made it makes it more personal and gives it impact. From the company's point of view, especially with GDPR, it's showing them that if they're not careful the company is going to be punished as well. They have to be more responsible with data. They shouldn't hold on to it for longer than they need to and, from all angles breaches, mistakes, should be reported straight away because things get worse, not better. So, from both sides, it's quite a strong message really.

The public also has to become more aware of what's happening out there. I set up a stall in a shopping mall, and I said to people that I could protect their identity if they gave me all of their personal information. And they did. They gave me all their card numbers, all the three-digit security numbers on the backs of their cards, their mother's maiden name, their passwords, absolutely everything anyone would need to steal someone's identity. And it was just me, standing there in a suit in a shopping mall with a stand and a clipboard. No one asked me how I, one guy in a suit with a stand and a clipboard, could protect them. I just told them I could and they believed me.

It was all filmed for a TV documentary so, of course, we told the people the truth in the end and destroyed all the information. But, even as I was setting the stall up, there was a queue of people waiting to give their information to me. It was being sold to them as free identity theft protection provided they gave me enough information to steal their identity. It doesn't even make sense. In the end, at least we made our point to these people and revealed to them how they need to be more careful in future. This time they were lucky because we really were the good guys.

Do organizations take data security seriously? Well, now they're likely taking it a little more seriously because they're coming to realize they can be punished for making mistakes. In the past they had the attitude of taking care of other peoples' data, but it was tied in with the mindset that, if there was a problem, then it wasn't really a problem for the company and all they had to do was sort it out. Now though, with the GDPR, they are coming to understand that if they're caught out making mistakes it will be a problem for the company and likely a big one because there are hefty financial penalties looming. They also know that if this happens the bad publicity isn't going to be good for their company either.

I think for many companies this means they're going to take data protection more seriously, although I doubt that in a lot of cases it's for the right reasons. Maybe there will also be some fireworks at the start. You could imagine that the ICO and other governing authorities would maybe try to find some organizations to make examples of. And, of course, the bigger the company the bigger the example will be.

Yet it does seem strange that it's only now identity theft of the masses is being viewed with a little more significance. When Channel 4 commissioned me to do the program about identity theft the production company told me I would have to steal the identity of somebody in authority to prove the point that identity theft was relatively easy. I must admit that I wasn't too happy about it, it just didn't seem like a good idea. But that was their prerequisite and I was basically told there would be no program without it.

What I did then was to get a birth certificate in the name of the then Home Secretary, Charles Clarke, MP. This allowed me to apply for a driving license in his name and, unbelievably, I got it in a matter of weeks. If I'd wanted I could have gone on to get a passport or anything else for that matter. For me the most surprising thing about it all was that it was just me doing it. How could I possibly be able to do this? But I could and it was easy and it shouldn't have been. Then again, that was supposed to be the point.

After that, things turned a bit nasty. Despite my informing both Scotland Yard and the Home Office what I'd done - the plan was to confront the Home Secretary with my 'new identity' in an interview with him - nobody seemed to be interested. Then they came and arrested me for it. Things could have got nastier still but the loophole, at least from my perspective, is that I wasn't doing it with any ulterior, criminal motive. What I was doing was in the public interest.

The thing is though, the Home Secretary at the time just wanted me thrown in jail for simply doing it, even though I'd proved a point. Some good did come out of it because what I did and how easily I'd done it - and likely because of who I'd done it too - the problem with driving licenses was highlighted and the application form had to be altered as a result. Hopefully it will have stopped it happening to other people.

It's quite ironic really, although things have changed a lot now, an ethical hacker would obviously be doing something like that with permission. Some companies are keen to find loopholes just like that and employ people to demonstrate them. But, as a good guy doing it, you can end up in a lot of trouble.

Taking everything into consideration, and although I understand you can't have a free-for-all on this stuff, at the same time it does feel that it's balanced in favor of the criminal. It seems ridiculous to persecute those who are trying to do good and letting those who have done bad go unchallenged. At some point it stops making sense.

Now we have A.I. on the horizon and, whatever this is going to do or mean for all of us, I know that A.I. cannot genuinely empathize. That, to me, is where the problem lies in having this type of mechanism or technology in place. It might be able to hold a conversation, or give you help if you're trying to fill in a form or whatever, but if you come up against problems, that's where I think it will fail.

You're going to have a machine that does not, in any way, fully understand human emotions. At least for me that's the hard part to imagine right now. To a certain extent we come across this now even with human beings and customer support. It's all, "I'm really sorry to hear about the problems you're having..." and, "What we suggest is ..." It's all very, very automated, detached and rehearsed. Of course, they aren't machines, but to many people they sound as if they might as well be because the genuine empathy obviously isn't there. When I go round and give talks to customer service teams, telling my story, they can put a face to a situation and it all suddenly becomes more real. The feedback I've had over the years is that they're more genuine when they speak to customers because they have the memory of what happened to me. But you're not going to have that type of empathy with circuitry.

The CISO PERSPECTIVE
Matthias Muhlert - CISO
(Manufacturing)

Matthias is an experienced CISO that truly understands the world of the hacker; in his early days he taught himself how to code along with studying the art of hacking systems, his tenacity and passion for self-learning continues to this day. I asked Matthias to talk about his experience as a corporate CISO.

Matthias Muhlert: Corporate CISO
"I've been in cybersecurity for 19 years now. First in I.T. security - antivirus, Intrusion Detection Systems (IDS), Intrusion Protection Systems (IPS) systems, firewalls and working toward the hacking perspective and teaching about it. And the last nine, in information security, looking at the bigger picture from a governance or policy perspective. I got quite good at Layer 2 hacking and worked globally for a while, now I'm based in Austria. With the hacker side of things I didn't go for certification, such as the CEH (Certified Ethical Hacker), I worked hands-on and just hacked stuff. Back then tools like Kali Linux didn't exist and I wrote a couple of exploits, but most of the time a proper shell script would do the job. I also did an extensive network testing script. It was hard work, reading up on BackTrack, analyzing your latest exploit and then reverse engineering it, but I enjoyed learning about the technical side from the hacker's perspective.

Different businesses though have different priorities. For example, banks don't really have any intellectual property like an industry does, which is where I'm working now. Banks are more focused on traceability and accountability. As a CISO I like to switch between the industries because they all have a different focus and you get to learn what is important to each business.

Communication is key to my role. I spend at least three hours a day in meetings and more often up to six. You have to really understand the business, but also be proficient in conveying the message of information security. A CISO needs to talk to HR, other compliance departments, development or corporate functions. So, for me, a lot of the job consists of conveying the message and getting people to understand. I also have to find time to manage my team and to make sure that they grow.

It's difficult to see where the role of the CISO will go from here and I'm hoping that the role will develop further and go into the management area. Personally I would find it difficult to go into general management and don't know how much benefit I would be. I report to the head of compliance and legal. Reporting to the CEO, well, that's difficult because he has a different agenda and objectives most of the time. He's hired to make sure things run smoothly and I'm hired to make sure they run securely and they are not always compatible. I'm not certain I would want to report to the CEO, but would prefer to report to the Chief Risk Officer or Chief Operations Officer who sit on the board.

I'm not certain if CISOs should sit on the board, it depends on the industry. For example, if your main source of income is Internet Technology, then the CISO should be on the board because it is one of your main risk drivers. Then there are other industries where security isn't the main source. Besides there is a diversity of people who call themselves CISOs and in reality it's many different things to different people and different organizations. Some CISOs are people who have been promoted from firewall admin. It's not that they aren't up to the job but really there should at least be some qualifications in there as well. I took the CISM and CISSP although I don't think more certification would be beneficial because if I don't know it by now then it can't help me.

I feel a responsibility to the organization and, if it was breached and it was because of something I'd overlooked, then I'd definitely feel responsible. If someone else signed off the risk though, then I would not feel responsible for it.

It's like the Susan Mauldin situation. There were so many conversations and arguments. Okay, so she did an art major in music. I know a lot of art guys who are great security guys because they have a different mindset and they think in a different way, their eye for detail is really great, so I was a little bit frustrated by the whole discussion.

Then again, it also depends how expensive the bullet is that you take. You sign up for a certain responsibility, right? You can't say, okay, I'm part of upper management and then afterward not be willing to take the responsibility. That doesn't really work for me.

The biggest threat to cybersecurity is the industrialization of cyber-crime. You have script kiddies who can do national attacks now. Then you had the Russian business network that came into play, who really professionalized the whole thing where you can buy DDOS attacks for a reasonable price, and they were totally open about it, so that was an interesting topic for me.

Then, if you look at ransomware attacks, in 2016 and especially 2017, they rose over 600%. The other thing that concerns me is integrity and where it can lead which we saw with attacks such as Stuxnet. You don't know if, say, an Excel sheet has been changed unless you check the MAC records each time - and no one can do that. You get an Excel sheet and you put the numbers into your system on the presumption that they are correct. The integrity of SCADA systems is even more complex to check. So from the CISO perspective, I think hackers will shift into integrity and they will be able to do some damage there.

Integrity breaches have though been around for ages. For example, Meltdown has been around since '95. What's new is that they are now on the one side exposing it to more attack surfaces and they're interconnecting it more. Because of this we need to put more and more lines between O.T. and I.T. which should not be there. So this is a new dimension.

For me, the most important part of the job is making the risks transparent to allow business decisions to be made in an informed manner. However, often I make the risk-bearer aware but he's not giving me his part of the informed decision back.

For me three motivational factors have to be in place for me to want to be in a particular CISO role because I have to believe I can be of benefit to the company. First of all, what autonomy do I have when it comes to cybersecurity decisions? I need to be the decision maker in that instance no matter where I roam in the organization. Then comes mastery, and I think a lot of security professionals will tell you the same. The more they learn, the more they understand they do not know. Mastery is a topic where you can learn every day. This is why I go to conferences because you get new input and new ideas every day. So you can master yourself, you can master your subject, and you can improve on that.

Last, but definitely not least, is purpose. I strongly believe that if I go to the office, then I serve a purpose for the company or something even bigger than the company, maybe also for the industry or the security community. So, if I have those three motivational aspects in place, it makes me want to be a CISO."

Chapter 7
CISO Fingerprinting: The Traits of the CISO

"I am not a product of my circumstances. I am a product of my decisions."
-     Stephen Covey

From speaking to many CISOs over the past fifteen or so years, and indeed taking my own experience of working as a Global CISO and Interim Head of Security across a diverse range of industries and sectors into account, it became clear that in addition to the diversity of the demands there are many styles of CISO and security leaders defending the cyber-realm.

These are brave men and women taking on a challenging, somewhat unique and, to some degree, misunderstood and under-appreciated role. The CISO requires a wide range of skills and a certain mindset to protect an organization's critical assets, data, and information from being compromised by a diverse range of threats, some of which emanate externally and others which are internal to the company.

Occasionally, CISOs are tasked to work in difficult environments and in different parts of the world where the rule of law is not as mature as it is in the west or across the developed world. Some must deal with corruption, coercion, and even the threat to their own lives or that of their families from criminal gangs or violent groups. These are, of course, the extremes and this book focuses more on the traditional aspects of the role operating in the context of circumstances considered closer to the norm for most of us.

It was meeting these characters and listening to their stories which inspired this book and indeed the title 'CISO: Defenders of the Cyber-Realm,' but the diverse range of skills required to do the job inspired the development of the CISO Fingerprinting model because it quickly became evident that the cybersecurity officer is, or should be, a breed apart from other managers or executives within organizations.

Not to put too fine a point on it, and while some have a low public profile, make no mistake all are in a position of influence or at least they should be. These are the men and women whose job it is to keep the lights on, the banks open, and food on the shelves, along with multiple other critical services that keep the nation and the millions of products, services and processes available for the continued smooth running of both the country and the organizations they represent.

As a culmination of these observations, we embarked on a program of critical and structured research and, very quickly, two things became clear. Firstly, the environments that our CISOs are operating in and asked to defend vary greatly. As a result, the activities which CISOs are required to perform are also extremely varied. However, we also discovered there are common, and likely more important, measurable aspects of the role that ultimately played a significant part in our analysis.

The second emerging concept was that despite the environmental diversity and the core leadership skills needed, four very distinct styles began to surface. Although it was clear that many CISOs come from a technical or I.T. background, a fact which is confirmed by our CISO interviews, three other strengths – strategic, operational and advisory – also became extremely relevant. This is not to say that any one individual will have a profile so binary that it is grounded in one particular style, but it demonstrated there will be a preference and leaning based on a number of factors such as experience, education, cultural, and environmental influences.

About the CISO Fingerprint

This CISO FINGERPRINT™ is a self-assessment tool and is not designed to be a test. As such there are no right or wrong answers. Neither is there a 'perfect' score since the values are not expressed as numbers but rather as a graphic representation. This can then be used to compare the relative fit, strengths, and bias to identified role specifications.

The results we see are just as varied as there are numbers of security officers out there, but there are common traits and themes which allow us to contrast and compare to one another. Requiring the honest feel for the values within each section is imperative for the matching model to work well, so the tool allows us to capture an indicative measure of the CISO's preferred style based on their own perception of their skills and expertise.

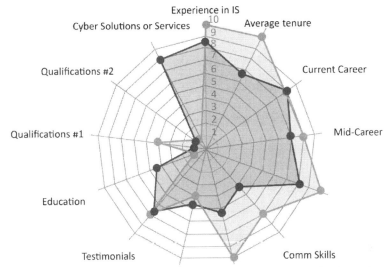

Image 1 – Example of a CISO Fingerprint – Individual against a benchmark – In this example, the inner score represents the benchmark.

Intuition, the Sea Within, and the Art of Being a CISO

The 'noise' of the external world has developed to the point that it is muting the sound of our inner world, and the implications of this constant stream of distraction mean our intuition is being suppressed. We are becoming more and more distracted by external stimuli, often in the form of entertainment, and we are becoming less connected interpersonally at a human level despite our virtual connections increasing. The more frequently we connect using technology, the less frequently we engage with the natural world and the impact of these changes have yet to be fully experienced.

Although intuition might for some be an elusive concept, in many cultures it holds great significance. The ancient Icelandic word for intuition is 'innsæi,' the translated meaning of which revolves around the concept of 'the sea within'. This is also described as the borderless nature of our inner world which is a constantly moving and infused world of vision, feelings, and imagination all beyond mere words. It is accepted as being inherent within the individual and an essential part of who we are, yet our current practices mean it is being suppressed.

The growth of invasive technologies has interrupted the way we have traditionally communicated and interacted over thousands of years not only with others but also with ourselves in respect of the inner talk or voice. Our natural ability to make intuitive decisions based on gut feelings is, if not disappearing, then certainly being impeded. Whatever the case, it would appear that fewer and fewer people are either becoming less intuitive or at least not listening in the same way we once used to. In many cases it would seem that our inner feelings of human intuition are actually being replaced by new artificial intuitive deities better known as Google, Bing or Safari.

Today, rather than following our intuition, most people need to verify everything before proceeding. Everything has to be validated, proven, rationalized, and reasoned before action is taken. Is this actually a sign that the inner sea is evaporating, that we have lost or are losing the ability to make spontaneous snap decisions because of the necessity to justify every move? Most employers would not consider intuition to be an integral force in business, despite the fact many of today's renowned entrepreneurs originally went with their intuition to make it to the top.

But how important is it when it comes to securing and protecting an organization from a cyber perspective? The ability to sense that something is not quite right and needs investigating seemed, to me at least, to be an essential trait in a good security professional. However, is that really the case? Is it even possible to measure this as a success factor? These are all questions I found myself asking when coming to understand what traits made a successful CISO.

In the pursuit of understanding these traits, my team started to develop the CISO Fingerprint™ which is a pragmatic application designed to quickly capture the essence of the person completing the self-perception assessment. What we found from this was a collective picture started to emerge which pointed to four key preferred styles of CISO which are underpinned by the general acceptance that having well-rounded leadership skills are a given fundamental in the makeup. Further investigation revealed that although CISOs tend to have elements of all four styles, which is only to be expected, the style to which they leaned the most strongly indicates to an organization how best to support their CISO or to match skills based on what is needed dependent on organizational requirements, the level of organizational maturity, and the organization's state of readiness in accepting what needs to be achieved.

Of course, what our research also revealed was many organizations do not understand how to access their own requirements and needs. As a result, we went on to the develop the CISO Footprint™ which provides insights into the cybersecurity profile of the organization and provides a matching tool to help ensure the right security leadership is in play at the right time.

Capturing the Essence of the CISO Fingerprint Styles

There are four key styles that emerged from the research and whilst no one style is necessarily attributed to each individual – to a greater or lesser degree we tend to be a mix of all – there does tend to be a prominent or preferred style to reflect the bias of the CISO at least from a self-rating perspective. The objective of the exercise here is to provide more insight into the crossover between the environment and the challenges the CISO faces and his or her security leadership style in coping and managing with the demands of the role.

The Four Styles of the CISO

TECHNICAL LEAD
This person often comes from an I.T. or I.S. background, either personally or professionally, and has a strong bias and passion towards the more technical and detailed aspects of cybersecurity. They may have a long list of industry certificates and accreditations to support and underpin their experience. Frequently the focus here is on tools and technology as the main element to mitigate cyber-risk and this person will typically develop a solid allegiance and affinity with technical and I.T./O.T. departments and system owners.

The external perception of this person is one who is seen as a technical expert and respected 'geek.' They tend to fit in well with the standard organizational paradigm because they often think and operate from a more conventional and conservative worldview. Forward planning is frequently a trait and they have medium- to longer-term drive and momentum. Focus is on ensuring systems and architectures are resilient and secure. Based on the profiles completed to date around 50% of the CISO community have a technical or I.T. background.

STRATEGY LEAD

This person often comes from a commercially-focused background; finding and developing appropriate solutions to business-related challenges or problems is critical. They view technology as an enabler or tool and a means to an end in getting the job done. Consequently, they are more inclined to be a consumer of technology than an enthusiast or technician. Frequently this person is seen to be a visionary, post-conventional thinker and has a driven leadership style. As a result, they have the ability to visualize and work with whole systems and processes across an enterprise. These are people who want to lead change and are not frightened by the challenges of doing so.

In the hierarchical organization they can often be misconceived as a negative disruptor to the status quo. This person sets the vision, develops the roadmap, and provides a holistic strategy to meet current and emerging challenges and will focus on ensuring the business, as an ecosystem, is secure.

As communicators they tend to interact well with the executive team having the ability to 'speak the language'. Correspondingly, they understand the business implications of cybersecurity and can articulate and present to the board to gain their support and backing. Overall, this individual aligns the organization with a clear set of objectives and can work with cross-departmental and functional teams to implement them. They also audit progress and maintain a progressive momentum while being adaptive, open, and approachable. Around 10% of CISOs profiled fall under this category.

OPERATIONAL LEAD
Those with operational lead strengths often come from a security-focused, operational role within the business and

are experienced in managing the day-to-day operational aspects of information and data security. They have a strong focus on understanding business needs which is underpinned by a good grasp on supporting technologies and functions such as the Security Operations Center (SoC) and/or Network Operations Center (NOC) or the I.T. support function.

This person is often a conventional thinker with the ability to effectively blend operational and security needs in a manner that balances a pragmatic approach with sometimes competing disciplines. They are most effective and indeed motivated in a steady state BAU (Business as Usual) environment where developing day-to-day security resilience aligned to operational efficiency is paramount. Our research showed 35% of CISOs are operating in this capacity.

ADVISORY

Often coming from a consultative background and taking the role of trusted adviser to the senior executive and main board, this individual usually has an in-depth knowledge not only of the cyber-risk landscape but also of the impact that a significant breach would or could have on the corporate infrastructure. They are skilled in areas such as post-breach recovery and managing the development of a cyber-resilient ecosystem.

This person articulates and sells the need to take cybersecurity seriously and is respected as a credible source of advice and guidance across the enterprise. They are capable of delivering both conventional and post-conventional strategies and solutions to meet security needs. When it comes to technology, they see it as part of the solution but understand that taking a more holistic approach is needed to beat the cyber-criminals, understanding the evolving risks which this encompasses. They are also effective in supporting other CISOs or to act as an independent or NED to provide oversight to the Board on the activities and approach taken by the incumbent CISO or security team. They can help achieve greater and faster progress and are useful in challenging the status quo where needed. Somewhere in the region of 5% of CISOs spend a portion of their time in this capacity.

Summarizing the Areas of Focus
Our research went on to define characteristics, experience, and traits of the CISO without relying on the norm of the static qualification which is a frequent prerequisite in any employment field but which, when it comes to the ever-changing world of cybersecurity and the complexities of human nature itself, is only applicable for a specific moment in time.

Clearly, the requirements of the organization, their level of corporate maturity in respect of cybersecurity, and the traits of the CISO are something which must be compatible to ensure secure defenses can be built against the bad actors.

To assist in doing this, I developed the 5M's model as a starting point in enabling organizations to become what we term 'Hacker Hardened™'.

1. MANAGE: HAVE THE RIGHT SECURITY LEADERSHIP IN PLACE

Managing the situation in a manner appropriate to the individual organization is essential. If we have learned nothing else, it is that 'one size does not fit all' when it comes to cybersecurity. Ensure your CISO or senior security leadership capabilities match all Footprint requirements and the organization provides the resources necessary to complement, deliver or lead the CISO office or support an efficient and effective security Target Operating Model (ToM) that resonates with the needs of the business.

2. MEASURE: WHAT GETS MEASURED GETS DONE

Capture your organization's current security posture and level of risk exposure by baselining your cyber and security control together with the organizational level of security maturity to define and inform your business strategy, policy, budget, and critical defensive projects and security capabilities. Provide the board with a level of reporting that makes decision-making more informed and easier when it comes to managing and accepting risk in the digital and security world.

3. MONITOR: WHAT YOU CAN'T SEE YOU CAN'T FIX

Investigate the real-time oversight of your security estate and in the process identify areas that are potentially open to exploitation through key monitoring factors. Monitoring for anomalies and changes in network behavior is an excellent way of identifying any possible breaches whether they are of the external or internal variety. This also provides much-needed insight for executives and allows for improved decision-making.

4. MITIGATE: PLUGGING THE GAPS AND CLOSING THE LOOPHOLES

Often, vulnerabilities in cybersecurity are best identified by a third party. Whether you are thinking of offering a 'bug bounty' to ethical hackers or employing a specialist company to perform penetration and adversarial Red Team Testing, frequently these options identify gaps across physical security, digital (cyber) security (I.T. & O.T./I.C.S.) and associated human factors. Prioritize mitigation strategies and solutions based on your level of risk appetite, the threat landscape, availability of budgets, and your cultural and resourcing requirements.

5. <u>MAINTAIN: KEEPING THINGS TIGHT IN A CHANGING LANDSCAPE</u>

Virtual or 'As-a-Service' on-going executive oversight and management of your security estate. Recognizing the business, legislative, and security threat landscape changes frequently and the need to maintain HACKER HARDENED(TM) status is ongoing.

Conventional and Post-Conventional Thinking

"No problem can be solved from the same level of consciousness that created it."

- Albert Einstein

Recognizing that cybersecurity continues to be a challenging phenomenon for most organizations and nation-states, we need security leaders that have the ability to look at the world through a lens that goes beyond conventional thinking. As Einstein's quote implies, taking a conventional approach to solving the challenges that the digital world imposes on society is not likely to achieve the outcomes needed to ensure our ongoing safety and security.

We need people who can think 'post-conventionally,' those that are truly transformational leaders, those that can define and implement strategies derived from a level of conscious awareness which would appear to be relatively scarce globally, let alone in the corporate world. In a sample of almost 500 well-educated, working adults in the United States, 90% were scored as holding conventional Action Logics and only 7% profiled as being post-conventional according to studies carried out by Professor William Torbert.[1]

Post-conventional individuals who have the ability to perceive and think about solutions to common problems in different ways are, in the eyes of this study, relatively rare. Those that have the ability to operate beyond conventional wisdom, the thought barriers, and glass ceilings that this level of thinking brings may be a good starting point in selecting the caliber of CISO needed to combat the rise in cyber-crime. But what does that mean in practice and how does it manifest itself in the 'real' world?

Some years ago, I discovered the Leadership Development Framework (LDF) and over time have found this particularly useful in understanding this transition in leadership and its utility and usefulness in the security world.[2]

The LDF articulates the transition from conventional leadership (what we learned through formal education) to post-conventional leadership. In applying this model, we are better able to understand where on the pre-conventional to post-conventional continuum a particular leader sits.

Developed by David Rooke and Professor Bill Torbert of the Carroll School of Management, the LDF postulates that adults experience stages of development which significantly affect their abilities to solve problems, interpret, and interact with their environment. These stages of development make meaning which lead to action – so each stage is called an Action Logic (A.L.). No one is fixed at their current A.L.; if motivated and supported, everyone is able to develop new ways of behaving. Under stress, someone may revert to an earlier A.L., but research shows that no one can access behaviors from a later logic level.

So, What Do the A.L.s Look Like?

There are nine, in sequence, seven of which I'll introduce briefly here.

Rooke and Torbert adapted the Washington University Sentence Completion Test (WUSCT) for managers in the 1980s and 1990s. The test was initially developed by Dr. Jane Loevinger as a test of 'ego development'[3], which in itself is one of the most widely used and validated instruments in psychometrics. Unlike many conventional assessments of this type, this approach does not force the individual being assessed to select a pre-prepared answer.

If you have ever completed a Conventional Psychometric Assessment, emphasis on the word 'conventional', you will understand what I mean – the *'select one of these four statements that most describes your style?'* type approach (errr… none of them or actually all of them given changing circumstances… right?). Instead, it presents thirty-six starting sentences which you are asked to complete.

As an example, you are asked to complete a sentence such as, "When a person steps out of line at work…" Or, "I can't stand people who…" It's a very different and intuitively more insightful approach to understanding the way leaders think and how they solve problems.

From the answers provided, the Leadership Development Profile (LDP) was developed and there have now been thousands of the 36-sentence completions. Results show that of the vast majority of those managers assessed, approaching 80%, across industries and organizational levels, fall in the Expert and Achiever Action Logics. The scoring is based on identifying patterns in the answers, which become more apparent as the data volume grows, and that allows expert assessment to identify and contrast the 'music' of the responses in a scoring matrix.

Here is my take on summarizing each A.L., in short form and with a cyber twist. For the full descriptions see, Torbert, Fisher, and Rooke's 2004 publication *'Action Inquiry; The Secret of Timely and Transforming Leadership'* published by Berrett-Koehler or visit Bill Torbert's website for details at http://www.williamrtorbert.com/action-inquiry/ or at https://www.gla.global/.

The first two in the sequence below are pre-conventional logic levels, three and four are conventional, which reflects the bulk of managers, and sit centrally on the bell curve, five is a transitionary A.L. into the post-conventional levels:

#1 Opportunist – Around 3% of Managers studied hold this Action Logic

Winning in the moment any way possible, self-oriented, short-term horizons, manipulative, mantra 'might makes right'. Our prisons are full of opportunists who ignore consequences in favor of the 'prize.' Many young hackers may also fall into this category which is reflected in timely action occurring when "I Win," or put another way when, "I crack the password or access that private database I was targeting."

#2 Diplomat – Less than 5% of Senior Managers studied hold this Action Logic

Avoiding overt conflict, obeys the norms of immediate group, consensus decision making, wants to belong, rarely rocks the boat, everyone's friend – one can imagine that Facebook likes are an important driver for this level of thinking. Tends to focus on routine tasks, being on time, and works on a one-week to three-month time horizon.

#3 Expert - 45% of total respondents assessed hold this Action Logic

A specialist who rules by logic and expertise; is immersed in the self-referential logic of their own belief system regarding it as the only valid way of thinking. Is interested in problem-solving; critical of self and others based on their belief system, chooses efficiency over effectiveness. Perfectionist; accepts feedback only from "objective" experts in their own field. Dogmatic; values decisions based on the incontrovertible facts. Wants to stand out and be unique as an expert, sense of obligation to wider, internally consistent moral order, consistently pursues improvement; is a strong individual contributor, works in the business. Plenty of this level of A.L. displayed on the technical side of cybersecurity and I.T. Security. A good number of the more technical CISOs may also be reflective of this A.L.

#4 Achiever - 35% of respondents assessed hold this Action Logic

Is an implementer who meets strategic goals; effectiveness and results-oriented; sets long-term goals; future is vivid, inspiring; welcomes behavioral feedback; feels like an initiator, not a 'pawn'; begins to appreciate complexity and systems; seeks increasing mutuality in relationships; feels guilt if does not meet own standards; blind to own shadow, to the subjectivity behind objectivity; seeks to find ways around problems in order to deliver, maybe unorthodox; adopts rather than creates goals. This and the following A.L.s, work ON the business.

Then there are the first 2 of the post-conventionals:

#5 Individualist - 11% hold this Action Logic

A catalyst/consultant leader who innovates processes, takes a relativistic position with fewer fixed truths; focuses on self, relationships and interaction with the system, less on goals; has an increased understanding of complexity, systems operating and working through relationships; has deep personal relationships; takes on a different role in different situations; increasingly questions own assumptions and those of others; attracted by change and difference more than by stability and similarity; increasingly aware of own shadow.

#6 Strategist - 5% hold this Action Logic

A synergistic integrator who creates personal and organizational transformations; links between principles, contracts, theories, and judgment; recognizes the importance of principle, contract, theory and judgment; creative at conflict resolution; process- and goal-oriented; aware of paradox and contradiction; aware that what one sees depends upon one's worldview; places high value on individuality, unique market niches, historical movements;

enjoys a variety of roles; has witty, existential humor; may be tempted by the Dark Side of power. From a CISO and cybersecurity perspective, perhaps one of the A.L.'s more adept at understanding the 'Dark Side' and the adversarial perspective. Great at looking at old problems in new, innovative, and transformational ways.

In conclusion, from a security perspective, strategists can be seen by other A.L.s as disruptors of the 'status quo.' This, however, is a manifestation of their pursuit of the development of a more resilient and secure environment and driving cultural change for the good of the business. Being able to understand and match an individual CISO or security leader's preferred style, supporting and recognizing their need to embrace the intuitive nature of the work and the level of Action Logic deployed in problem-solving; all factors that can help in ensuring you have the right person with the Fingerprint profile necessary for success in the role.

Add solid business acumen, well-rounded executive skills, and the ability to cope with continuous self-education along with buckets of resolve and the commitment necessary to deal with the daily living of the threat of a significant hack, and you start to understand the role.

Security is a journey and never a destination – just when you think you have all the bases covered and appropriately locked down, along comes a new threat, a change in legislation or technology that requires a refresh of the security controls in place.

So, the review of each focus area above should involve the organization's Risk Committee – the first question should be "What has changed in our security risk posture since our last review?" Followed by, "What do we need to do to maintain or improve our current position?" And so on.

We next need to understand the maturity of the environment that our CISO will operate within – enter the CISO Footprint.

About The CISO Footprint

Having developed the CISO Fingerprint™ which is very much focused on the individual as a security leader, the next logical step in understanding the role was to assess the environments that CISOs are operating within. Some are working in parts of the world where they have to survive (literally) in a highly corrupt environment and where exposing the goings-on may cost them more than just their jobs.

So, ignoring the extremes for now and working with the more 'normal' and regulated environments of the developed world, I designed and developed an application that would, in short order, quickly capture the essence and maturity of an organization's security posture and provide some indication as to the security culture. This has been designed to give mainly small- to medium-sized organizations a starting point in reviewing their security needs and to help match this to appropriate CISO skills.

The CISO Footprint is a 30-question construct built around the 5M's of Manage, Monitor, Measure, Mitigate and Maintain, with an additional focus on 'approach' which seeks to capture cultural aspects.

It's rare for two organizations to have the exact same profile or, in this case, Footprint. Whilst there are common themes and trends across industries, we find that some organizations are more mature and resilient in their approach to cyber and security in general. Whilst many others, despite the growing level of risk awareness across executive teams, remain overly exposed to exploitation by adversaries and the impact that a significant cyber-breach can and does have. Once completed, this Footprint is 'yours' based on your perception and answers to the short questionnaire that you have completed.

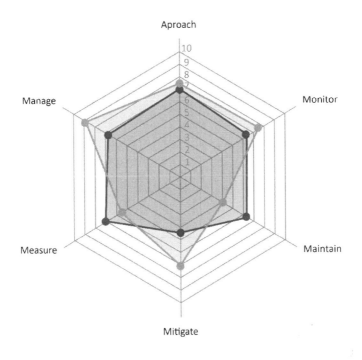

Image 2 – Example of a CISO Footprint – organization against a benchmark – In this example, the inner score is the benchmark

The Footprint is no more than a snapshot in time, based on your current scenario, perspectives, and work environment. This is susceptible to change at many levels; from changing business needs, operational architectures, legislative and compliance drivers, as well as an evolving and dynamic threat landscape.

We recommend that you revisit the CISO Footprint at least a couple of times a year to update your results and to measure any change.

In addition to capturing a view of your 'APPROACH' to managing cybersecurity in your organization, the Footprint focuses primarily on the ABG 5M Framework and the capabilities that sit behind them. This ensures you have the necessary components to demonstrate at least a base level of security risk management in a manner that allows for adaptive change to meet new challenges. Behind each of the 5M points on the spider graph lies a more detailed review or capability.

At ABG we look from a CISO perspective to have a balanced score across the 6 points on the graph. A high score would indicate and demonstrate your confidence in that specific area; you feel there is sufficient maturity and capability to avoid or mitigate a breach and to comply with the latest legislation (e.g. NIS NIST, GDPR, HIPPA, PCI DSS... or others appropriate to your region or industry). A low score or any imbalance or distortion in the graph indicates that further investigation is required as a potential area for exploitation may exist.

This is really a quick 'thumb in the air' view to capture a sense of your level of security maturity. Needless to say, we recommend an independent assessment to provide additional insight and to complement and substantiate the graph results.

As we grow the database for both the CISO Fingerprint and the CISO Footprint, we achieve greater insight and comparisons across industry. This allows us to create a benchmark and is a useful means to help at a local, detailed level but also in shaping industry and nationwide solutions to common challenges faced by all in the ever-expanding digital world.

The combination of the two profiles helps organizations gain an understanding of the maturity of their current environment and then helps ensure the appropriate skill sets are applied to meet the immediate needs of the organization – all with the objective of reducing risk across the business.

Both tools can be accessed on the AscotBarclay.com website.

Interview with Industry
Bharat Thakrar – Cyber Security Technologist
(Global Services)

I was pleased to be able to sit with Bharat and enjoy a coffee conversation that took us deep into his 14 years of experience in the cybersecurity industry. Today Bharat is Head of Business Continuity and Resilience Services for a well-known global services firm and offers a personal view on his take towards the CISO role in today's global economy.

Bharat Thakar: Cyber Security Technologist

"I'm Bharat Thakrar, I understand technical security, but when I go into organizations there seems to be an over-focus on it. Yet the board is less interested and almost to the extent that it's a side issue for them. What they want to know is, "Is my organization secure? Am I likely to get breached? Are we doing everything we can if we get breached, and are we prepared for that?" In large organizations with a big security function the CISO might have a lot of influence, but in mid-size organizations that's missing, and often there isn't a direct link. The person in charge is either the head of I.T. or reports to a security manager, but again, he's technical. Many of these organizations actually have an advisory board, or non-exec board, who have a risk oversight responsibility. A lot of the time though they see that as a purely financial risk oversight, whereas a cyber-breach might actually bring the company to its knees. But in their minds there isn't a direct connection between a breach occurring and the company going down the tubes.

I think we need to champion this cause to say, "Look, that is directly central to your brief here," and that's missing. Whether they think cyber is too technical, or that it's a technical risk, I don't know. Because it hasn't happened these guys aren't connecting the dots and are missing the point. No-one has sat down with them and said, "Look, let me remove all the technical terminology and relate this in terms of what could go wrong. Our information is online, none of that can be guaranteed, but we can improve our defenses." Having set information – a book, or a program – explaining things in non-technical language that they can relate to - would help.

If the CISO or board don't take cyber seriously then, even if there's a non-exec function, there isn't direction from the top to say, "We need to put attention on this."

Budgeting for cybersecurity is an expensive business. On an ongoing basis we need to keep investing because hackers and scammers are getting good, and we've got to be able to meet that to keep our security posture and maturity improving year on year, meaning investment needs to be made. When the security manager goes to the board and says, "I need investment," the Chief Financial Officer (CFO) says, "You need £100,000? How much are you going to reduce the risk? Are we going to get our risk from 35% to 25%? Explain in terms I can understand." At the moment security managers aren't able to do that. If you look at Return on Investment (ROI) when it comes to Google, they give accurate information to their clients. They can say, "Look, because you created that ad on this page, your hit rate has gone from 23% to 59%." If you measure the sales over time then you can directly see the correlation between the additional investment in ads and the additional sales revenue. Whereas our guy is encumbered by the current, fairly vague notions, of reduced risk, and it's not an answer we can give.

The solutions lie in two or three areas. One is greater awareness of the fact that security is a cost. It's not revenue generating. There is indirect revenue generating, in the sense that if you can demonstrate you are a more secure organization than the other 20 companies you're competing with, and get that information across to clients, then they're more likely to stay with you and you don't lose that loyalty.

We also need to understand the risk management techniques. It's not always impact versus probability because that's a very blunt instrument. We need to be able to translate that into financial terms in a much more precise way, to say, "These additional investments are leading …" But this is an ongoing thing, it's not a one-off, you have to improve over a period of time.

It's also about the metrics providing the connection between security and the board. Are they understandable, do they pinpoint from a financial and business perspective, do they show the improvement in the company's security posture?

There are two additional areas that I've spent some time on. One is threat intelligence and I've chaired a couple of conferences on that. The other area that I've been taking an interest in is the Internet of Things. It might not be new, but the wave of technological change that's coming in the next two or three years is going to be astounding. We've got research from the likes of Cisco saying that 50 billion devices are going to be connected to the IoT by 2020, just over a year away. And 500 billion devices within another five to seven years beyond that.

Our homes are totally going to be connected, our cars will be connected, we'll be wearing wearables, and that's just on a personal level. We're going through the most massive change, and I don't think the security function is ready for this.

Then there is a commercial imperative. My company can't be too much behind the curve. Look at what's happening with the retail sector at the moment... they're being driven by a digital revolution.

But that's just today, the next three or four years are going to be like a step change. If organizations are struggling, then the attack surface for the hacker has multiplied five, ten times. If I'm a criminal making money from drugs or whatever, it's worth me giving that up and getting online. The tools are available, you don't need to be computer literate. Help desks are available, online hacking as a service is readily there. The attack surface is going to expand and this is a huge issue.

We can automate a lot of things, but the hacker is also going to find automation tools very cheap. Instead of him sending botnets to 100 or 200 targets, he can scale up.

If I've learned anything from 20-25 years of cybersecurity it's that there is no silver bullet. You have to do the hard work, the hard slog. No organization can have a shortcut out of this. The companies who put time in, put investment in, do things in a structured, logical manner, will be the ones who benefit. They'll stay secure for longer.

There are also concerns about A.I. and machine learning that could get us into hot water because, of all the A.I. material I've looked at very few highlight the security risk. Collecting data quickly is important, but are we doing it with effective cybersecurity controls? It certainly doesn't seem to be part of the story at the moment.

When it comes to cyber-crime there was a time when the good guys had the upper hand. At the moment, we don't. And solutions don't always have to be about technology. Incorporating technology with a more mature approach will give us an ability to manage this, rather than always being behind the curve. It is possible to manage it, and be clear about the value of it, although you will never be able to predict everything. If we focus our resources on that, it doesn't really matter if the hackers come into the garden, the courtyard and onto the veranda, they won't get into the house.

It's a combination of process, leadership, and the right technology."

Chapter 8
Emerging Threats: Future View

"I don't want to really scare you, but it was alarming how many people I talked to who are highly placed in AI who have retreats that are sort of 'bug-out' houses to which they could flee if it all hits the fan."

- James Barrat (with Washington Post)

The threat landscape has evolved with technology and technology has advanced at a speed far greater than most would have ever considered possible. Despite this bringing with it more potential competitive advantage and social interaction, albeit of the virtual kind, it has also brought with it increased risk. As of yet, we have failed to establish with any degree of certainty just how damaging those risks could be.

When it comes to enterprise, though, the problems are becoming clearer, despite their being pitiful few solutions to what is developing into a critical situation. For the CISO and the companies they attempt to defend, the scenario is simpler to define – as more devices and individual human interactions are added to networks there is a corresponding increase in the number of potential problems for them to manage.

What we find when we examine the situation more closely is that in many cases the original threats security officers faced are still in existence today. The only difference is they have simply become more sophisticated over time. What we also find is that this drive in sophistication is not only due to technological advances but also because the nature of what the bad actors seek has changed.

Historically, we know that threats in the world of cyber came first with geopolitical spying and warfare tactics in general. Then the hackers got involved, initially just to see if they could. Today emerging threats, at least in respect of devices, more frequently depend on whether the intention is to:

• Obtain data
• Obtain money
• Cause disruption

As more and more aspects of our lives are being drawn into the technological maze, the goal of the bad actors, in general, has changed. Where once disruption was often the objective, money then became the driving force. This, in many ways, was no different to gaining access by stealing bank cards in the physical world, but then data itself became the market. Everybody wanted it and for their own legitimate or nefarious reasons. There was no need now to risk taking the final step of actually stealing funds because the monetization of data meant this was the source of income. The more the public could be convinced to part with it, the more it increased in value and became the major target for anyone with an interest whether they be marketers, lone wolf or nation-backed hackers or geopolitical spies.

The hacker then evolved, not only in skill level but also in how they needed to operate. They might once have been primarily kids with too much talent and the same amount of curiosity to match, but today they have grown into organized gangs sometimes working on behalf of nations in what is now being termed 'cyber-warfare'.

On the surface it would seem, at least for the most part, most devices being used today have their foundations in the original mechanisms. However, the environment has changed to the point of being unrecognizable in respect of several essential elements:

- It has become more difficult to trace the perpetrator; attribution remains a challenge.
- The ways in which the devices are used depends on market demands and the target element.
- The convergence of O.T. and I.T. has narrowed 'air gapping' or eradicated it and increased the number of vulnerabilities in critical infrastructure systems.
- The increase in the number of connected devices has correspondingly increased the number of vulnerabilities in systems and expanded the threat landscape.
- The potential for third-party (users of connected devices) negligence has not been taken into consideration at a significant enough level.
- Emerging technology is set to change the landscape completely by increasing the kinds of devices available to both the good and bad actors.

The Emergence of Disruptive Technologies

Disruptive technologies are those which are not only innovative but are predicted to displace those already in existence and, as the name suggests, create a new industry and so disrupt the status quo. Although the term Disruptive Technology might sound like hi-tech jargon, in reality, it isn't actually a new concept at all. In fact, we could view cars as being a disruptive technology which displaced horse transport on the roads; photography as being a disruptive technology which eventually displaced the artist in replicating scenes and portraits. Cinema too was a disruptive technology when it replaced theater as the main mode of entertainment and the advent of the telephone was disruptive in many aspects, not least in affecting the main methods of existing communication.

In many situations, disruptive technologies might be viewed with more than a little apprehension, some which are reasonable and some less so, but no matter what the opinion at the time, the end result is if they are adopted they change the way in which we live our lives forever.

Today, disruptive technologies are emerging all around us. They are set to alter the course of the way we live if, of course, we choose to adopt them. They will be linked to everything we use, buy, manufacture, and even grow. And, of course, underpinning all these developments we must turn our attention to developments in Artificial Intelligence (A.I.), Artificial General Intelligence (A.G.I) and Machine Learning (M.L.).

The fields in which disruptive technologies have the potential to be useful cannot be denied. For example, face recognition software has already been utilized by law enforcement in apprehending suspects and criminals. The benefits to healthcare have even more pertinence, particularly when it comes to A.I. imaging diagnostics and the multitude of medial mobile applications such as those designed for diabetes management. Similar mobile apps can also provide medical professionals with essential information about a patient's condition, and the development of patient data software allows a host of medical authorities access to relevant information about a specific patient.

Outside of all the professional field applications, of course, we also have technologies which apply specifically to the Internet of Things (I.o.T.). We are faced with a variety of gadgets which range from telling us what's stocked in the fridge to menu apps in restaurants. Then, within industry itself, we have the Industrial Internet of Things (I.I.o.T.) which are devices providing the means to improve production and safety when it comes to sensors and other monitoring instruments.

Yet, outside of the undefinable benefits, and even in cases where the benefits could be considered dubious, what these emerging disruptive technologies also bring is a huge increase in the risk of threats not only on a personal level but also to industry and to national infrastructures in general.

The threats can come in many forms and the first aspect to consider is what happens when these things, in the way that technology tends to, go wrong even without third-party interference. Although it might not result in a critical situation if a mobile menu app suddenly decides to serve you with milkshakes instead of Chardonnay, things would start to take on a more sinister tone if facial recognition technology started identifying the wrong suspect or diabetic apps began to give out the wrong readings.

In the U.S., the Food and Drug Administration (F.D.A.) are known for their encouragement of the development of mobile applications, particularly where they can be used to advance healthcare practices. The F.D.A. is also the authority responsible for safety and takes a 'risk-based approach' to the assessment of such devices, mainly at the level of functionality. We might then be reassured that, at least on some level, such devices are manufactured to minimum safety standards. However, as we have discussed earlier in this book, most technical devices are not designed with security in mind when it comes to hacking and compliance-based manufacturing rarely cuts the mustard when the chips are down.

Most would consider assessing technical devices for functionality and failing to consider how well protected they are against deliberate interference is an incident waiting to happen. If we include the fact that many of these devices also have the ability to be used to take down either one or more aspects of our national infrastructure, even those truly enamored by the technology might be influenced enough to sit up and take notice.

By allowing devices which are in the hands of private individuals to cross the line between I.T. and O.T. sectors, which is exactly what is happening, particularly in fields such as medicine whether the devices are in the hands of staff or patients, then the threat landscape expands to the point where it becomes unmanageable and has the potential to become extremely dangerous to large swathes of society and maybe even nations as a whole.

At this point, it is worth remembering that most breaches are actually achieved not through problems with technology but because of the thoughtless acts or errors of individual people. Whether those thoughtless acts include using repetitive passwords, clicking on a link, opening an email message or browsing on a directed website, they happen every single day and not only do they continue to occur, they actually occur with increasing frequency despite all the warnings given.

Few people can be more aware of the fallibility of the human animal than the CISO and we know that within an organization much of their time is taken up by trying to raise security awareness of employees in general as well as managers and board members. Yet what is also becoming clear is that few individuals actually take on board the seriousness of such issues and this is proven over and over again when we look at how many breaches occur as a direct result of individuals inadvertently opening Internet access doors.

Clearly CISOs can have no direct influence on third parties who are using apps in a personal capacity. For example, diabetic patients who connect with organizational systems where one person might make a single error that has the ability to lock or maybe crash healthcare systems.

So, when it comes to risk assessment or compliance in general, the situation as it stands might reassure us that technological safety guidelines are being met when it comes to functionality, and we might also reassure ourselves that staff within an organization are being made security aware, but the greatest risk may well turn out to be third parties who are outside of the currently considered risk arena, located somewhere along the supply chain.

These issues should be considered by health authorities such as the F.D.A. because they are aware of the nature of healthcare being part and parcel of the critical infrastructure of a nation, but this rarely appears to be the case. Neither are these same issues likely to be promoted by I.T. solution providers since they are selling the products. Investors too, who are only looking at financial returns as the objective, are also highly unlikely to concern themselves with problems that are out of their field of vision.

The new legislation arising, at least in Europe in the form of the GDPR and NIS, is attempting to make sure companies understand the significance of embracing cybersecurity and strict financial penalties now loom over those who fail to comply. Unfortunately, as with all punishments, it is something undertaken after the event and most companies seem to have lost sight of the real reasons for such laws being introduced. In some cases, organizations who might be affected seem less concerned about increasing their cybersecurity and more so with trying to circumvent the legislation by finding loopholes in it. Seeing the legislation for what it really is – an attempt to increase involvement in protecting their own businesses – rarely appears to be appreciated. One has to assume that if organizations truly understood the precarious situation they face in respect of hackers, they would spend a lot more time, effort, and money on increasing cybersecurity and a lot less employing those involved in the business of law to try and find ways around it.

The risks are proving to be a cause for concern in some quarters and none is raising eyebrows more than A.I. and M.L., which are technologies where the terminology is often used interchangeably. And, although it's only recently that A.I. has hit mainstream discussion it has actually been around for a long time.

A.I. allows for tasks to be performed by machines that have characteristics of human intelligence such as the ability to plan, memorize objects, learn sounds, and understand languages. Machine learning, on the other hand is, according to Arthur Samuel (1959), *"The ability to learn without being explicitly programmed."* This means that A.I. technology can exist without machine learning being part of the application.

Although we might automatically think of the Schwarzenegger Terminator robots when discussing A.I. in its most basic forms, we have actually come to know it very well and interact with it on a daily basis. Newsfeeds, for example, such as those provided to you by Facebook and other social media sites, are dependent on A.I. technology, as are all targeted ads. The Google search engine is A.I. dependent and Apple's Siri and other digital assistants are A.I. powered. Artificial Intelligence is and has been for some time, part of our everyday lives.

Recent developments in A.I. are a great bone of contention with some, despite the fact that those in favor of it are currently in the majority. However, the dissenters are not simply layperson naysayers voicing an uninformed opinion but are those with the skills and capacity to critically analyze. Frequently they are noted game-changers within their respective fields, and names such as the late Stephen Hawking and the effervescent Elon Musk are the two that automatically spring to mind. But, whether they are household names or otherwise, such specialists are often extremely concerned that the dangers as well as the benefits are not being taken into consideration.

Laypersons also often report that they are distrustful of A.I. despite the fact that they are probably using it every day; science is now going to lengths to decrease concerns, although this often doesn't pan out quite as planned. Even with the advances made, A.I. as we currently know it is still in its infancy. Some experts in the field believe it will take hundreds of years before we get to A.G.I or Artificial General Intelligence, a level that matches human cognitive reasoning and machines come closer to matching our creative thinking abilities.

It is a controversial topic as even those professionals who study 'intelligence' find it difficult to agree on the real definition of the word. Some say that worrying about A.I. is a little like worrying about humankind over-populating Mars – it's so far into the future it's not worthy of concern. When it comes to Machine Learning, teaching a supercomputer, such as Watson, to beat a Chess World Champion as a single task is impressive, but when that same computer is asked mid-game to take on a five-year-old at noughts and crosses or tic-tac-toe, without any reprogramming it would likely struggle.

The Medical Miracle?

Currently, medicine is the field which has seen the greatest expansion of A.I. and, although it is embraced by some, it is the subject of much consternation with medical professionals who often take yet another perspective when it comes to critical analysis. Two sectors which have had recent experience of A.I. technologies are that of surgery and diagnostics.

Where surgery might have fewer concerns, in respect of diagnostics it has not been voiced as a total success and it's the 'how?' factor that usually takes center stage. For example, IBM's Watson for Oncology, a supercomputer which promised to provide quality recommendations for the treatment of cancers; in cases where Watson agreed with specialists the professionals concerned decided, perhaps quite reasonably, there was little value in the technological diagnostics. However, when Watson disagreed with specialists, understandably, they wanted to know not only if the conclusions were likely to be accurate but exactly how they had been reached. Because no one actually understands how these machines learn and ultimately reach their conclusions – remember that Arthur Samuel told us right at the start this is about technology having "the ability to learn without being specifically programmed" – then the questions the doctors were asking simply could not be answered.

A similar problem arose among patients. Quite rightly most would argue that these people attended a professional to access their personal skills and training. Yet, when they were also faced with medical recommendations provided by a machine, they went on to ask not only how the recommendations were reached but also why and how their clinician had achieved an alternative solution. Again, the doctors simply couldn't answer such questions and the real truth of the matter is that no one can.

This raises concerns about how to communicate to patients that it is not their doctor who might be deciding on a particular treatment regimen, but a machine, and then how it might be possible to justify particular courses of treatment.

The Lawyer's Biggest Nightmare?
Another potential problem that has started to surface relates to what happens when things go wrong in situations involving medical A.I. such as Watson. The first problem being that there may well not be any way to actually prove anything went wrong with equipment because it is designed to learn without human involvement. How, then, will we ascertain, much like the case with 'time bomb' malware, if this isn't a natural course of events until it's too late? In short, will anyone notice or even question the situation before great harm has been done?

Of course, machines, just like humans, have the capability of going wrong without any third-party intervention, but it is also possible that hackers, no matter what their motives, could infiltrate this kind of technology and reconfigure it to be destructive without anyone really noticing a problem exists.

Other questions have also been raised that stand outside of the practical applications and this includes the financial aspects. Who, for example, is going to fund the equipment? How are insurance companies going to cover for accidents, or will they even agree to in cases where the 'how' can never be proven? Where will the invasive practices of hackers fit into the equation and where will the financial and legal responsibility lie?

An Emerging Monster?
In the natural course of events, when it comes to safety, most devices are risk assessed according to current standards. Yet, despite the risks to safety being even greater when it comes to the intentional hacking of the same devices, this would appear to be very low on the list of priorities for most of the authorities involved. Because emerging technologies reach across the boundaries of both I.T. and O.T., the capacity to cause a breakdown within critical infrastructure sectors becomes ever greater. So, the 'air-gapping' and segregation of systems which was once all important and should be now more than ever, seems to have disappeared off the radar of all but a lonely few.

There have already been a few hiccups in the development of A.I. or at least issues which have caused the raising of a few eyebrows. Facebook were developing a chatbot A.I. interface that was originally reported in mainstream media to have been dropped because the bots were actually chatting between themselves in a language not understood by the developers. As it turned out, Facebook said this was not the case and the program was abandoned simply because the chatbots were not able to do what they were designed for – to communicate effectively with the user.

Yet Google also found that their translating system, which utilizes similar A.I. technology, started to use its own language as it translated from one language to another. The 'middle' language it uses is the one which essentially belongs to the bots. Google have been unconcerned about this development and, as far as I am aware, continue to let the system play nicely on its own.

When it comes to A.I. and M.L. concerns appear to have foundations in two separate perspectives. Firstly, we have those expressing apprehension that machines which can learn without being programmed to do so may well oust the human from our dominant species position. Secondly, the minority voice is concerned not about what A.I. will do on its own but what those with bad intentions will make it do when they get access to these systems.

Opening Pandora's Box

Although we might often use the saying 'open Pandora's Box' in the context of letting loose problems which are difficult to contain, few are likely to recall that in Greek mythology Pandora herself was created to tempt men. This she did and in turn was bestowed with many gifts, including the one of curiosity. After being given an urn (not a box) by Zeus and told not to open it, her curiosity, as you just knew it would, got the better of her and Pandora let out all manner of evils to wreak destruction on man. Once out, they could no longer be controlled.

There are perhaps many morals associated with the myth but the main takeaway, in this case, is how humankind's curiosity, when temptation is put in our path, and the bright, shiny, whizzy technology certainly equates to the urn placed before Pandora, can bring forth uncontrollable destruction. Of course, today we have other sayings such as 'curiosity killed the cat,' 'opening a can of worms' or even, when it comes to the law, 'opening the floodgates of litigation' to show that once certain actions, for whatever reason, have been performed, things can never be the same again.

What we also might forget as we forge forward with technology and focus only on its advantages to society is that hackers too can develop their own programs. This is something that has happened over and over again, particularly in the last 15 years, and yet as the new technology continues to emerge it is something only a few people consider. Lessons, it would seem, are still not being learned despite such threats now having the ability to encompass the critical infrastructure of many nations.

Often those who warn of catastrophic danger are accused of using scaremonger tactics and it seems to be a throw-away applied by those whose ability to think critically and assess facts is seriously impaired. The realities of hacker attacks affecting devices, in particular those affecting critical infrastructures, must be taken more seriously because attacks by hackers on critical infrastructure systems are already taking place and becoming more frequent.[1]

The defense put forward is that emerging technology can and will prevent such attacks from taking place. The presumption here though would seem to be that independent hackers are now developing their own A.I. and machine learning devices in a pre-emptive move that will overcome the defenses being put in place.

But A.I. does not stand alone when it comes to emerging technologies because it is holding hands with blockchain, and nanotechnology is following hard on its heels.

Nanotechnology

Even though many people believe nanotechnology to be another emerging concept, just like A.I., it has actually been around for a long time. The term 'Nano' refers only to the fact that the field uses matter on a minute scale, usually with at least one dimension of a particle measuring 1 to 100 nanometers and with a single nanometer being the equivalent of 10 angstroms. No wiser? Rest assured, few are. Well, here is something to give the numbers a little scale because a sheet of paper is around 100,000 nanometers thick. This makes nanometers really, really, really small.

The technology aspect of nanotechnology can also be a little confusing because it actually relates to multiple disciplines. For example, materials made from nanoparticles have been around for a long time and are known as nanomaterials in their own right. There are also many others, such as organic chemistry, energy storage, electronics, and biomaterials, to name but a few. When it comes to computing in general, nanocomputers are those which are incredibly small and these aspects of the field can also be combined with others resulting in an overall picture of nanotechnology of the future.

The potential of nanotechnology is currently being investigated and one area which is proving to stir up much interest is that of geotagging, or the placing of tracking or tagging devices in products. This means in future anything you buy could have a nanocomputer inserted into it which will identify not only where it is currently located but where it was made, how it was transported, and which retailer or wholesaler sold it.

Anything could have its life journey recorded which certainly has the potential for many benefits. Theft of property and cash, for example, might be a thing of the past if nanotechnology became part of the product. Coins impregnated with a traceable graphite compound are already being manufactured; one of the main benefits proposed is that it will prevent the possibility of counterfeiting. Clothes and other products that are geotagged would have the ability to be tracked if stolen from shops, retailers or even homes, so the advantages appear to be incalculable.

Yet, no matter what reasons are given there are other sides to the geotagging coin and not only those which are denominations of currency. Geotagging on a mass scale would mean that everything we come into contact with, from currency to cosmetics, has the potential not only to be monitored as a product but also to track the owner. It might be they have the possibility to record your whereabouts and many other things about you from your temperature to your mood or even your intentions.

In inanimate objects, we could perhaps call geotagging 'tracking', but in human terms we would likely call it 'surveillance.' Although many might already be concerned about the levels of surveillance we are experiencing today, it is pretty basic by nanotechnology standards. We may have our Internet movements recorded by cookies and social media or any other websites that might want to learn a lot more about us, but nanotechnology can extend things far beyond the Internet and more so when combined with the I.o.T.

Today, we are often told that no matter what source data is being collected, it is for our own benefit and more often than not because it's necessary to enable interested parties to provide us with suitable targeted advertising. Of course, as the Cambridge Analytica drama revealed advertising, at least of products and services, might well be the least important driving factor when it comes to data collection. Advertising in itself may generate revenue for those who are selling it and selling the data to support it, but in so far as it being economically viable in a wholesale sense, the benefits are actually difficult to define.

We know that Google, for example, can tell advertisers they have increased hit rates from one percentage to another because a particular ad attracted more viewers, but does it really increase sales for the majority of companies at the end of the day? For example, since the advent of preferential research and targeted advertising, has the U.S. seen a dramatic increase in its wealth as a nation? Has it seen more jobs created or the economy soar to record highs?

Putting the advertising red-herring to one side for a second, it might be wiser to look at emerging nanotechnology as being the ultimate in surveillance. Would we really be comfortable buying products which might be capable of recording not only what we're seeing and thinking but also experiencing? At best this is liberty compromised by those we do trust and perhaps shouldn't, and at worst this is the ultimate weapon if it falls into the hands of those we do not.

If history has revealed nothing else to us it's that many lives have been saved simply because we had the ability to hide our identity when situations demanded it. And, of course, we have to consider that even without our own allies and trusted sources inflicting nanotechnological devices upon us for their own reasons, our enemies, or even potential enemies, have the ability to use nanotechnology to infiltrate like nothing else before it – and they are, without doubt, in the process of developing their own.

Nanotechnology on its own would at first appear to have both pros and cons. However, some are concerned that developments being made in this field are coinciding with other emerging technologies and not least that of A.I. The 'what if's' in this case often relate to nanotechnology being developed with A.I. capabilities and having the ultimate ability of not only being unseen by the human eye but also being able to learn and develop in the process. Couple this with the fact that the technologies as a whole are likely to be omnipresent and pervasive to the point that control or the ability to opt out or even switch off would seem unlikely, then populations in general may have huge problems on their hands.

The pros and cons of nanotechnology are, for the most part, incalculable for now. And, as one of our interviewees quite rightly pointed out, who is watching the watchers?

Blockchain

For most people, Blockchain is a bit of a mind-bender. We might come to understand relatively quickly that bitcoin or cryptocurrencies use something called the blockchain to be transferred from one person to another. But, apart from having a few abstract references to even more abstractions which few understand and even fewer can explain, that is usually where our level of understanding comes to a screeching halt. And, since no one is willing to hold their hand up and say, "I think the Emperor is as nude as a vulture's nut,' things rarely go any further.

The blockchain itself is actually an amalgamation of a set of technologies which, like most other things on the Internet, allow you to encrypt and encode data, but it's from here on in that things get more than a little confusing. This is because there is no centralized source, nothing apparently traveling directly from A through to B, and that is because everything is collected by not one computer, but a network of them. If you are talking cryptocurrency then the big news of the day is if money needs to be transferred from one point to another, this can be done in the full and certain knowledge that millions of calculations are performed to ensure the currency is actually available. It is done through all the decentralized units that grab hold of it and thus ensure it is not only checked by one authority, such as a bank, but by many.

The transactions made are all lumped together and, when the calculations are made, you get your cash (or rather cryptocurrency) and the chain moves on to the next block. The fact that these calculations not only take time as the blocks build but also use an enormous amount of electricity that might often hold more value than the money being transferred... well... it's a snag. The other snag, of course, is that because it is decentralized, holding someone accountable for anything that does go wrong is a virtual impossibility.

But blockchain is about more than just currency; it's about record keeping in general and, we are told, it will not only carry all the information anyone needs to know about us as individuals but also about those we might want to check up on. If you want to ensure that your vote for the Republicans was actually cast, then just go on a blockchain to check. If you want to know who owns a particular property, then go on a blockchain to check. Want to know your credit score, or maybe your neighbor's? Simply go on a blockchain.

Centralized authoritarianism, we are told, will become a thing of the past. A blockchain will hold all the information we need and it will be correct, easily accessible, and its integrity will be assured. Of course, you might not want your neighbors to know, or your boss, or your ex, but if everyone else wants convenience just as much as you do then you can't expect to have your cake and eat it. We are also assured that information put onto a blockchain won't be erasable or perhaps even amendable since it will come from a decentralized source. So, unlike the way in which the current Internet is structured, everything on a blockchain will be absolutely true, without error, and will provide us with an even more effective means of communication than we have today. Working on the presumption that, when it was inputted, it was correct, of course.

Some people love it and think it is the future. Others are distinctly more cautious. However, neither side is what they most often should be – objective.

How important blockchain will be to our future remains to be seen, but there is no doubt it is open to both error and abuse. Rarely do we see articles discussing what will happen when the hackers find ways to manipulate or abuse a blockchain, which of course, they most certainly will, but only when the cost of doing so makes it worthwhile. And, although we have seen propaganda bot trolls discussed in the context of their ability to influence users of the Internet but not a blockchain, we rarely see discussions about the damage trolls of the physical kind, who proliferate the forums and chat rooms, might cause. Taking on board that social engineering, whatever the form, is one of the most powerful weapons the bad actors have in our extremely active virtual social world, we should not dismiss the physical intruder lightly.

Some journalists have been noted to welcome the advent of blockchain claiming it will minimize the risk of misinformation and fake news. Maybe it will or maybe it won't, but there has been a way for journalists to achieve this same end for many, many years, although more recently the advent of misinformation is evidence in itself that it has fallen by the wayside. It is called performing due diligence and is what real investigative journalism is all about. Blockchain may prove to be a stepping stone towards some newer and more secure online platform. It may even be at the core of the next generation of the Internet. To get there, however, Blockchain needs to become much more power efficient than it is at present and this challenge has sparked a race to get to 'green blockchain.' If that does happen, then whoever cracks that particular challenge is set to reap significant commercial rewards.

Due Diligence

When discussing the development of emerging technology, whether looking at blockchain, nanotechnology or anything else, the term 'risk assessment' is often in play. In other words, what are the risks as well as the benefits? The problem with risk assessment in respect of hacking is that it is rarely approached with the same enthusiasm and attention to detail as the benefits of, for example, the evaluation of a new software. Today we hear of software and devices even being allowed to leave the manufacturers with vulnerabilities exposed. In some cases, we know that manufacturers have made the devices with those vulnerabilities built-in. Yet the risks for all those involved, which is basically everyone, have the potential to be massive and catastrophic in the way we live as individuals and also in the way we put ourselves as nations, at risk.

Maybe it's time to stop thinking in terms of risk assessment because few in the business of sales provide an honest assessment when it comes to the products they are selling. Neither do manufacturers nor designers consider the cons to any great degree. Scientists too, although it is their job to view things objectively, are often carried along with the tide of enthusiasm for what technology might do *for* us, without considering what it might do *to* us.

Perhaps we might start to think that everyone involved, at every step of the way, should be performing what in law is referred to as due diligence, but in practice is simply responsible behavior. From those who have the concept, through to those who write articles about the subject, and everyone in between, to be seen to be performing due diligence and being objective in their assessment.

No sane person would, for example, elect to say that the invention of fire was a bad thing. Man making fire has been something most would admit is extraordinarily useful. But we all know that fire is dangerous, it cannot be allowed to enter into our lives without constraints being put in place. In today's world, we fare much better than our ancestors because we also live with the knowledge that we have the ability to call on organized, equipped, and skilled firefighters to tackle fire when something goes wrong. Even then, even with all our skills and equipment, many lives are lost each year to fire that has got out of control and, in some cases, it is clear the correct due diligence has not been performed. One of the most recent examples is perhaps the Grenfell Tower fire which ended over 70 lives after substandard insulation was fitted to the exterior of the building.[2]

Yet we are inviting, and in many ways embracing, emerging technologies without looking at any of the potential catastrophes which might occur. If we took the same approach in respect of fire hazards, most would consider that approach to be at best irresponsible and at worst delusional. Due diligence has to be performed to ensure that products and services are as safe as they possibly can be when designing, manufacturing, selling, installing, and using goods that involve the use of fire, and the repercussions when this does not happen are extreme. We would be wise to hold the same standards when it comes to something as potentially invasive and dangerous as, say, nanotechnology.

When it comes to the hacker activities, we know that over the years tracing the perpetrators has become increasingly difficult and it is often something we rely on to prevent an escalation of problems. Should a blockchain be invaded and disrupted, an objective onlooker would conclude that technology has just made it easier to start a fire that we cannot even access to put out.

Interview with Industry
Kevin Gjerstad – CTO
(Energy & Utilities Application Development)

Kevin is a visionary Chief Technology Officer (CTO) and a global thought leader when it comes to positioning technology as a business enabler. With a foundation of experience built during his many years at Microsoft, Kevin has a penchant for identifying technology trends that will have a global impact. Today from his Norway base he leads a team of Data Scientists, Machine Learning, Security, and Cloud Computing experts in the pursuit of innovation and technological breakthrough. I asked Kevin to provide a view of how these new ventures are likely to impact society and the commercial world.

Kevin Gjerstad – Chief Technology Officer:
"I'm actually from Seattle and, after college, I got a job at Microsoft in the early '90s. I worked on the mission-critical products at that time, and Gates was constantly having reviews with product teams. There were probably ten occasions where I was in meetings with Bill and for maybe five of those I was presenting to him. It was an experience for sure. We worked on Windows 95 and XP, the .NET platform and early versions of A.I. technologies around speech and handwriting recognition. It was the very early days of A.I. We always thought it would happen so now it's very exciting to see the arc of improvement.

When it comes to technology and jobs, as with other revolutions, the changes can open up opportunities that didn't exist before. So, it's not just the loss of jobs, there's a bunch of new things that spring up from it. The challenge isn't so much the disruption in the short to medium term, it's the pace of change. If you have change where you go from the horse to the steam engine, the steam engine to combustion engine and so on, that's happening over decades – still fast by human standards – but now everything's accelerating and these changes are sweeping across causing disruptions in occupations. How do you train for that next job?

The other aspect is, when machines get to the point where they're faster and better at learning and doing things than we can be - where retraining a machine will be more efficient than training a human - that will start to provoke questions about the extent to which we keep humans employed versus machines? These are implications for how we all live in this world. Do we all share the fruits of this robotic future or is it the haves and the have-nots to the extreme?

But, on the ethics side of things, the fact that A.I. and these advanced tools can be used to challenge our security or could be used in war in ways that are impossible for us to combat or deal with, means we could be opening up a real Pandora's Box.

Blockchain has hit the ultimate hype status by association with bitcoin and it's very hard to get to the nut of the thing. The idea of a distributed ledger, where there's no centralizing authority controlling things and where the transactions are secure and they can't be tampered with, that sounds great. And it could be applied to finance, it could be applied to energy, trading, many things. The challenge of course is that the technology doesn't scale, it consumes vast amounts of ever-increasing energy. These two aspects do seem in conflict with each other and appear difficult to solve. It would be great if I had a distributed ledger that was super secure and couldn't be tampered with and could scale and be sustainable, but we are not quite there yet. We built a prototype at Powel and can do blockchain for energy trading, and we continue to test the technology but there is an ethical question as to whether we should do block chaining at all, as it uses so much energy. If you think climate change is at all real, and a challenge for this planet and humanity, then you can't seriously get behind blockchain right now.

With A.I. and privacy, if these devices we carry around are tracking everything we're doing and creating graphs of everyone we meet and everything we do, there's the raw danger of somebody knowing too much about you and having the ability for programs to generate a profile about you. Then there is the danger that this data is used with programs that learn how to manipulate you without you knowing about it. Cambridge Analytica could be an example. So, when you take these incredibly powerful, essentially marketing tools, and you apply A.I. technologies with massive amounts of detailed data about you, then I could manipulate you into believing or acting in a certain way which obviously would be of great interest to the political elite or those with special interests.

The technological acceleration is dramatic in terms of pace and impact, but our ability to absorb such things has a natural brake. So, society will reach a point where it can't change much faster and the technology can fly off the wall. In history, when you look at these periods where there's been great technological change it often results in social unrest, conflict, and revolutions. People displaced, people living on the streets, etc.

If or when we get to the point of super intelligence, a million times smarter than humans, which could be achieved very quickly if we reach that singularity point. So, climate change for a sentient robot that's a million times smarter than the human, could probably solve a climate crisis quite easily. Maybe in that scenario you would say, I welcome my A.I. overlords with open arms. That's the best possible scenario, that we end up manufacturing our own salvation in terms of a benign A.I. deity. Or, in the shorter term, some sort of A.I. technology helps us solve some of these existential problems in ways that we couldn't imagine. That's the positive scenario.

The pessimistic scenario; that we lose control of it and build A.I. tools that essentially end our existence. Because an A.I. program will fulfill its mission if it's programmed to do something and possibly all the way to some extreme although logical end. For example, if a super intelligent A.I. were created to solve the climate change problem, we might not like the solution. Maybe it says human life must be preserved, and so that's a tenet as part of its program, but still you might get unintended consequences. With a program optimized to solve the problem the first thing it would do is reduce the size of the human population, because we're the problem, not the climate.

A huge part of the objectives CISOs face around cybersecurity and keeping an organization safe is the company culture and managing people. There's the budget and technology aspect, but maybe 80 percent is just people management and helping them understand the process. We have all the tools now and if you could flick a switch in everybody's brain we would be so much more secure tomorrow. But we've got to reach all those brains one by one, that's the challenge. It's not just the malicious forces that you've got to worry about with cybersecurity, it's all those other components as well. Getting people to think a little more about the big picture is the real challenge."

Chapter 9
Critical Infrastructure Attack

"Why are experts so polite, patient, and forgiving when talking about cybersecurity and national security?"
- James Scott, Senior Fellow Institute for Critical Infrastructure Technology

As a developing scenario, what we have seen is the merging of technologies, enterprise, and individual lives. Yet there is also another aspect to consider, one that has the potential to affect everything to a devastating degree and from which there is little chance of swift recovery even if alternative solutions are found quickly.

This book has stressed from the outset that cybertechnology now lies at the very core of our society and, outside of the problems faced by private enterprise, we have ultimately become reliant on it to regulate, supply, protect, and maintain what is known as the 'critical national infrastructure' no matter where you live in the world. Although critical national infrastructure sectors might vary slightly from country to country, and a national infrastructure sector is not necessarily critical, the definition of an impact to these sectors remains pretty much the same.

We often see similar wording repeated but the general premise still exists: critical national infrastructure industries or organizations are ones where disruption to, or the destruction of the integrity of services, could possibly result in a significant loss of life or casualties either through disruption to economic stability and social factors or where it might threaten the defenses or general running of a country.

The scholarly phraseology actually means, in reality, if any of these sectors or organizations are affected, whether on a local, national or global scale, the results can not only be chaotic but have the potential to be catastrophic. To show it in a clearer, perhaps more practical light, we have to examine what would happen if medical facilities were to be affected, or if communication systems were to be attacked. What would be the likely result if freight transportation were to fail, or food production facilities were in some way disrupted or even contaminated? The ways in which life can be put under threat are myriad and range from losing access to money through to having no water to drink.

Yet despite the seriousness of the situations, questions asked less frequently are: what if more than one sector was affected at the same time? What if those same functions failed not only in one region, or even one country, but in several? The effects then, depending on their reach, would expand beyond the catastrophic and become of apocalyptic proportions and near impossible to manage.

Critical national infrastructure failures ultimately have the capacity to costs lives and lots of them. But surprisingly enough, it is getting increasingly difficult to protect these sectors in the way it once was and only a short time ago. Indeed, most CSOs, CISOs, and governing bodies would likely agree that it would be preferable, at least in the technological sense, to return to an era where it was possible to more clearly distinguish between critical and commercial systems. This would enable stringent cybersecurity measures to be put in place and reduce many of the vectors or avenues which might result in a cyber-attack on essential sectors and organizations. Yet what this book has proven time and again is increasing convergence between these two worlds and, because of this, our critical infrastructure systems are becoming less secure rather than more.

For many years, critical infrastructure systems were specifically governed by what today is referred to as Operational Technology (O.T.) as opposed to Information Technology (I.T.) which is at the foundation of private commercial systems. Operational technology is a term used to include the Industrial Control Systems (I.C.S.) and Building Management Systems (B.M.S.) used to supply, control, power, monitor, heat, cool, start or even shut down operations when necessary. It is distinct and normally separate from the Information Technology used in business and this distinction, or division between the two, comes under the auspice of what is known as 'air-gapping' and is essentially a safety measure.

In a scenario such as this, what affects I.T. – where the majority of hacks have historically taken place – should in theory not affect O.T. Critical infrastructures in areas such as the nuclear Industry which may have a higher level of protection than others. However, in general terms around basic controls and cyber hygiene factors, O.T. security is considered to be some 20 years being the world of I.T. security.

Hardcoded passwords, unrestricted outbound and publicly accessible Internet access to and from O.T. systems, and poor patching practices are all prevalent in the operational technology space. Conversely, the focus has traditionally been on the big hacks that have hit information technology systems, so the impression is that it is far more vulnerable to cyber-attack than those systems in the industrial and critical infrastructure world. These systems are, however, converging fast and as they do the risk of a serious security breach escalates with each new connection.

The Jurassic Link

Michael Crichton drew us a great picture of O.T. when he wrote Jurassic Park.[1] The fictitious Isla Nublar where the dinosaur park was located was run by an operations system that controlled everything from security fencing through to stabilizing individual laboratory environments, tracking the animals, and counting them.

The Jurassic Park O.T. system functioned in complete isolation from any other. There were no incoming or outgoing messages, no computerized ordering to outside sources, no way, in fact, that any external force could interact with the island's cybertechnology as it monitored, controlled, and secured its own operation. Isla Nublar, at first glance, appeared to be an operational technology dream, at least that appeared to be the message Michael Crichton was trying to get across... if it hadn't been for the insider subterfuge performed by the character Dennis Nedry when he turned it all off. Jurassic Park will certainly be remembered the iconic movie about dinosaurs, but the overall premise was, in fact, that we can never be in full control even when we think we have all the bases covered. The monsters will somehow find a way into the wild, it's just that in the digital world the 'monsters' are often more difficult to find and move around the globe at lightning speed.

In the real world when it comes to the critical infrastructure sectors, they might often be perceived by the masses as those being under the control of national governments and, indeed, some of them such as specific military and defense programs often are. In truth though, the majority of critical infrastructure sectors are run by private enterprise where the main aim is not protection but to make a profit.

Financial institutions, for example, are part of a nation's critical infrastructure, but they are run by the private sector. Yet, if banks are attacked by hackers and the money supply is disrupted as a result, not only are the private elements affected but clearly the critical infrastructure of a country can begin to fail. Here we also get an additional clue as to why governments often step in to help individual financial institutions when they're failing, no matter what the reason.

Others, such as telecommunications, water services, and transport, also fall between the two stools of critical infrastructure sectors and private enterprise, as do energy suppliers, chemical, and food production facilities, some of which come under the definition of Public-Private Partnerships. Now we start to see not only a convergence between O.T. systems, which are prevalent and absolutely essential in critical infrastructure organizations and that of I.T. which dominates private enterprise, but also a direct conflict of interest when it comes to the business plans of the organizations concerned.

Critical infrastructure sectors are meant to keep a country running, private enterprise is in it for the money, and an increasing number of I.T. devices are becoming necessary to provide private organizations with competitive advantage just to keep up with the game. The only problem is that such devices are at serious risk of being compromised on a regular basis which in turn puts our national infrastructures at risk where the sectors cross boundaries.

Outside of the technological issues it is perhaps easier to see the picture more clearly if we take the issue of defense and ask ourselves if we would like it to be run by the private sector. Do we really want, for example, an army to be governed by a body whose primary interest is in making a profit and, just as important, keeping shareholders happy and maintaining a reasonable share price?

Would we want an army who were issued with devices, perhaps apps, that we suspected could be compromised by hackers, maybe even those from another country with geopolitical intentions? Would we want shareholders deciding or even dictating what kind of weapons forces were armed with based on cost alone and knowing that it is in the financial interests of those same shareholders to keep costs low?

The Commercialization of Critical Infrastructure Sectors

The private sector has embraced emerging I.T. technology as a means to assist the functionality of the business and as a way to indirectly make money from the devices because data collection has become an additional name in the game. Many organizations now, whether they are insurance companies with a physical presence through to forums where you discuss your kids, your favorite cars, or your health issues, data collection has been embarked upon as a way to make extra money and this is the same data that hackers are after either for exactly the same reason or others which might be much more sinister.

What we have is a potentially cyclical situation completing when we finally understand and accept that the technology we are sold as personal devices are not only those which collect the data which is valuable to others but which are also the same mechanisms allowing hackers further in-roads to steal the information.

A similar, yet more complex situation is arising when we look at the operational technology environment because here the paths become intertwined with what's being protected – data versus operational security – and because there is a conflict of interests when businesses straddle the private (I.T. systems) and critical national infrastructure (O.T. systems) sectors.

To maintain efficient functionality of businesses and in the interests of possible competitive advantage, these converging companies are making choices which increasingly place the O.T. systems in an ever-weakening position by adopting I.T. devices and embracing the Internet of Things. As this tendency increases, we are becoming placed in a situation where the 'air-gap' which was once deemed so significant and which has protected lives of many people has not only been narrowed but in many cases has disappeared altogether.

Taking our Jurassic Park analogy one step further, we have moved from an isolated operating system to one where the visitors arrive and can connect to it via a multitude of apps, messaging systems, and linked web pages. Correspondingly, what we can see for certain is that technological advances have just made the job of Mr Nedry and Co. a whole lot easier. Even in the world of fiction, this story would be a hard one for the entertainment seeker to take seriously – but then truth is always said to be stranger than fiction.

But for the CISO employed in these industries the practicalities of the game are much less entertaining. Not only do they face having to keep the Operational Technologies safe, now they must contend with keeping a multitude of Information Technologies safe, particularly those emerging from the I.o.T. which also include Smart buildings and developments – a fact which we know at the moment is essentially impossible to achieve. To make matters worse many of these devices are in the hands of the general public who give not a jot about cybersecurity.

Even when it comes to legislation, further conflicts of interest arise and this is most apparent when you look not at the GDPR which governs data but at the NIS which governs operational security. Huge penalties can be applied in both situations and when it comes to private companies working within the critical national infrastructure sectors, they can attract penalties arising from both these aspects of the law. Yet the demands of private enterprise are dictating that such organizations put themselves in the potential firing line by embracing more and more I.T. technologies which assist with collection of the 'data gold' on the one hand and operational efficacy on the other.

It's The Little Things That Matter
Most breaches, whether they are committed against the private or public sectors, commence with subtle social engineering. There are no fireworks, no sudden changes, no flag-waving frontmen leading the onslaught. What the hackers rely on, and what often happens, is that someone is a little silly or lax and they, or their superiors, would prefer

that the fact they passed on an email or opened an unauthorized link or any other small matter is kept small.

No worries, no problems, no disciplinary procedures, just a simple mistake that is best kept quiet by either the perpetrator or the close-knit colleagues around them. Yet this is exactly what the hackers rely on because, as we have come to learn, social engineering is only the key being placed in the lock. If it is left there, they can return at a later date to commence the real attack.

We saw in our interview with Bennett Arron how difficult it is for people to get such 'small' matters taken seriously or to see them actioned and, if the truth were told, many might not even be recorded. As a result, most of these incidents go completely under the radar and if they are undertaken as the initial stages of a cyber-attack this is allowed to continue unchecked.

These physical 'micro' breaches have led many organizations into deeper waters, but by then, of course, it's all too late and this is where the new legislation will really kick in – at the end rather than at the beginning. When this happens in respect of I.T., data is lost and lives are damaged. When this happens in respect of O.T., both data and lives are at risk.

When we look at the private sector and critical infrastructure sectors, what we see stretching before us is a continual line of conflicts of interests and the consistent narrowing of the 'air gap' between the two sectors. For those involved in cybersecurity, and particularly those in industries operating at critical infrastructure level, the concerns are increasing because legislation aside, companies themselves are making cybersecurity more difficult to implement with each passing day.

Are We Really At Risk?

Both across the globe and nationally we have seen the potential implications of successful attacks on national infrastructures among the many thousands of attempted hacks which occur. In recent years we have seen notable attacks occur on the Ukraine power companies as well as those in the U.S. However, many other countries have also seen their critical national infrastructure sectors coming under an increasing number of attacks that have been disruptive if not destructive.

In 2016, reports began to emerge relating to an attack on a German nuclear facility that occurred some two or three years previously.[2] Although specific details of the case are scant, perhaps for obvious reasons. In 2014 it was discovered that malware had compromised over 30 systems in the control room of the Monju Nuclear Power Plant in Japan after an employee had installed a free application.[3]

South Korea has also seen problems with cyber-attacks on nuclear facilities, a recent one being in 2014 when the Korea Hydro and Nuclear Plant Co Ltd. saw hackers retrieve data from the facilities systems.[4] This was on the back of other attacks which took place in 2013 which resulted, among other things, in bringing down the servers of two major banks.[5]

More recently though the U.K. – Northern Ireland and Wales in particular – found their grids under attack. Although the ultimate target was EirGrid, the wholesale supplier who moves energy supplies around Northern Ireland but who also have routers in Wales, the initial compromise began through Vodafone. The hackers, which were believed to be state-sponsored, gained access to the telecommunications network and then installed a virtual wiretap on the EirGrid system. This enabled them to read all the encrypted data and to set up a 'man in the middle' style hack.

Although the initial infiltration began back in April 2017, the full implications of the hack were not discovered and revealed until several months later.[6] This breach and many others like it are now considered by many experts to be proof of concept hacks rather than intending to cause damage. And even where outages have been caused, such as with the series of Ukraine hacks, there is a general consensus developing that the attacks are pre-emptive strikes and the real damage could have been much, much worse.[7]

There have been some efforts to reassure the public that in cases such as electricity supplies at least, a mass power outage throughout the U.S. would be impossible. Professionals within the industry explain how the system is distributed, or if you prefer 'air-gapped,' with three grids comprising of 1,000 electricity operators and how the control systems within the grids are highly complex and difficult to figure out if you do not work within the industry.[8] Additionally, because electricity systems are consistently disrupted by weather of all types on a regular basis, there are 'redundancies' built-in to these systems, meaning the supplies can regularly be re-routed.

Confidence within the industry at least would appear to be high when it comes to the belief that hackers have the ability to simply 'switch off' supplies to the United States. Experts also explain that hackers would have to 'try very, very hard' to disrupt electricity supplies and that, without insider knowledge, it would be virtually impossible. They do though admit that it is possible to enter the system in reverse by gaining access through technologies such as bill paying facilities, which is a nice example of I.T. and I.o.T. of the private sector crossing the critical infrastructure boundary into O.T. land.

They too suggest the recent attacks were not attempts to disrupt the systems but were actually attempts at reconnaissance and trying to 'understand' the system for a possible future attack. A situation which, to be quite honest, is hardly reassuring. Yet when we take all this into consideration and combine it with the evidence that around 75% of hacks necessitate physical infiltration of the organization at least in the initial or preparatory stages, then the Dennis Nedry factor suddenly starts to come into the equation and the possibility of widespread disruption begins to emerge as a real possibility.

We also know that, whether we are talking Black Hat hackers who work for monetary gain or those of the geopolitical variety, these groups are highly organized and extremely well-funded. As a result, 'trying hard' is something they do as a matter of course during their daily lives and not just as part of their working day. In fact, they often eat and breathe 'trying hard' when it comes to hacking in general. We also know from the Stuxnet situation, the German factory, and many other attacks, that hacks can result in physical destruction and often without the cause being identified for long periods of time. What the Ukraine situation also evidenced is just like the attack on Sony in the private sector, hackers often follow through with support attacks which delay identification of the breach, reporting of issues, and resolution of the problems.

There is also an additional aspect to consider which very much ties in with the idea that hackers would have to 'try very, very hard' to infiltrate systems. This is because the presumption is nearly always made that the hackers are continually playing a game of 'catch-up' when it comes to emerging technology. Few consider the fact that hackers today are so well-funded and well-versed they are quite capable of developing their own technologies outside of those currently used to make pre-emptive strikes.

There is also another fallibility and this is where there are broad security discrepancies between the critical national infrastructure sectors. Electricity supplies, much like the aviation industry, are at the high-end when it comes to cybersecurity awareness. Others, though, such as water services, are not so well-equipped to fend off attacks. Although it is currently only hearsay because the water company concerned have never officially revealed their name much less admitted to being compromised, a vendor reported that a water services supplier had likely been hacked and the proportion of chemical components added to water supplies had been altered. Whether the story is true or not may never become clear, however what the vendor's investigations revealed is that even though they are part of the critical national infrastructure, water supply systems are often not defended with the same high levels of integrity as many other O.T. industries.

But even this situation is nothing new because as far back as 2011 it was reported that hackers obtained login names and passwords before accessing a water utility system in Illinois U.S. They then turned a pump on and off repeatedly resulting in it eventually burning out and causing disruptions to the water supply to thousands of people. This was on the back of reports claiming that another hacker had gained access to the control systems of a second water utility.[10]

Even though we discuss how the I.T. and O.T. sectors are merging, or in some cases how CNI sectors are adopting I.I.O.T. technology which might not be as secure as one would like it to be, there are those who, from the baseline, still don't appear to be taking the game seriously. Although many countries have, for example, health services which straddle the private and public sectors, some such as the U.K. see their National Health Service as being publicly run. We would expect then, as a single critical national infrastructure sector, for this to be a prime example of how to secure an O.T. operation. Unfortunately, the picture we get reveals nothing of the kind and if the 2017 drive-by WannaCry attack was anything to go by, indications are that cybersecurity is somewhere at the bottom of the list of priorities rather than being placed at the top. And, once again, we see human error being the root cause of the breach.

This one example alone should knock on the head the idea that many managers, directors or executives hold is that cybersecurity is a technical issue. But is that really the case? Maybe the simple fact that it was allowed to happen in the first place only serves to reinforce that fact that most of the people in power still think it is?

An Incomprehensible Future?
When it comes to cybersecurity breaches the risks for all of us are perhaps beyond our comprehension and only extend to our vision on the horizon. For the private company it may, at worst, mean closure. For the individual it could mean a life thrown into chaos. When it comes to the critical national infrastructure breaches it might result in lost lives, economic disaster, and social turmoil which is often not even understood by those who run the individual organizations.

Few understand the true implications of CNIs being affected by a cyber-attack. What we see most frequently are governing bodies counting costs not in the specific number of lives that might be lost, but how much it might affect a nation financially – the main concerns usually involving calculations of the problem as a percentage of GDP. Even here though we hit another problem because when we look at GDP percentages, they are rarely high enough to trigger cause for concern within the business or even investors.

However, as a document published by the U.K. Parliamentary Office of Science and Technology in May 2017[11] revealed, the sums involved are often extremely difficult to calculate accurately. The research they provided actually estimated costs to the U.K. in sterling, as opposed to a percentage of GDP, and they came in at anything between £1bn and £27bn per year, which is a pretty broad range by anyone's standards, and likely reflects that no one really knows the damage that might be inflicted.[12]

Yet attacks on CNI sectors would be far more devastating for many on a personal level and this possibility should be considered in light of the knowledge that the same document stated there are currently around 60 high-level cyber-attacks per month which have the potential to affect the critical national infrastructure of the U.K.

Scaremongering

As I touched upon briefly in an earlier chapter, when matters of critical infrastructure failures are discussed a frequent accusation cast around is that of 'scaremongering.' Surprisingly enough, particularly when we see it discussed by those claiming professional capacity, this aspersion is often made by those who are educated in one subject or another. As a consequence, they have gone through formal academic training which from start to conclusion requires them to look at the pros and cons of every topic and field studied and to apply objectivity to their observations to ensure they critically analyze any given situation.

At no point, as far as I am aware, do students of any subject consider investigating the cons of a subject to be 'scaremongering,' and neither do they comment as such in their essays, dissertation or thesis. In reality, though, even where a scholar is trying to prove a hypothesis, what can often happen is that investigating the cons causes a shift in mindset from the original stance; a situation which some might find particularly disconcerting. Let's face it, those accusing others of scaremongering when they haven't investigated the potential negative aspects of any situation are taking a cheap shot. It is the adult equivalent of rattling a door knocker and running away.

We can also look at many articles on the Internet or attend conferences and, for the most part, see that only benefits of emerging technologies are discussed or, less frequently, the disadvantages. Rarely do we find those willing to do as they were taught and discuss both pros and cons within the same document to allow for objective and informed conclusions to be reached.

Finally, and perhaps most importantly when it comes to the threat landscape, most private organizations are adopting technology appropriate for their business and this includes all the aspects that we have previously discussed including the adoption of A.I. Remember that when it comes to cybersecurity the all-pervading mindset at the moment is not if an organization will be breached, but merely a matter of when. And when it comes to industries which cross into the public sector national infrastructure threat, can we really afford to be so complacent?

They Hit So Many Times, You Think You're Surrounded

Although we've had fair warning, in situations such as the Ukraine hacks where multiple sectors were attacked simultaneously, the strategy when it comes to defense is not one which receives rigorous attention. Most national authorities often view a critical infrastructure attack as affecting only one organization or sector and plan accordingly. What they rarely consider is what would happen if more than one sector was hit. The assumption is also often made that services would be restored quickly. And even that is often backed up by the belief that if services were to be affected on a national level then help would be on hand from other allies. Yet these are scenarios which, in reality, can never be guaranteed.

The CISO Perspective
Andrew Rose - CISO
(Critical Infrastructure)

Below are insights from an experienced CISO working in the critical Infrastructure space. I asked Andrew to provide his view on the differences and, indeed, the relationship between safety and security in the aviation sector.

Andrew Rose: CISO and Head of Cybersecurity:

"Across industry there's still a perceived difference between safety and cybersecurity, but it's closing fast because people in the safety industry realize that security is another aspect of safety. Safety has, unlike cybersecurity, been around since the start of flight - even the Wright brothers put a seat belt on the Kitty Hawk - and it's had a long time to mature, refine processes, get the right metrics, and grow large experienced teams. Safety is of course embedded everywhere in the Aviation sector's culture. The pace of change between the two worlds needs to be recognized as probably the biggest difference – changes to safety-related topics tend to move slowly and safety solutions are methodically tested, taking time to consider every possible outcome or implication, and testing to incredibly fine margins; cybersecurity has much more dynamic drivers and demands much more agile solutions. There are many different styles of CISO and it's impossible now for a CISO to know everything about all aspects of cybersecurity. Security also has aspects of being an 'art rather than a science' and this makes broad industry experience essential as it feeds your intuition which can lead you down paths which suddenly open up other doors to improving matters. I would encourage new CISOs to come into cybersecurity as it's such a broad topic – from encryption and forensics, to culture and legal compliance – and it's constantly

challenging. It's simply the most exciting and interesting industry there is."

A Caribbean Perspective
Dr. Rupert A. Francis, Captain-Retired.

Adviser to the Minister of Foreign Affairs Jamaica and Global Lead Diaspora Crime Reduction Task Force

"Having personally spent several years dedicated to the protection and security of our beloved island nation often called, "The Pearl of the Caribbean" and having seen the community here face numerous threats from the environment and criminal activity and prevailed. I am now convinced that Jamaica now faces the most significant threat of all, Defending herself and her people from risks emanating from the Cyber-Realm. Therefore we must be proactive, not reactive. Simply put, Jamaica and the wider Caribbean have faced and are facing serious threats to our: Personal, economic, social, cultural, religious, educational and political lives. In the cyber-world "An ounce of Prevention is better than a pound of Cure." Jamaica is waking up to the realities of the digital world, and the benefits and the challenges it offers. We need to educate, train and inspire our youth to take up the mantle and become the defenders and the architects of a future that Jamaica can continue to be proud of."

The CISO Perspective
Sue McCauley – Group CISO
(VP Strategy IOTSA)

Sue is unique in many ways, not least of which is the fact that she is a woman working in the male-dominated world of operational security technology. Sue knows her stuff and as a CISO, strategist, and cybersecurity leader she has the ability to map and structure viable approaches to improving security. I asked Sue what it is about this industry that attracts her interest and focus and specifically where the influence of I.o.T sits within the environment.

Sue McCauley: CISO
"I'm Sue McCauley, Vice President of the International Operational Technology Security Association (IOTSA). The reason I originally got involved with this organization is because I have a fundamental interest in protecting the critical infrastructure of the U.K. So, when I say that, what I mean is from a national infrastructure perspective and from a business infrastructure perspective, because both are extremely important to U.K. security and business continuity.

Very often cybersecurity alone is seen to be a very male-oriented environment, and operational technology is even more so. However, my background has been working predominantly with central government organizations, quite often Defense environments. As you might imagine they can be male-dominated, but they're also quite dynamic and I enjoy that atmosphere. My interest in operational technology specifically was triggered when I started a Masters' degree in cybersecurity and one of the very first topics we covered was Stuxnet. For me, Stuxnet opened an entirely new world of discovery in cybersecurity. It was a fascinating story, with some terrific insights into how new 'nukes' could be projected into the world of our critical infrastructure and, without too much effort from those involved, cause extreme damage. No matter who the bad actors are, whether criminal gangs, nation-states, who are trying to cause disruption or other hacker organizations trying to make some kind of profit, there are some easy targets in the O.T. arena. It is an established fact that some recent cyberattacks have been deliberately targeted at critical infrastructure safety systems. So, for me it's about looking at how we can build the cyber resilience to protect them.

Although the IOTSA is a relatively new organization, we are looking to build our membership to create a collaboration platform where we look at all of the different threats and vulnerabilities in operational technology. This will enable us to start building a bridge between the I.T. and the O.T. world. Currently we have a situation where I.T. is very much the domain where cybersecurity is well-managed. O.T. on the other hand has traditionally been a segregated world of SCADA and industrial control systems and PLCs where engineers have been looking after the assets. O.T. has traditionally been segmented from I.T. But, very much in the last 10 years, it has become increasingly converged with the I.T. environment and connected to the internet and that's when you start to get the risks coming across. In reality then, what we are trying to do is to bring that depth of cyber knowledge to the engineering community which will enable them to start looking at what the real threats are and also to mitigate them, by building cyber resilience.

Risks to O.T. are currently registered as a Tier 1 risk on the U.K.'s National Risk Register and that is one of the reasons why the European Community developed the E.U. Network and Information Systems (NIS) Directive. This means the protection of critical infrastructure physical assets have been incorporated into the Directive. This is in terms not only of networks and I.T., but the actual operational technologies which support our critical national infrastructure requiring operators of essential services to manage the threats, vulnerabilities and risks that are being posed to our O.T. assets.

From a new technologies perspective, the biggest threat to O.T. is the proliferation of I.o.T the Internet of Things, devices, components and sensors, which all have a connection to the Internet, but lack security features. It's through the Internet that you find the threats coming through to those operational technology environments and so the Internet connection poses the biggest risk. Currently there is a great push for Industry 4.0 initiatives, which is about converging I.T., I.o.T. and O.T., in order to build efficiencies into our manufacturing industries. These initiatives incorporate technologies like AI and Machine Learning and, although that is a great thing, in many ways they increase the threats and risks. This means we must find ways to manage operational technology securely, and we are not there yet by any means.

A.I. and ML provide increasing ways of developing efficiencies in manufacturing environments, but it's about how we merge these technologies securely and facilitate the join-up of cyber physical production systems and manage the vulnerabilities brought into play by that convergence.

Although there are many associations out there that focus on the collaboration of the I.T. world, to my knowledge the I.O.T.S.A. is the only organization that is focusing on operational technologies. This evidences the massive gap between O.T. and I.T. systems, and the differences are substantial. Where I.T. focuses on information, in O.T. Process is king and certainty in terms of systems that must be available 24/7. The availability of operational technologies is fundamental to what they deliver; think about traffic systems, banking, utilities – they're always 'on'. They have to be or there would be chaos.

But the bringing together of safety and (cyber) security that may actually cause conflict with each other. For example, in normal activity if a critical infrastructure system is going to fail, it fails in a safe position so that people don't get hurt. Whereas if you are looking at it from a security perspective it may work in a completely different fashion. Professor Hankin at RITICS describes that if we take the Underground as an example, if you wanted the barriers to fail-safe, they would fail open so the people could escape. If you wanted them to fail secure, because you didn't want people to run out without paying, you'd want them to fail closed. So those two aspects safety and security, are opposed to each other.

Although there are few women in cybersecurity, on a personal level, I certainly don't look at career opportunities in terms of gender orientation. If something interests you then that should be a good enough reason to develop a career. I do though think that women look at things more holistically than men do, taking a more rounded approach and men tend to look at things in greater depth. Perhaps I'm being stereotypical here, and that statement is not mean to be disparaging to either sex. When I was studying for my degree, the intake was predominately male and there were only four females in that cohort. Yet, even in the way that we studied, the guys really focused in on specific areas and specific points and being quite detailed on the technical issues. When it came to the women they looked at things from a much more holistic perspective and viewed the subjects more broadly. At one stage I worked with a fellow student on a collaborative piece of work. He very much focused in on the technical aspects whereas I brought in the wider environment, including the financial, commercial, resourcing, and everything around that. When it came to the way we worked together, it resulted in the outcome being very balanced.

I firmly believe that everybody should earn the position that they are given and it shouldn't just be accorded to somebody because they are female or because they are male. I think people have to earn the right to be in a particular post and, when you are in that post, you better be ready to stand up and take all of the responsibility that goes with it. If that means you end up being sacked because you didn't do a job properly, then that's just part of what you signed up for. What I wouldn't want is to be treated any differently to a guy who was taking on a position just because I was a woman. If I'm going to take on that role, I may bring different flavors to it and a different quality to it. I think the kind of things that women can bring to an organization are the long-term vision, the strategic positioning and a transformational overview. From my personal skill set, that would also include employee engagement and inclusive stakeholder management. In general, it benefits the business as a whole, to look at what it is delivering within the community and how you can build an organization that functions for the greater good.

When it comes to the IOTSA that's about how we can build the knowledge, awareness and capabilities to give our critical infrastructure Engineers and Boards the ability to comprehend and address the risks posed by vulnerable operational technologies, which currently are not being managed securely."

Chapter 10
So, You've Got Nothing to Hide?

"Life is composed of lights and shadows, and we would be untruthful, insincere, and saccharine if we tried to pretend there were no shadows."
- Walt Disney

Much of what has been discussed in this book revolves around the push and pull factors of individual privacy. And, although we might view the term as most often referring to official surveillance or the breaking of laws, the spectrum is far, far wider than that.

The markets, whether legitimate or otherwise, have discovered that our personal information is worth something to someone, somewhere and like it or not, our private lives and our most intimate details now have a price on their heads. Because of this, much of what consumers are sold, whether it be in the private, social, or public sector, is often data scraping wrapped up in a premise that is in some way said to benefit us, but which, in truth, usually benefits someone else a lot more.

Of course, the benefits to others may not always be of the financial kind and the statement is usually applied to the far end of the geopolitical spectrum when referring to surveillance. But there can now be little doubt that hacking our data or even duping us into providing it willingly is beneficial to many parties. Even individual governments, and likely those we trust, collect data which, although might have little or no value today, may be valuable for many reasons tomorrow.

If history has shown us nothing else, it is whoever is in control of the masses usually wins the war. And even if they don't, the masses are obliterated in the process anyway. Data that may seem to have no consequence today may become useful at some future point, although most of it is just noise. However, if you collect everything then one day somewhere in that huge pile of human data excrement, you have all the history, background, and personal details of our future leaders and those that may become persons of interest. To whom and for what reason? Well, that's the question!

Individuals within companies also have much to lose when it comes to privacy and intellectual property theft because although we might speak of organizations as being single entities, they're not. What any organization is, at its very core, is a community grown out of the knowledge and labor of individual people. Yet, simply because this knowledge exists, research and development are also often a target either from competitors or even geopolitical hacking.

Frequently, when it comes to the collection of data we hear the following phrase voiced by nameless, faceless individuals who frequent the world of the Internet or, as it happened, when I was delivering a keynote talk at an industry event. The subject was State Level Surveillance at an EU Conference in Brussels around the time of the Snowden revelations and someone I now know to be a journalist shouted out from the back row: *"Why worry if you have nothing to hide?"*

The implication behind this statement does suggest that those who are doing nothing to contravene laws should have nothing to fear if the minutiae of their lives were to be explored. Yet we are no longer discussing the more extreme ends of the spectrum because the surveillance now starts with the trifles of our lives and demands that we examine the situation in greater detail.

Most people consider it reasonable that marketers want to establish our purchasing preferences in an effort to increase sales. And it is this one simplistic argument that is most frequently put forward by those who are now collecting our data. If the marketing argument needs further strengthening, then we will see the word 'research' or even 'researchers' being thrown into the equation because, after all, we equate research with something that will, in some way, further benefit the public good.

We know now that this might not be the case and even professional and respected researchers, such as Alexander Nix, the former CEO of Cambridge Analytica, will collect data for purposes outside of selling us targeted products or contributing to the public good. Yet often, because the intentions behind the collection may not be as ethical as we might either believe or hope, the information being compiled delves much deeper than identifying our purchasing preferences.

Whether they are known 'bad guys' or unscrupulous 'good guys', would those who say they have nothing to hide really think the same way if the bad actors gained access to private information that perhaps even their nearest and dearest are unaware of or they themselves have forgotten over the years?

For example, would those who have nothing to hide be concerned if strangers learned they had erectile dysfunction or were unable to have children? Would they want their driving speed to be monitored by authorities every time they got in the car? Would they consider it reasonable that a stranger could identify their location at any given moment in time and who they were in the company of? What about someone, somewhere, reading every text message or email they send? Is it reasonable that a stranger should covertly learn of childhood sexual abuse and be allowed to include the information in part of a study without their knowledge? Or maybe that they're having a long-term affair or that their partner had a one night stand a couple of months ago?

Would they really be comfortable with someone learning of their true sexual preferences or that one of their kids is taking drugs? Do they want people to know they slapped their child that morning even though they promote non-physical discipline on a 'perfect parenting' forum? Do they really want others to know that they have moved on from erotic magazines and now surf the porn sites on a regular basis? Do they want people to know that they didn't really get all the qualifications or grades they lay claim to? Do they want all and sundry to know what they really earn, or that they got a dressing down at work for messing up or that they were fired from a previous position? Maybe they would not be happy for the world to know that they find the man who lives across the street far more attractive than they do their wife, or that they have four glasses of wine when they get home from work rather than the one they usually admit to? Do they not care that the authorities may easily learn they ran a red light on the way to work or perhaps forgot to put on their seatbelt or used their cell phone while driving?

Do the people who say, "Why worry if you have nothing to hide?" really understand the implications of what they are saying and the totalitarian existence they are welcoming in with open arms?

More importantly, do they realize that these are the activities not of the 'bad actors' but of the 'good actors' in the game? It is perhaps unimaginable, at least to those in the democratic west, what might happen when the 'bad actors' get hold of the same information.

This is the minutiae of our lives and solidly reflects our existence as individuals and makes us what we are. We are not perfect and cannot match up in reality to the virtual illusions that we spread on the Internet. We are rarely natural, pouting beauties or six-pack touting bucks who never lose their temper, stick to a diet rigidly, always keep to our New Year resolutions, have perfectly harmonious relationships, never say a bad word against anyone, and have never, ever, ever had a duvet day or one glass of wine too many.

If then, you still think you have 'nothing to hide' you might actually consider that you are closer to A.I. than you ever could be to a wonderful, distinctive, yet inherently flawed, human being. Or maybe those that hold this view, and there are plenty, just consider that the rest of us are actually stupid enough to believe that there are 'perfect people' out there?

Throwing Away Our Rights?

Privacy is defined by Merriam-Webster, America's most trusted online dictionary, as being 'freedom of unauthorized intrusion'. Under article 8 of the European Convention on Human Rights, it is 'the right to respect for your family life and private life, your home and your correspondence'. Yet when it comes to the 'nothing to hide' side of the coin, the presumption is that we might, just might, be involved in illegal activities and so these freedoms are ignored.

Of course, most people don't willingly and knowingly break the law, although they might nibble the edges on a regular basis with minor misdemeanors depending on what kind of day they are having or even where they reside in the world. But, wherever you live, what is legal today may not be tomorrow. Laws change frequently within and across every country of the world. What's legal in one is not always legal in another and might even attract the death penalty.

In other words, information you might have been happy to share with the world yesterday may be the same thing you would prefer to keep private tomorrow. Even today you might travel to another part of the world and suddenly discover, for whatever reason, that you arrive as a criminal. In most western countries democracies are pretty stable and so the laws don't regularly careen from one extreme to the other. But as we have become more enlightened we realize that other cultures and populations may not be quite as lucky and, for them, there is much they need to hide to ensure physical safety; who are we that have those rights to declare others should forsake them?

Often, when it comes to understanding the importance of privacy, empathy is the name of the game. We must learn to understand others, to walk in their shoes, to enable us to realize the risks we or our descendants might one day face. Yet privacy is the right of most and to say we don't want it is tantamount to rejecting the freedoms for which many have fought and under which we are lucky enough to live.

Exploitation

Throughout modern history man has exploited his fellow humans to put himself in a position of advantage. Whether we're talking about serfdom, slavery or simply a paid workforce, our history books resound with exploitation of the skills and labor of others. Today, though, what was once of value often no longer exists. Industrial revolutions, agricultural revolutions, and now technological revolutions have devalued, if not the cost of labor and skills, then certainly the need for it in the same amounts.

In some cases, the source might have shifted. For example, in the U.K. there were once 174 coal mines employing 200,000 men and now there are only three deep pits employing 2,000 in total.[1] Now where coal is needed it is imported from lands where the labor required to produce it costs less. In other cases, such as the market for sheep and wool, textile technology and synthetics have simply displaced demand and the labor required to produce it is no longer required.

Today, we see another source of exploitation emerging – this time there are no costs involved in employing a workforce. Personal data is now a source material much the same as coal or wool. Yet it is provided freely, there's no charge, and it can be used to make money and create a power base for others, particularly those who are willing to stoop to the lower levels on the ethical scale.

The data of each individual who has any kind of interaction with technology, whether buying at a supermarket, managing finances through a bank or browsing a website on the Internet, is offering up their private information which has a value to someone somewhere. Our private lives, and privacy itself, has now been designated a monetary value.

In many cases, this trade in our information is actually covert and it hides behind the principle that we are being provided with something for free and that the collection of data is to benefit us in isolation. How many times do we hear that social media sites, for example, are 'free to use' and that they are collecting information simply to send you 'targeted advertising'? Such companies would appear to be doing us a big favor, right?

But the game is not limited to social media sites, it involves most any other where they will not let you browse without collecting cookies and most certainly where they 'require' information to register. Many websites, at varying levels of involvement, are trying to make a profit even where it is not obviously so. I know, I know, you thought all these places where you could go and discuss common problems and interests were being run by the most altruistic people on earth. Yet we would be far closer to the truth if we looked at such sites as profit-making enterprises, and in some cases, even where they are registered as companies they have no 'apparent' means of making money and keeping the site running – not even through selling advertising.

Maybe it's time to turn the tables rather than relying purely on legislation or being placed in a position where we are told we should not expect to use a site for free even though it advertises itself as such. After all, supermarkets have been indirectly paying for customer information for years through their loyalty card schemes, so maybe we should be asking websites, "How much will you pay me for the data I'm providing?" Rather than letting them have their cake and eat it.

Data Collection - So You Really Don't Care?

If you haven't quite understood that data, whether personal, sensitive or corporate is a big deal yet, then perhaps it is worthwhile looking at what is being collected and by what methods.

Corporate data, by definition, is privileged and protected. Only a fool would want competitors getting their hands on research and development projects or any other corporate information which might lose them competitive advantage. Yet by the same token, and in myriad ways, many organizations are offering an increasing number of ways to access their data and systems simply by having an 'online presence' in many venues.

On an individual level, a whole new industry and market has been developed founded on personal data and the more sensitive the information is the higher the value. Be aware that when someone is asking you to provide something as innocuous as your favorite book, the reason is because that information can be monetized.

Although the Cambridge Analytica scandal was one to hit the headlines it is by no means alone. But what it has done is offer up the chance to examine more closely who is collecting what and why.

If a company intends to monetize data rather than simply track trends, the avenues open to them are multiple and often highly complex. The bottom line, however, is that the more they collect and the more sensitive it is, as it aggregates, the more valuable it becomes. And we are all subjected to this socially acceptable and legitimized form of surveillance from the moment we switch on our computers and start to browse.

At a base level, and before you even touch your keyboard, your browser reports back which type you are using, your unique IP address, and approximate location. It can tell which computer system you are running or whether you are on a mobile, OS, CPU or GPU. Some systems can tell which links you click on and track your every movement across the Web. They might also tell what your display resolution is, what plug-ins you have, and they certainly record when you press a 'like' button.

Some specific sites will monitor your mouse movements around the site (have you noticed how, on some websites, if you even stray near the icons suggesting you might leave a pop-up will appear saying something like, 'Before you go...' ?) and see where you click or how you press the keys; more pressure on one key less on another, your typical typing mistakes and corrections, each providing a unique signature that tells the computer (and others) it's you.

They will check what default language your computer is running on and the fonts that are installed, and just to make sure they know exactly how you view the Internet world they will also check your monitor color depth and likely your screen size. Why? Well, one reason is to do with ensuring your system is optimized to improve the user experience, but as with all these things it is open to abuse and exploitation where the will to do so exists.

Cookies are a variety of those little bots I spoke about earlier in the book and, although sold to you as being helpful they can be invasive little so-and-so's; they are a fragment of information which a website deposits on your hard drive the first time you visit. On the plus side, they might record what you have previously looked at or remind you what you last bought, but they are frequently a lot more help to the site you are visiting. This is often reflected by the fact that up until recently at least, most sites will not allow you to browse unless you agree for their own little cookie to invade your hard drive. It was a case of opt in or opt off, so to speak.

Now, new regulation has made it more difficult to do this and quite likely because although most agree that cookies often improve site functionality, they can act as two types and one is a lot less user-friendly than the other. First party cookies are ones where, when you visit a site, it puts out an identifiable cookie specific to a domain and the information can only be viewed by that owner. There are also third-party cookies. What happens in this case is when you visit a site it doesn't drop a first party identifiable cookie on to your hard drive linked to the site address, it drops a different one instead linked to another domain. This means that the information can be picked up when you visit other sites and it can track your movements and pick up information as you browse the net. This can then be injected across multiple sites and used in conjunction with other tracking technologies. Let's face it, some cookies are a lot sweeter than others.

Remember though, at this point you haven't even been asked to input any personal information. Yet all this data has been extracted and correlated and put together in a nice little basket, either without your knowledge or with your implied rather than explicit consent. Then, when you do volunteer information, in many cases it is out of necessity, for example, when you are buying products on websites.

Others though encourage you to provide a lot more detail. For example, when you join forums or social media sites. And how many millions of us have uploaded our detailed resumes to a central recruitment engine such as Monster? At the very least you might provide your name, age, gender, full date of birth, the name of your company or employer, your telephone numbers, your email address. On some sites they may request that you 'fill in a profile' and you volunteer which schools you attended, place of birth, current country, city, town or even the street.

You'll tell of your first workplace, your current occupation, the qualifications you obtained, your favorite sport, hobby, movies or books. You might tell the name of your spouse, your marital status, your gender and even your sexual preferences. You may well give out your ex's name, those of your kids, their dates of birth and where they go to school. Maybe you will be asked your political preferences, which sport you prefer, the team you support and what your favorite charities are. You might be asked if you want the site to 'connect to your email account' or other related sites.

Indirectly, of course, you are then linked to family, friends and their friends, likely your colleagues and maybe some clients just for good measure. There are then the contacts you make through your bank, your insurance company, maybe shopping companies you use. In fact, anyone and everyone you have ever had an email connection with. Then, as you browse the net everything will be recorded from what you search for on Google through to which YouTube videos you watch. As you chat with your contacts you will tell who your friends are and often those who aren't. You will at least record and report on important incidents in your life and often those that are much more trivial. You will tell what you eat, where you go on vacation, when you are sick, happy, depressed or thinking of getting a divorce.

Some of the information requested, though, at least when it is taken in isolation seems pretty innocuous. Some less so. And some leaves you wondering why they would want to know? Only recently, and likely as a result of the newly implemented GDPR, I received an email from a 'charity' health site I am a member of. On reading the terms and conditions I was shocked to discover that they had awarded themselves the capacity to 'contact and communicate with family and friends' of members. Why, I asked myself, particularly in an environment where all things medical are usually considered confidential, would a health charity feel the need to either know the details of family and friends of members, much less communicate with them? And where would they be getting that information in the first place other than through any discussions taking place on their forum or links to other websites because it certainly wasn't a prerequisite to provide it when joining the site?

Think about it – this is more information than a doctor is allowed to ask and even then it's usually only for contact purposes in an emergency.

Many people, particularly those who say they have nothing to hide, will dismiss all the above as being of little consequence. It doesn't matter if anyone knows which car I want to buy, or what wine we drank at Christmas lunch, or if we have just lost our job, or the wife has just run off with the best friend. Nothing matters to them and the reason for that is clear – because they haven't suffered the ill effects of it yet and likely don't have the imagination or judgment to see what might happen if they do. They assume that it will not happen to them and they have no fear because they have no experience of the devastation it might cause.

The bottom line here is clear – if you don't value your privacy, then you can't expect anyone else to either. By the same token, you cannot tell other people to forgo their privacy rights simply because you do and particularly if you have no negative experiences or a balanced argument to back up those opinions.

Alex Stamos, the Facebook CISO, had both insight and judgment and clearly saw the potential damage which can be inflicted when user trust is exploited. Yet still there are many millions of people who are comfortable in parting with the minutiae of their lives as they continue to place trust in the hands of those who have already abused it. But even when it comes to the Cambridge Analytica drama we know that this is still only skimming the surface of data collection; the real intention is not just to build the recognized tools of the marketing trade but is also related to the emerging field of psychographics. This is where emotional data is extracted from subjects to enable emotive targeting and, some would argue, psychological manipulation to a level and degree that we have never before experienced.

The basic foundation of psychographics is the 'OCEAN' model which measures personalities across five aspects:

- Openness
- Conscientiousness
- Extraversion
- Agreeableness
- Neuroticism

This is most easily done by establishing your likes or dislikes when it comes to the comments you make, images you post or even videos you watch. Where you see a 'like' button, you can almost certainly guarantee that someone, somewhere, is monitoring your emotional responses so you can be targeted with individually designed advertisements based on your emotional biases.

When this information is combined with everything else that has been collected about you, whether through the Internet, third-party organizations or data brokers, the amount of detail companies have about individuals becomes close to extraordinary and this is why the Cambridge Analytica saga became so very, very interesting.

Michal Kosinski discovered that what people 'liked' on sites such as Facebook were essential to discovering the personality of individuals.[2] His research revealed that:

- 70 likes were enough to exceed what an individual's friends knew about them.
- 150 likes were enough to exceed what an individual's parents knew about them.
- 300 likes were enough to exceed what an individual's partner knew about them.
- 300 and more likes surpassed what an individual thinks they know about themselves.

The direction that data collection and marketing in general is taking is that not only do organizations want to know what you do, but they also want to know what you are thinking about so they can manipulate your emotions to produce their required outcomes. And this is where Mr Stamos and the Russian misinformation saga, together with the Cambridge Analytica drama, all became rolled into one and why we see the warnings by the incorruptible CISO starting to come true.

There has been much debate regarding the real effectiveness of psychographics, but in truth that is only part of the argument. The real point to be discussed is that third parties are being allowed access and compile such in-depth information in the first place, when we do have rights to privacy that should not be overruled by use of simple contract law.

Today misinformation is the name of the game and it is often difficult to know whether what you are reading is authentic. As few will have failed to notice, propaganda also seems to be playing an increasing role in reporting no matter what or who is the source of the information. This is leading, among others, marketers and advertisers to take an active role not in creating desire for products but attempting to use thought processes to manipulate the biases of individuals or even to switch belief systems completely.

This means that when it comes to situations such as political parties, politicians have no need to promote broad policies or to appeal to a particular demographic. All they have to do is simply design campaign strategies that will appeal to the individual and to target those same people via the Internet.

It may still be marketing, but not as we know it.

Data Brokers

Because the Internet is so central to the world of data collection, what we often forget is that we also exist outside of it and many of our details are available in the physical world too. Data brokers, sometimes referred to as Credit Reference Agencies, only appeared on the scene within the last 15 years or so, but they collect information on millions of individuals all over the world and not only from the Web. They also check out census records, motor vehicle licensing, court reports, bank card transaction lists, consumer purchase records, media reports, and even health service records.

The data, along with all they have found out about you through the Internet, comprises thousands of pieces of information and it is then packaged up and sold on to other organizations or individuals who are willing to pay. By now it should be very clear you are a commodity.

Whether they like the title or not, Cambridge Analytica were a data broker holding over 200 million personal profiles based on 5,000 data sets. So too are companies like Experian and Acxiom; they hold data indefinitely, they are not obligated to reveal where they obtained the information, and neither are they obliged to reveal who they sell it on to.

Meanwhile, those they have collected the data on – the rest of us – frequently pay them to prove to other interested parties that we have a clean credit record. In 2013, the U.S. Senate Committee published a review relating to the industry and one of their main findings concluded that, "Data brokers operate behind a veil of secrecy".[3] Data brokers will reveal who is financially vulnerable, who is suffering from HIV, who has been sexually abused, who is registered physically disabled. There are no limits on what information they can glean and will part with, provided, of course, the price is right. Nothing but nothing is out of bounds. And if you are on a list, which you will be, then somebody out there will know your greatest secrets.

Of course, we haven't yet touched upon those who are normally considered to be the 'bad actors' in the game, because hackers too are data brokers even if they aren't registered as legitimate companies. Then again, when we look at what the 'good actors' are up to, maybe the hackers are the least of our worries.

The CISO Perspective
Tim Grieveson - CIO/CISO
(Former Chief Cyber Strategist HP)

Tim brings a wealth of experience from across industry having operated as CIO for a division of one of the largest private organizations on the globe, where operating in hostile environments comes with the territory, and as a former advisor to the global CISO community whilst at Hewlett Packard. I asked Tim to provide some thoughts on the direction of data privacy as a concept and the impacts of GDPR, the Data Protection Act 2018, and legislation on the corporate world.

Tim Grieveson: CIO/CISO

"When it comes to privacy I talk of it as the data piranha because the bad guys are not simply going after one target. Instead of taking credit card details, they are stealing people's entire lives. They take healthcare records, bank account details, spending history, and build a package which becomes much more damaging to the individual and causes significant impact.

An example might be their ability to get credit. The bad actors could already have been applying for credit cards, loans, or taking out goods and services in their (or your) name, resulting in the victim not being able to get credit and possibly a financial loss. You also have difficulty in removing data once it's been compromised, which can be extremely tough and challenging. It can impact careers, because the victim may work in a regulated role where they can't have a negative credit history. It could also be even wider than that. Credit ratings could be compromised for governments or countries. Imagine if a series of breaches occurred on the U.K. Government and their ability to gain credit was impacted. That's significant for any country or state.

As an individual one of the challenges is that often you have to prove it wasn't you. My son had his card details stolen from an online website and had a devil of a job to demonstrate it wasn't his purchase. Another challenge is that you don't even know you've been hacked and only find out sometime later. I've been hacked when I took money out of a cash-point and within hours a number of cards were replicated. Now I'm very careful where I use my card and never share my pin number. Fortunately, the bank saw the irregular payments and immediately froze the account, so I do think they are getting better. However, in many cases the customers don't know. The older generation wouldn't think about that necessarily, but the younger ones aren't any better. I see people booking holidays, and cars while sat in a crowded train carriage. They are sharing when they are going on holiday, what their home address is, and what their bank account details are.

When it comes to social media certainly Generation X and Generation Y are much, much smarter and they are using it better, but often they do not see privacy in the same way that we, as security professionals, do. That said, I think the onus should be on the social media companies such as Facebook and the Google's of the world, to take responsibility.

Yet, as we know from recent events, they have shared data without our knowledge. We do sign up to it, we do click on the next, next, next button, but we don't read it because it's long and complex, but somewhere in there it does say they have the right to sell, use, and harvest your data. Organizations do need to be much more transparent about it. But they only become transparent when they have an inevitable breach or leak.

It's not a victimless crime because ultimately somebody pays, whether with insurance premiums or bank charges. And there can be terrible impacts on people who need to pay their mortgage or insurances or get food for their family. The victims are there.

The 'If you've got nothing to hide' argument doesn't really play out. I have nothing to hide but we all have private information we wouldn't give bad actors and people who may not be as moral as we are. Besides, cyber-crime and cyber-theft, it's very lucrative, so there are always going to be people stealing your data. I use social media, but consider what I put out. Could people build a picture of me? Of course they could. But the responsibility is to consider what you put where and minimize the impact of it.

Like other people, I subscribe to many accounts and so do my children. But I also subscribe to a credit bureau service which checks my credit history. I also make sure I change my passwords regularly and don't have the same passwords for every account. I minimize my online activities when purchasing things, using third parties. I'll use paid credit cards when I go on holiday, or have a number of cards.

You never know if a password has been compromised so change them regularly and make them complex. Use two-factor authentication or digital signature. If you get alerts don't use the link in the email. Log in the normal way because you don't know if it's a phishing attack. Some are very sophisticated and look genuine, things unusual? For example, the email address from HMRC or wherever, is it correct? Are there spelling mistakes, is the data there, are they asking you for information you wouldn't normally share? They shouldn't be asking for your passwords etc. Verify the email with the bank or third party. Make sure you are always thinking, 'Is this genuine?' If in doubt ignore or delete if it is genuine you will be contacted in more traditional ways.

We also need to challenge vendors making sure they are bringing security in because it's about people, process, and technology. You need all three of them. For example, are they using encryption, clear text, two-factor authentication, taking care of our data? That's where GDPR is really, really, important because it brings together and harmonizes responsibility and accountability. There's a responsibility for them to notify if there are breaches with fines and sanctions. They can also lose their license to do business and ability to process data.

With the Dixons hack the ICO will be looking closely even though the breach happened before GDPR was introduced, and they will be extremely probing in terms of what processes were in place. Where they protecting the data in an appropriate manner? If it transpires that the appropriate protection wasn't in place, then surely they will be fined and their ability to process data might be affected which could have wider implications for the business.

It's also possible that the regulators will show their teeth and look for targets to focus the minds of other firms to be responsible. Although they should have been responsible with data for years because the Data Protection Act has been in place since 1998.

Today a breach is basically inevitable. The bad guys are getting much, much smarter and it's a very, lucrative market. I think my figures say $1.2trillion in the market by 2020. If I'm a bad actor I will attack the technology, but I will also attack the social side. Where the individual's wife goes to work, or gym, or school for the children. They build up that social picture of everything which is more difficult to protect than the technology. So we need to have a wider view of security and not just on the systems, the network, the widgets, that could be connected. We need to think about the non-connected devices, things that build good security posture. I've been thinking for a long time about security in terms of Health and Safety. It needs to be everybody's responsibility and built into our culture. In certain countries cyber-warriors are trained at school because they start early. We're associated with a couple of Universities, Coventry and the MBA in Cybersecurity, and there are others are starting to get involved too.

Most training courses are not aimed at security people, but I.T. people who already know the problem. Really though we need to educate the wider community, the SME market, non-executive directors, the chief fire interlocuters, the marketing officer. Cyber Health and Safety is everyone's responsibility.

We need to become datacentric. Understand the data you have, the assets you need to protect, understand the value of them. Because if you know what value you've got - and you can't protect everything - you can focus and prioritize on the things that are important to you. See GDPR not as a big scary compliance, but it's ability to optimize your business. See it as generating new markets.

Support your CISO and make them part of your organization. Don't beat them with a stick when there's a breach. Help them to help you. Help security to enable your business and not disable it."

Chapter 11
The Voice Of The Vendor

"We are addicted to our thoughts. We cannot change anything if
we cannot change our thinking."
- Santosh Kalwar

Throughout this book we have experienced a range of views from across industry but what of those vendors that we depend upon to build, deliver, and integrate the technology solutions that underpin our defensive platforms? Whilst no single vendor can represent the overall industry, Justin Coker aims to provide an unbiased view based on his personal and extensive industry experience.

Justin Coker - VP EMEA Skybox Solutions:
My name is Justin Coker. I'm Vice President for Europe, Middle East and Africa (EMEA) for Skybox Security and I've been in the security management industry for 20 years. I'm pleased to share some of my personal insights from a

vendor's perspective, and I'm also in the fortunate position of having regular discussions with CISOs from many different walks of life and businesses. This means I can join the dots across industries and sectors and provide a more holistic view of some of the more significant cybersecurity challenges.

The questions CISOs ask have stayed the same throughout my time in this job. They want to go to their board with the ability to answer some apparently very simple questions. "How secure are we? What is our risk posture? Are we spending enough on security? What do we need to plan for? How compliant are we?" Yet, despite those questions remaining the same, answering them has become much more difficult. That's because the complexity has grown immensely, and there are variables which create a 'perfect storm' for cybersecurity management.

Historically there has always been a challenge for CISOs in communicating to their board, because many cybersecurity leaders come from technical backgrounds and haven't had a grounding in C-level discussions or understanding of the business. Ultimately, that really hasn't boded well for them, particularly in communications where they are prone to simply drop in a technical report or use fear, uncertainty and doubt (FUD) arguments to sway opinions.

The impact of this has been that a lot of organizations, including top market leaders, often make good faith investments in multiple technologies that will never meet expectations. These shortcomings are often rooted in the fact that such investments aren't aligned with the larger business objectives. As such, it's no surprise that we have seen a good many CISOs from a technical background being progressively replaced by those who are more business focused. It's akin to a changing of the guard.

Too Much Technology

Technology is only part of the solution, and probably one which has been pushed way too much; it should be a combination of people, process, technology and strategy — not just technology in isolation. However, the vendor landscape keeps on expanding and this has not helped the situation. When I started back in 1998, there were probably fewer than 50 security vendors. Now, if you look at the latest data from Momentum Cyber, there are around 2300 security vendors. You only have to visit InfoSec in London, one of the largest security events in Europe, and you're swamped with a flood of new vendors each year. A relative of mine who recently become a CTO spent a day there reviewing security options on behalf of his company, and came out completely bewildered. Part of the problem is that the vendors use industry "buzz words" and present similar messages across multiple technologies. Also, often the boundaries are blurred. "Risk" and "vulnerability" are classic cases – these terms are often confused.

The Bigger Picture

The reason I've stayed with Skybox Security for 13 years is that they have a very clear mission of delivering the holistic, big-picture view to organizations. This is on target because CISOs and senior execs are generally visual people. Sage advice from Sun Tzu's The Art of War, written 2,500 years ago, and Napoleon's strategies from the early 1800s, say that if you are going to defend something, you need to see the battlefield from an elevated position. That's very logical to me — you need to know where your resources are best deployed, and your view will inform your strategy on how to best defend your primary objectives.

The other thing that is very different about my firm is that it takes a very proactive view on security rather than being reactive. In many ways, the industry seems to be 95 percent reactive and maybe 5 percent proactive. It feels like the industry is driving the car the wrong way round, staring into the rear-view mirrors instead of focusing on the front windscreen. This means that we need to find a way to encourage security leaders to think differently and look ahead to understand and solve the situations we face. As Sun Tzu said, we have to understand ourselves as well as our enemies because — if we don't we will lose every battle.

Different Concepts

The concept of modeling also seems very logical to me as I had a background in computer-aided design (CAD). Modeling isn't clever, it isn't new. In fact, modeling has been around for a long time — it just hadn't been applied to the security industry. When you've got lots of data and complexity, lots of different technologies, modeling is a very smart way to put that together, especially when you have silos in organizations that need to be connected. It's no different than what happened in the engineering industry when you had lots of different types of data that went in to, for example, building a car or an aircraft. CAD brought all those together into an objective, singular reference model, and the same can be done in our industry.

Collaboration and Communication

When it comes to the safety side of security, one of the best comparisons to make is between the airline and medical industries and their approaches to collaboration, communication and overall safety management. Both of these sectors are dealing with risk management but have very different processes. I have a passion for aviation, and one of the most impressive things about the industry is that it has a very international, open-body of processes and people around the technology they use. They share and have a very good feedback loop. So, whenever there is an incident, it's always open, investigated thoroughly and information is available for people to use and learn. It's not the same in the medical industry. There isn't as much of a good feedback loop, and certainly the information isn't often shared — either between the hospitals or around the world.

Sharing is something which is also probably missing in our industry, and we need to join up better as far as collaboration between vendors, CISOs and system integrators to create a stronger ecosystem. No matter what your involvement, our enemy is united against us, and ultimately we are all part of the same defense mechanism.

Few people make the connection between cybersecurity risks and personal risk. When you are going on an aircraft or into hospital for a procedure you inherently, subconsciously *feel* risk. You understand that your life is 'in their hands' and it's beyond your control. Therefore, you have to rely on professionals and procedures in place to make sure no one messes up. The same doesn't apply in our industry. People have not made the fundamental connection that one day, they may be in a hospital bed and — as the result of a hack — their patient records might disappear at a critical moment. Or they may be driving along a street when the red light unexpectedly changes to green and they are hit by another car. Or it could be that a factory or processing plant blows up near them, or maybe a pill that they are taking has got the wrong compound in it. Maybe they think it's just for the movies, that it isn't something that's going to impact them, and therefore they don't worry about it.

When it comes to the threat landscape, an important factor is that our industry is very siloed. Historically, the CISO or the information security officer has predominantly been looking at the IT systems they are directly responsible for. Increasingly we realize that the attack surface is broader than that. It covers not just physical IT, but could include services in the cloud, hybrid or virtual networks. It could also include operational technology (OT) networks such as industrial control systems (ICS) and supervisory control and data acquisition (SCADA) systems, or maybe the smart buildings most of us frequent these days. For example, it could be that a heating, ventilation and air conditioning (HVAC) system was taken down deliberately, and there is a knock-on issue that the data center will power down in a matter of minutes. If you are a bad guy wanting to cause trouble and thinking outside of the box, why not attack the smart building infrastructure rather than trying to get through the IT network? This actually happened in a well-publicized data breach with Target, the U.S. retailer. It was later reported that the attack was traced back to stolen credentials from their HVAC vendor. What we need to do is look from the top of the hill at all the possible ways in which you can be attacked, but we also need to have a very good understanding of the threats. We have to use intelligence from the dark web and look at threat sources. With WannaCry, for example, the attack that badly impacted the U.K. National Health Service (NHS) and others, we were fortunate enough to be able to marry up the threat horizon and the attack surfaces of our clients to predict the risk a month in advance.

Whizzy Things and Silver Bullets

Whizzy Things and Silver Bullets

I certainly think we need to get the balance right in the industry and not only move away from just being reactive but also from being dazzled by the next whizzy or hyped shiny silver tech bullet. Talking to a lot of CISOs recently, they have been saying, why do we need to worry about a string of zero-day attacks when known vulnerabilities and open misconfigurations — the proverbial doors and windows — are open anyway? And why, if you think about it logically, would the bad guys use expensive, scarce zero-day resources when they can just get in through open configurations and vulnerabilities? If you look at the Verizon Data Breach Investigations Report, going back several years now it's been saying that over 90 percent of the anonymous breaches have come from known vulnerabilities, misconfigurations and basic 'open doors and windows.'

We've done analysis and looked at the common vulnerabilities that are used by rootkits and hacker toolkits, and often they share the same vulnerabilities. These are not new vulnerabilities, they are certainly not zero-day, and can be 18 months old in general. So really the Achilles' heel of the enemy is using technology that we know about and we can block. And when we talk to CISOs, they know they are not going to become impenetrable fortresses, but they can make themselves very resilient, especially to cybercrime. Remember, although cybercriminals have resources, it also costs them money as well. Ultimately, if you can make yourself very resilient or less likely to be breached, then they may just give up and go to the next organization down the road that takes security less seriously than you do and thus costs less to attack.

There are many forces at play suggesting we do lots of different things involving lots of bright, shiny, whizzy technologies. This combined with the fact there is a great deal of money going into the cybersecurity market is why there are 2,300 vendors. Everyone wants to find the silver bullet that can propel them to a quick exit, yet often it's the simple things that move you from a poor security posture to a much better one.

These 2,300 vendors provide a lot of overlap. There is a single 'cyberscape' chart from Momentum Cyber, and there are fewer categories than you might think — just over a dozen — with a huge amount of overlap among them. So much of the issue of chasing silver bullets is about the natural loss of focus. The simple analogy is that it's easy to get distracted about the next new whizzy thing and to forget about the basics of shutting the doors and windows, particularly if a brand-new, shiny 'silver bullet' technology has come out. It's also about raw capitalism playing out, not something sinister.

Bring in the Women!

As we think differently, it's a good thing to have a healthy gender balance in any team. So I aim, within our organization, to get the balance right between the number of male and female staff, and it's certainly rewarded us. If you look at the common ways in which men and women think, women tend to be more proactive and men, more reactive. If we had more women in the industry, they would probably do a better job of shutting the 'doors and windows' and setting us on the much needed, more proactive path. Surely there would still be a need to put out fires when incidents do occur. Both aspects are important, but I think in the future of the industry, there will be more jobs for the proactive-minded than firefighters.

In our business, it's very much about looking after customers. That's part of the challenge we've had, where vendors are pressured because of the raw economics to get to an exit as fast as possible. And, to be fair, they have to be very mission oriented in what they are going to do, how they will get there and succeed as fast as possible. This means you don't have a lot of time for cooperation, but the job is not about just switching on a product and off you go. We have deliberately employed a balance of genders and found that some of the women we've employed are very, very good at getting their heads around the complexity of making sure clients are well looked after. They ensure that we circle back, understand any problems and get the return on investments made.

The View From the Top of the Hill

When we talk about the silver bullet mentality, it's often a practice of having a lot of controls in isolation, and not of controls that have any context holistically of the battlefield. If we look at intrusion prevention systems (IPS) for example, often we find when we do a full model and look at all the controls, the IPS have been bought, plugged in, switched on, but they are in the wrong place. That is a classic example of an expected return on investment (ROI) not being received on that particular technology because it was not implemented with the context of the security environment in mind. What we are doing more frequently now is trying to look at a three- to five-year window and embedding our proactive security management as a strategic concept. This means organizations can look at a series of milestones that will allow them to change the balance of the modus operandi from more reactive firefighting to a more proactive approach, including in how and why security investments are made.

That has a lot of benefits because, as with the medical industry, if you understand something early you can deal with it before it becomes terminal or serious. So really we're trying not just to look at technology but think of the whole premise of that technology and the people and process. We're seeing some very interesting organizations now that are looking at that type of modeling capability to empower their business and to re-engineer their processes. We are working with some of the biggest organizations in the world that are now using our threat-centric cybersecurity management. This means they can focus on one to five percent of the vulnerabilities in their network that are actually a critical attack vector and the ones that are at the heart of their business. These can then receive a very high focus, heading off any significant incidents before they happen, and then everything else is scheduled and patched as part of the 'business as usual' process. As an additional example, we are also working with a large telecommunications company who are looking to fundamentally shift their security operations center (SOC) from a reactive modus operandi to a proactive one and, again, there are some big number savings in that in terms of people, costs and efficiency.

What we have to remember is that a lot of these more traditional technologies, like security information and event management (SIEM) systems for example, create so much noise it can result in breaches being missed. It's great if you are looking at it from a compliance or forensic perspective, where you can go back and find out what's happened, but from a situational awareness perspective, it's not giving you the radar view of what's coming. Although SIEM is viewed as a situational awareness and a governance, risk and compliance (GRC) tool, it was originally built purely as a compliance tool. Although it may have context in vulnerabilities or assets, it has no context of the access across the network. It doesn't see the network access map. If you run attack simulations then you can understand where all the open attack vectors are into the network before they happen. That's the ability which has been lost. Instead of being up on the hill like Napoleon, they're stuck down in the trenches, reacting and firefighting.

We Are Fighting a Battle in Cyberspace

If we look at the people fighting the battle, I think we have to be more holistic and think carefully about the army we assemble and who is capable of taking on our adversaries. If we understand the enemy, and know they can be creative and think outside the box, then we have to be able to think like that too. We have to be one step ahead, particularly because we can only defend — we can't attack. So if we can't use our creativity to understand, for example, the HVAC system, then they are going to out-maneuver us and outsmart us. It's not just about intelligence. It's about getting a balance of different people, left- and right-brain thinkers, creatives and logicians, men and women. We also have to readdress this false sense of security that we are not connected to anything that might damage or hurt us. Even if the risk is not directed at us personally today, our kids could suffer from our actions within our lifetime.

But I think, if we look at it in accord with Maslow's hierarchy of needs, we are all in that high part of the pyramid — the safe, happy place. We are all doing okay, we have got good jobs, we're able to provide for our families, so we are in that happy place where we don't need to rock the boat or change anything. But there's a lot of change going on in the world right now. In the West we are fairly comfortable, but there are parts of the world where there are some pretty good hackers who don't have the same lifestyle or perception of things as we do here and we have to recognize that.

When it comes to adversaries, there are obviously at least two key elements and possibly three: the criminal fraternity, which includes organized crime, the nation-state actors, and also the hacktivists. If you look at the criminal fraternity it's become very, very organized and, like any organization, it's become specialized. For example, if you look at malware or ransomware, it's very easy to get on ransomware as a service (RaaS) site. You place the input where you want to fire the ransomware, you set your bitcoin value, and you set the consequences. Then all you have to do is press the button and wait for the bitcoins to come in. That doesn't take a genius to operate and you can get very quick rewards, so people will think, why not? If you look at the attack resources, there are vendors, service providers and specialists and you can quickly assemble an army. Previously, it was very difficult to do that. That's the organized crime side, and we mustn't underestimate how quickly it's growing. There are various estimates of how much cybercrime makes, usually in the hundreds of billions of dollars. One thing we know for sure is that cybercrime is growing much quicker than our industry and so is the balance of economic power behind it. It would be interesting to see the difference between how much is spent on defense compared to how much the bad actors are grossing.

Then there's obviously nation states and a group of other categories which could be called hacktivists or fundamentalists. In the end, though, it's just a different set of motives. The toolsets they have and their ability to cause damage are somewhat ubiquitous, and nation states will have better access to weaponry such as zero-days. These are vulnerabilities that have been identified and announced as exploitable risks but where a patch or fix is not yet available.

But, as I said before, our adversaries don't need zero-days to start doing some damage. If you go on to the open source sites and look at SCADA vulnerabilities that are out there, it's very, very scary seeing the number and type of devices available, what they are configured to do, what they control, and then also see what the vulnerabilities are in these critical systems. Shodan is one example of such a tool, and it gives you — and the hackers — all this information, including in some cases the exact geo-location of a vulnerable device. So the technology is there that allows you to assemble an army, assemble the weapons, and then it's a case of where you point it.

There have been a number of recent articles from industry commentators suggesting the Russian activity in the Ukraine and the two successive attacks over the winter period were possibly a proof-of-concept exercise, and they weren't necessarily doing the damage they could have. This means we have to consider and anticipate that these types of attacks could escalate; then we contain and limit any damage. It's not about presuming that what happened in the past will be the same as what happens in the future — the impacts may be much more severe.

We need to connect back to the sensible logic of risk management as a human being. Things don't need to be space-age, it doesn't need to be whizzy. Let's just look at the basics holistically. Look at shutting the doors and windows, making sure we understand the battlefield, and also that we have a view of the technology. Make sure we can assemble our defenses and people so they are not in silos. Make sure we can direct that situation and communicate it to the board in plain language that they can understand. We need to paint a picture for them about risk and compliance that ideally they can see, just like a command-and-control view for a military operation.

We need to get away from this overloaded and reactive view that won't scale and wouldn't be enough even with a skilled team. Yes, you will have some AI and technology to assist you in that, but fundamentally there is still a mass of data there. We need to focus on what really matters and try to get ahead of the curve. We need to stop focusing just on technology and also make it about the right balance of people, culture, and defending yourself as much as possible. You may be breached, but then it's about having the right processes around managing that breach.

Protect Our Privacy

When it comes to privacy, you need to go back in time — not forwards — and put yourself in the mindset of Sun Tzu 2,500 years ago: know yourself and your enemies. It's never too late to make sure people are aware about security in general. We must also push security awareness and education for the next generation and make them aware it's not just good guys who are going to get that data. As we've seen with the Cambridge Analytica leak, your data could end up in the hands of the wrong people who might use it for reasons you hadn't intended. We know now that massive amounts of data have been compromised but to what depth might depend on which generation you belong to. My generation has some stuff out there, but we don't live and breathe our lives through full social media exposure, and you certainly won't see me posting what I'm eating for breakfast.

I'm reminded of a TED Talk that Mikko Hyppönen, the Finnish security guru, gave around some of the big storage facilities being built by certain Western governments, and I think he mentioned that one of the facilities was the size of an IKEA superstore. You can imagine how much storage you can get on a small USB stick you can buy from a shop, much less one the size of IKEA!

We must always remember that information is power and it's valuable. If you can find information, and everyone has it, that has a value. Not just because of the criminal side to extract dollars or pounds, but also it could be used in espionage. It could be competitor information or, for example, like the Ashley Madison hack, used for blackmail.

Where Are We Headed?

If you put everything out there about your day-to-day life on the internet, and everything is visible, that does have some clear benefits with our friends and family and in a good society made up of and run by good people. On top of this 'digital footprint' we leave, we are seeing more and more examples of CCTV cameras going up around us, more of a surveillance society evolving across the globe. For example, there was a recent story in the press about a criminal being arrested at a pop concert in China using facial recognition technology.

Sometimes you have to ask yourself where this is all leading, what does the future look like? Politics is ever-changing, and there are several examples now of 'strong man' leaders or dictators. If you start with this mass of internet data, coupled with CCTV surveillance, then add the threat of propaganda via 'fake news' and the ability for technology to hijack the fidelity of audio and video clips, democracy itself and free press and speech are at risk — the foundations of our modern-day society!

You could argue that today, unlike in WWII, there couldn't be a French-style resistance movement any longer because the 'overlords' would know exactly where you were. It's very difficult to go off the grid, and even reality TV shows, where contestants are tasked with 'disappearing' for as long as they can to beat the 'trackers,' reflect the fact that it's almost impossible to do so.

Now, to a large degree, we are all tagged and tracked whether it's through our mobile or some other IoT, GPS-enabled device such as a fitness band or watch, and that situation is getting worse.

At one extreme, there is a readily available online video, *Slaughterbots*, and the concept of a swarm of killer bots which in effect could be launched to assassinate select targets through smart weaponry. We've heard this technology, 'smart weaponry,' talked about, and we know that there are drones, not just predators, but lots of small drones that could be launched from fighter jets. Then they work in swarms and have the capabilities to find and track individuals and assassinate them. This is the ultimate scenario. If we get to singularity and AI computers want to get us, we are in big trouble. It probably won't be like Terminator, it will be a lot more efficient, and based on today's capabilities it's likely we, the human race, would have little chance against such an adversary.

We need to question where it could go wrong. A lot of the leading thinkers are concerned about the programming going into AI and that it might not be being done appropriately or at least without due consideration being given to the 'what if? or 'what could possibly go wrong?' scenarios.

I'm not a security futurologist, but I was lucky enough to present alongside one of the best in the industry, Bruce Schneier, about eight years ago when he was security futurologist at British Telecom Group. These days when I am looking for a future perspective he's one of my go-to sources.

In Summary

Cybergeddon hasn't happened yet. We still have the opportunity to look at what we've learned so far and try to be prepared and guide the outcomes.

There is also a great opportunity to do many things because we have the technology and capabilities that our enemies don't have. Some of our organizations are much bigger than any enemy organization could ever be, and at the moment the balance of power is on our side — if we choose to apply it.

We can't be complacent and we can't wait too long. We have to make sure we address risk, just like we've always done. Then there's no reason why we can't have a profitable, happy, functioning world and still be safe. There's no reason to think we can't have safe online and cyber environments where people feel relatively secure, much like we have when getting on an aircraft.

As a collective ecosystem of users, vendors, governments and organizations across all sectors, we are not doing a good enough job. This is on our watch and we should connect better and improve cooperation in order to make the world a safer place. We can make a difference. We can reduce the attack surfaces making it more difficult and costly for our adversaries, encouraging them to go somewhere else or do something different. But at the moment it's easy pickings, and all that does is encourage more of the same, and it becomes self-perpetuating.

So, in short, it's not all doom and gloom. There are lots of things that are improving. Technology is an evolution and obviously we are learning all the time. I just think, as Einstein said, applying the same thing and expecting a different outcome is insanity. We need to keep evolving, keep adapting, thinking differently, and then we can do some great things.

Just by using Pareto's principal, the 80/20 rule, can really put some perspective on things. Look at the 20 percent of things that really matter, that you can do right now, and that's going to reduce your risk by 80 percent. That's the way we need to be thinking. Know where to focus, step back and don't get stuck in the weeds, work as one big team with a united purpose to protect our critical national infrastructure from those who want to disrupt it. Then, we can really make a difference!

The Academic Perspective
Professor Raj Roy
(Cranfield University)

"I'm Professor Raj Roy, Director of Manufacturing at Cranfield University. I also lead the Through-life Engineering Services Research Centre. We are interested in cybersecurity for engineering systems, such as manufacturing, because there are recent reports published by E.E.F. in the U.K. which identify that 48% of British manufacturers are regularly hacked. Manufacturing is 10% of GDP, so that gives you an idea of how big the problem is, and it's 50% of export. So we have a big stake in the global market to protect our Intellectual Property because that's what it's really about, and some countries are trying to expedite their aerospace growth with technologies from us. This makes it very important for us to fight against.

But the problem happens in multiple countries not just one, and it varies from subject to subject, from sector to sector. It is not only about critical national infrastructure sectors but also private manufacturing operations. Our manufacturing systems, machine tools, databases of activity systems are hacked. It's routine and from many hostile agencies, countries, and individuals. And manufacturing is going to change in the future. It will use more digital technologies and the way of working, designing, evaluating, manufacturing products, will become even more vulnerable to cyber-threats. There will be cyber-attacks on those machines, to steal ideas, data, intellectual properties, so other companies can do it faster or better. Or they will interrupt services for hostile reasons. But the future is about making machines, designing machines, which are fundamentally more secure than they are today. I would like to see more safety and security features built into the hardware, the architecture electronics, and mechanical systems of machines.

Soon customers are going to demand that equipment remains safe over a period of time and manufacturers will have to take that responsibility. It's already happening that we sell time in a machine. Imagine you don't have to buy a car, just pay for the per-hour use. In London there are companies doing it now, and it will happen in manufacturing. Then manufacturers will have to take responsibility for the security of these machines over a long period of time and for its entire life.

Think about it, there are products we work with, aircraft, automotive, which have a 25+ year life. So you have to protect those long term, that's one challenge.

Another is that when we have more time, when we are an advanced civilization and do less work, our personal data will be very relevant for people to come and study and intervene in our personal life - in our health, in our body. Imagine people in the future will actually be chipped. Could that be hacked? Could somebody actually hack into that chip like they do today on industrial control systems? If you imagine that we will have internal industrial control systems which will directly interact with our body, our brains. What would happen if someone took control of that?

I think human beings have to become more intelligent in an increasingly mechanized world. One way to do this is to embed electronics into us and I think that will come. Initially it will be by way of medication, for example with epileptic, neural reactions or signals that can be fought with some electronic devices. And I think that will become mainstream for entertainment purposes, for general capability enhancement purposes, and it is the long-term future. So the current human being is the raw form of human being, which needs to be industrialized in the future.

My first motivation is to inspire creative thinking. I use the word audacity to think so long distance and far away. To have the opportunity to think very, very, long term. It inspires some short-term research, short-term development, to reach that goal, and that's what we want to do. So, we want to raise the ambition of people to really push for technology which will change life forever, in the long term, and not just for one group of people.

I also think that holography will play an important part. The ability to send your image somewhere else. You will be able to stand in front of a computer in your house and send your digital version to another part of the world. This technology is available already, but it's very expensive. I've heard that in North and South Korea they are using some of it.

But I believe as a human being if we start thinking long-term, that gives us some purpose, some direction. My intention, my objective, is to create thinkers in the world who will challenge the status quo and who will globally drive new ways of making products to serve human needs.

There is a government report from the Department of Digital, Culture, Media, and Sport called Secure by Design. This is about designing machines, designing systems, which are fundamentally more secure and not relying entirely on the software and updating it. Then there is the whole area of cyberization of manufacturing where manufacturers remain responsible for maintenance of the asset and guaranteed performance. Imagine if we said my mobile had to work more than 1% of the time for a year or they have to pay me £500. That will change the game. Performance-based payment. Then they will be monitoring my mobile. They will redesign it in such as way that it doesn't break. And, even if it breaks, they will give me a warning - your mobile is having problems, bring it to the dealer and we will look at it and repair it before it breaks - because now they cannot afford for it to break. And that's the future, becoming servitized. With this servitization, digital technology becomes an essential monitor. They must send data continually for the health of the mobile phone. But in turn that attracts more cyber-threat attention.

The system will become so complex humans will not be able to protect it. So think about autonomous agents software, fighting the cyber-threats automatically. Whether it's your mobile phone, your watch, everything, there will be software trying to protect it, like our human white cells. So we draw a similar analogy to creating an immune system which will continuously fight, and it will get better over time so that new threats can be stopped.

We launch an MSc from October 2018 called Cyber Security Manufacturing, to address that. To prepare the next generation manufacturing engineers who are knowledgeable enough to protect their assets.

Currently I don't think there is strong awareness although the government is keen to increase that awareness within manufacturing and engineering communities. But there aren't major changes happening in the curriculum. I do not see tools and techniques coming up in the public domain and commercial business in particular.

The defense and security world is ahead of the game and we need to bring in that knowledge and make it available to several complex engineering sectors like aerospace, transport, shipbuilding, biomedical, health sectors, food. All of them need cyber-secure manufacturing."

Professor Richard Benham

(Founder National MBA in Cybersecurity)

"Establishing the UK's National MBA in Cybersecurity was an instrumental step in plugging the education gap for technically oriented CISO's and security managers generally. Cybersecurity is an issue that needs the full attention of leaders across organizations and businesses of all sizes, and this is a message supported by the Institute of Directors (IoD) as well as the UK's Digital Minister Matt Hancock MP. There is a strong alignment around the notion that as a society we must embrace the benefits of the internet, however, we ignore the risks that the online world presents at our peril!"

Amber Pedroncelli

(Manger Strategic Initiatives E-Council)

"EC-Council's Certified CISO (C|CISO) program was created to fill a gap in the information security certification and training market and now with some 1,700 C|CISOs around the globe is an established industry certification for security leaders. There has long been a push in the industry for information security to be taken seriously at the C-Level. Companies around the world have begun to understand the importance of having a CISO, and any company worth its salt today has at least one. In many cases, competent security managers have been promoted to the C-Level with the expectation that they learn C-Level skills on the job. This approach undoubtedly puts companies' information assets at unnecessary risk, but finding experienced information security professionals with in-depth business acumen ready to earn respect in the C Suite is difficult.

The C|CISO program prepares information security managers to take on an executive role with confidence and helps those already in the role bring together the disparate knowledge needed to thrive as a CISO. The C|CISO aims to bridge the gap between the executive management knowledge that CISOs need and the technical knowledge that many aspiring CISOs have. This can be a crucial gap as a practitioner endeavors to move from mid-management to upper, executive management roles. Much of this is traditionally learned as on the job training, but the C|CISO Training Program can, for some, be the key to a successful transition to the highest ranks of information security management.

Each segment of the program was developed with the aspiring CISO in mind and looks to transfer the knowledge of seasoned professionals to the next generation in the areas that are most critical in the development and maintenance of a successful information security program."

Chapter 12
In at The Start: Meet the First CISO

"Try not to become a man of success. Rather become a man of value."

- Albert Einstein

Earlier I mentioned Steve Katz, who was already involved in information security back in the 1970s and is renowned for being the first ever CISO. I had the pleasure of speaking with the man who set the original bar for safety in the industry - by being the first to design system quality assurance protocols recommending the incorporation of user IDs and passwords - to ask him about cybersecurity at the start, what changes he's seen, and how the role of the CISO has evolved.

Steve has lived and worked through all the developments and changes to the Internet and cybersecurity and is the first to admit that the role of the early information security officer is no longer comparable to the CISO position today. Back then Steve began his career with Citi Bank in the 1970s and was later head-hunted by Morgan Guaranty (now J.P. Morgan), because of his reputation and already long experience in data security, to set up a security department which he eventually went on to lead. Then, in the mid-1990s, Citi Bank decided they wanted him back again.

Today, Steve is probably one of the most experienced CISOs in the world and he has some interesting insights and observations into the business. His primary stance is what it always has been in that the CISO should always be viewed as a 'business enabler' rather than a technical or security expert. He accepts that even today many organizations still do not think this way - and he knows that things have to change.

Despite Steve admitting he's happy with the way he has performed in the sector he does have remaining frustrations with some organizations, industries, and even the sector as a whole, often because they're not acting on advice. He goes on to say that even today recommendations he made back in the 1990s have not been implemented and thinks now is the time for organizations to start listening. Of course, this also begs the question that had such ideas been integrated into systems much earlier, things might not be as precarious as they are now. After all, despite passwords and IDs being a general irritation the world over, without Steve's original concept the situation would have been much, much worse.

Steve also speaks with passion about the importance of CISO interaction with the board and executive management; how information security should be viewed by companies as being a business rather than technological issue, building security and application code and, of course, how vulnerabilities require an immediate fix. For some though, it might be at least a little reassuring to learn how even those at the top of their game have sometimes struggled to get their ideas actioned. Steve does also make the point that it might be naivety on the part of the CISO in expecting ideas to be taken on board first time around - although a couple of decades should be long enough for even the most resistant of executives to come around to that way of thinking.

On the other hand, however, when it comes to breaches, Steve is adamant that most CISOs need to understand that the business only becomes owner of the risk when the officer in charge has done everything they possibly can to forewarn of vulnerabilities which may well lead to a potential hack. He also has staunch beliefs about the way a CISO should tackle the issue when it comes to situations indicating an immediate threat and points out that a CISO might well have to put their neck on the line in order to get the message across to the guys in the hot seat.

Perhaps quite sensibly, he points out when there is no other option, sometimes CISOs should have the courage to go over the head of those they directly report to in order to communicate with the main board - because that's where the ownership of the risk, regardless of the reporting structure, ultimately resides. And, as he goes on to say, although it might well result in the CISO losing his job, the alternative - doing nothing - may well result in a major breach which could also end in the CISO getting fired. Being brave, doing the right thing, taking the necessary action, and escalating issues to the required level should, for the CISO, always trump personal interests, suggests Steve.

This, 'heads I win, tails you lose' situation is one which many CISOs face and was the primary rationale for writing this book. Ensuring that the board gets the message can be virtually impossible for many CISOs and fraught with career pitfalls. Even when they're successful, one information security officer reaching one executive or organization is hardly going to change the world of cybersecurity. But, by involving many executives and managers, by providing them with the real-world challenges they and their CISOs face in an easy to read format has the potential to touch many minds at once.

The importance of effective communication of the right message is reinforced by Steve as he recalls advice given early on in his career when he was told, *"There are times when you need to make a decision, and times when you need to make a recommendation. Make sure you know the difference."*

Like many others in the cybersecurity field, Steve also believes that too many companies fail to establish what key skills they're looking for in a CISO. But he then goes on to say that many CISOs tend to rest on the skills they had when they originally entered the field, yet fail to recognize these might not be the same ones required to deal with the current environment or the challenges coming over the horizon. He explains that those with technology backgrounds often try to fix everything with technology, and those with audit skills will try and fix things using compliance, but points out that the primary skills needed today are soft skills which can be utilized to work with business leaders and the board.

Of all the issues facing the CISO and their organizations, Steve admits that the threat landscape has changed to the point where it's unrecognizable. He recalls that, back in the day, most of the hackers were youngsters out to create a bit of mischief rather than the state-sponsored groups which many CISOs face today. He also points out that computer crime is almost set up as being a separate line of business, particularly when it comes to data harvesting, because the customers are out there waiting for it, and often the hackers are funded up front with perhaps bitcoin or the equivalent.

On top of that, he explains many of the hackers are well trained and skilled, particularly in the far-flung corners of Eastern Europe, Russia, Asia and North Korea. What he goes on to point out is that not only is the likelihood of being caught pretty remote, but the punishments attached to it are rarely acting as deterrents. One reason for this, he thinks, is that it's difficult for people to get their heads around the fact that the prosecutions are about somebody stealing something - even if it's information - but that the information is still there after it's been stolen. He also observes that when someone does get caught they are usually incarcerated in a blaze of publicity - and isn't that what our own hacker explained is a primary motivating factor - kudos by the bucket load? Then the same hackers go on to earn money from their notoriety, which as Steve points out, is hardly a deterrent.

Steve also has some strong views on data collection in general and they are, for the most part, compatible with our comments in an earlier chapter. Outside of hackers and even the social media sites who, if only out of necessity because of the current problems, are now coming out and clearly stating their business models operate around data collection in one way or another, many other organizations are also involved but going quietly under the radar. Steve discusses this as being a form of advanced market research but points out that the 'customer' should be told by the organization collecting the data that they are in fact 'the product,' and that their information is being sold or otherwise traded in some way.

He also makes the observation that people should be given the option to opt out, which is in part what GDPR has started to offer. Although he does make the point that in the current environment, people are giving this information away all too easily and often without question. Yet Steve also makes a clear distinction between those companies who collect data out of necessity and those who capture it out of necessity and then go on to resell it - whether they be an insurance company, a financial services company or any other. This, Steve believes, is absolutely wrong and is perhaps one of the few times that company regulation should be introduced to stop this kind of practice in its tracks.

Transparency, along with ethical activities, he thinks should become the norm for most companies. How successful GDPR or any other equitable legislation that has been introduced will go toward reducing these practices remains to be seen. Given though what we discussed about this subject in an earlier chapter, one thing which could push some companies away from this practice is to make it a legal requirement not only for customers to opt in to this kind of data collection, but also for the companies trading it to pay the people who they are collecting it from. After all, store loyalty cards, which some think are where the trend was set, have long since rewarded customers for the marketing data they provide, so why should other companies and even Internet forums be able to collect free information without telling users they are doing so and then trade it for a profit?

All these things go toward building an increasingly complex threat landscape with an ever-expanding number of vulnerabilities and this emphasizes the requirement for the CISO to be viewed as a business enabler. It is the complexity of the message and scenario that, Steve believes, needs to be transmitted effectively to each and every organization. Without this, Steve is adamant that boards cannot do what they need to - establish how much risk they are prepared to take on by at least assessing the level of risk and potential impact a breach may have in respect of effect on the company, competition, clients, and compliance.

Is it really worth the risk of taking on extra profit for trading data and making your organization a more attractive proposition for hackers, only to establish that if GDPR is brought into the frame the company may well close as a result? Steve goes on to point out that a company needs to assess the risk-balance scenario as they would do with any other aspect of the organization. Cyber, he states, should be no different to any other potential risk failure achieved through assessment and analysis to determine not only the risk appetite of the organization but also that the business is matching CISO and appetite appropriately.

Given all the information that Steve provides, he often asks only one simple question of those wannabe's who want to enter the world of cybersecurity, "Why do you want to be a CISO?" This, he assures us, is a question that must be answered satisfactorily and not least because often those entering the field don't get to use the skills that may have got them the job in the first place. Most CISOs, he explains, have a strong skill set built over many years, whether they are based in technology, auditing, business or whatever, but they're not going to be the primary skills used in the role.

For today's CISOs other, soft skills, are paramount, and those new to the post quickly learn they have to be diplomats, evangelists, marketers, committed to lifelong learning, the person who has to work with a board, as well as being the business enabler. Confidence too, is essential, as they have to go to business leaders and explain the level of risk in a language that bypasses all the technological and security jargon, to enable executives to understand. Even then, the requirements are not complete because over and above everything else the CISO has to have courage.

Courage to stand up to those in power when conflicts arise and tell them they're moving forward with something which goes against his or her recommendations. This, Steve also goes on to say, carries even more weight when the CISO is prepared to put it in writing. But, at the end of the day, Steve also points out that someone who fits these criteria will likely derive more enjoyment out of being a CISO than any other position.

Plain talking then, from the man who has been around from the start and who has seen the landscape evolve from script kiddies entertaining themselves by hacking for fun, to one where cyber-crime has essentially become an extremely rewarding profession performed by very sophisticated hackers. Today, he explains, even when sophistication is lacking there is a large amount of software available to help those wanting to perform activities such as phishing or ransomware attacks. Just as importantly though, as we have come to learn, there are many hackers who are, if not state-sponsored, then at least state condoned and approved by the nations involved. His main concern here is that this particular type of hack continues to spiral almost unabated, making corporate intellectual property theft big business. Whether the intention is to gain information which will give one organization or nation the intellectual advantage or whether they intend to simply disadvantage the competition by initiating malware attacks, this is seen to be the biggest growing threat to enterprise.

Finally, of course, what Steve has also seen is a massive growth in espionage in general.

Surprisingly, being the first CISO is not what Steve wants to be remembered for or what he thinks is important. Rather, he believes his greatest contribution is his mentoring and coaching of a large number of CISOs over the years. In

Steve's eyes, paying it forward and leaving behind skilled CISOs who can contribute much to the world of cybersecurity is far more important than personal accolades and this is the legacy that he really wants to leave behind. But, before we finished talking and with the subject of lifelong learning taking center stage, he also left me with another, vital piece of CISO advice:

"Never be seen as the smartest person in the room… if it gets to the point where you think you are, then it's time to move to another room."

Chapter References

Preface

1. Vint Cerf: https://internethalloffame.org/inductees/vint-cerf

Chapter 1: The World of the CISO

1. Osterman Research Report Summary. July 2017. Second Annual State of Ransomware Reports: *US Survey Results*.
2. Naraine. R. February 2012. ZDnet: *Nortel hacking attack went unnoticed for almost 10 years*. 14 February 2012.
3. Bernard. T.S., Hsu. T., Perlroth. N., Lieber. R. September 7 2017. New York Times: *Equifax Says Cyberattack May Have Affected 143 Million In the U.S.*
4. Perlroth. N. October 3 2017. New York Times: *All 3 Billion Yahoo Accounts Were Affected by the 2013 Attack.*
5. Treanor. J. November 8 2016. The Guardian: *Tesco Bank cyber-thieves stole £2.5m from 9,000 people.*

6. Taylor. N.P. July 10 2015. FierceBiotech: *Financially motivated hackers break into 3 major pharma companies in 18 months.*
7. BBC News. 27 October 2017. *NHS 'could have prevented' WannaCry ransomware attack.*
8. Zetter. K. August 2015. Wired: *A cyberattack has caused confirmed damage for the second time ever.*
9. Zetter. K. 2014.Wired: *An unprecedented look at Stuxnet, the World's first digital weapon.*
10. Straka. C. October 2014. Food Quality and Safety: *Cybersecurity in Food.*
11. Meredith S. October 2018. CNBC: *Here's everything you need to know about the Cambridge Analytica Scandal.*
12. Ryan. December 2015. 2016. Cybrary: *Cyber Security Job Trends Report.*
13. Bekker. G. March 2018. BrightTalk NEB Webinar Presentation: *What will it take to stop the breaches?*
14. *Ibid*
15. Cooney. M. November 2016. Network World: *IBM: Many companies still unprepared for cyber attacks.*
16. *Ibid*
17. Walling. R. 2006. *Personality Traits of the Best Software Developers.*
18. HM Government. 2015. *Information Security Breaches Survey.*
19. Needs Mind map reference if one goes in.

Chapter 2: Who Took a Bullet?

1. Menn. J. 2016. Reuters. *Yahoo secretly scanned customer emails for U.S. intelligence.* October 4 2016.

2. Kastrenakes. J. 2018. The Verge.com: *Facebook's security chief is leaving after clash over Russian misinformation.* March 19 2018.
3. Shields. T., Necomer. E. 2018. Bloomberg.com. *Uber's 2016 Breach Affected More Than 20 Million U.S. Users.* 12 April 2018.
4. Wieczner. J. 2017. Fortune.com: *Equifax CEO Richard Smith Who Oversaw Breach to Collect $90 Million.* September 26 2017.
5. Sweney. M. 2017. The Guardian.com: *TalkTalk chief executive Dido Harding to step down.* 1 February 2017.
6. Boorstin. J. 2015. CNBC: *The Sony Hack: One year later.* 24 November 2015.
7. Furness. H. 2017. Telegraph.co.uk: *Gerald Ratner's Wife: I told him not to make that joke.* 17 September 2017
8. Arends. B. 2017. Marketwatch.com: *Equifax hired a music major as chief security officer and she has just retired.* September 15 2017.
9. Fox-Brewster. T. 2017. Forbes.com: *A Brief History of Equifax Security Fails.* September 8 2017.

Chapter 3: The Threat Landscape - Then and Now

1. https://securelist.com/threats/a-brief-history-of-hacking/
2. http://money.cnn.com/2000/11/09/technology/overview/
3. Katz. S. 2017. Security Current Newsletter. 21 December 2017
4. YouTube - Forensic Files - Hack Attack
5. https://en.wikipedia.org/wiki/MafiaBoy
6. 1991 Congressional Subcommittee on Technology and Competitiveness and the Committee on Science, Space and Technology. Winn Schwartau.

7. https://www.statista.com/statistics/289167/mobile-phone-penetration-in-the-uk/
8. Goodwin R. March 2017. *The History of Mobile Phones from 1973 to 2008.*
9. https://securelist.com/threats/a-brief-history-of-hacking/
10. https://www.theemaillaundry.com/mechanics-impersonation-attacks/

Chapter 4: Interview with a Hacker: A View from the Dark Side

No references

Chapter 5: A Different Breed?

1. Segan. S. ABC News: *Hacker Women are Few but Strong.*
2. Davis. J. 2013. *Jake Davis on Being Arrested and Banned from the Internet.* Video. October 2013.
3. WeinSchenk S. Ph.D. 2012 Psychology Today. Brain-Wise: *Why We're All Addicted to Texts, Twitter and Google.* September 2013.
4. Stevenson S. 2016. Sleep Smarter. Hay House UK Ltd. London.
5. Hegman. S. 2014. Adweek: *Study: 40% of Adults Experience Cyberbullying.* 23 October 2014.
6. Davis. C., Conlan. T. 2015. The Guardian.com: *Woman killed herself after being doorstepped over McCann trolling.* 20 March 2015.

Chapter 6: Bennett Arron - A Victimless Crime

1. Arron. B. 2015. Heard the One About Identity Theft? Silly Papi Ltd. September 2015.

Chapter 7: CISO Fingerprinting and Footprinting

1. Rooke, David & Torbert, William. (2005). *Transformations of Leadership*. Harvard business review. 83. 66-76, 133.
2. Ibid
3. Loevinger. J. 1976. Ego Development. San Francisco. Jossey-Bass

Chapter 8: Emerging Threats: A Future View

1. Martin. A.J. 2018. Sky News. *UK Infrastructure Being Targeted by Hackers*. 6 April 2018.
2. BBC News. Grenfell Tower: *What Happened?* 18 June 2018

Chapter 9: Critical Infrastructure Attack

1. Crichton. M. 1990 Jurassic Park. Alfred A. Knopf. 20 November 1990
2. Zetter. K. August 2015. Wired: *A cyberattack has caused confirmed damage for the second time ever. 2015.*
3. Paganini. P. 2014. Security Affairs. Co. *Malware based attack hit Japanese Monju Nuclear Power Plant*. 10 January 2014.
4. Paganini. P. 2014. Security Affairs. Co. *Nuclear plant in South Korea hacked*. 24 December 2014.
5. *Ibid*
6. McMahon. C. 2017. Independent.ie. Irish News: *EirGrid targeted by 'state sponsored' hackers leaving networks exposed to 'devious attacks.'* 6 August 2017.
7. Greenberg. A. 2017. Wired. Crash Override. *The Malware that took down a power grid*. 6 December 2017

8. Bump. P. 2016 . Washington Post: *Why Russian hackers aren't poised to plunge the United States into darkness*. March 2016

9. Carlton. R. 2016. Slideshare.net. *Scenarios from the Field*. Verizon.

10. BBC.com. Technology. *Hackers Hit US Water Treatment Systems*. 21 November 2011.

11. Houses of Parliament. PostNote number 554 May 2017. *Cyber Security of UK Infrastructure*.

12. *ibid*

Chapter 10: So, You've Got Nothing To Hide?

1. Statistica 2018.

2. Kosinski. M. 2015. Stanford Business School. *Computers are better judges of your personality than friends*. 23 January 2015

3. United States Senate. 2013. Committee on Commerce, Science, and Transportation. Office of Oversight and Investigations Majority Staff: *A Review of the Data Broker Industry: Collection, Use, and Sale of Consumer Data for Marketing Purposes*. 18 December 2013.

Chapter 11: Voice of the Vendor

1. *The top 10 vulnerabilities account for 85% of successful exploit traffic . . . the other 15% consists of over 900 CVEs, which are also being exploited in the wild."* Data Breach Investigations Report, Verizon, 2016

2. Mikko Hypponen, How the NSA betrayed the world's trust – time to act, TEDx Brussels, October 2013: https://www.ted.com/talks/mikko_hypponen_how_the_nsa_betrayed_the_world_s_trust_time_to_act#t-158577

Chapter 12 – The First CISO

No references

The CISO Defenders Cybersecurity Glossary

This glossary is by no means exhaustive. For a comprehensive, jargon-busting list of cybersecurity industry terms visit:

https://www.getsafeonline.org/jargon-buster/

Backup: Ensuring all important data is stored in a secure, offline location to protect it from being lost if a computer is hacked.

Black hat hacker: A person who uses programming skills to cause damage to a computer system, steal data and in general conduct illegal cyber activities.

Botnet: A grouping of computer systems, potentially anywhere in the world, that has been infected by a malicious piece of software. This software allows them to be networked together by the hacker (or bot-herder), giving them full control of all the "bots" in the network to conduct malicious tasks, including denial of service attacks (see below).

Breach: The moment a hacker successfully exploits a vulnerability in a computer or device and gains access to its files and network.

Brute force attack: A technique a hacker can use to break into a computer system. They do this by attempting to "guess" its password (either manually or using a computer software application that searches all dictionary words and terms).

Cloud: A technology that allows us to access our files through the internet regardless of where we are the world.

Command-and-control server: An application that controls all bots in a botnet (see above). The hacker will send a command through this server, which then relays it to all compromised computers in the network.

CISO: Chief Information Security Officer, an organization or company official typically assigned to protecting the firm from digital attacks or compromises by internal and external adversaries and those that would do it, its customers, staff and stakeholders harm.

CSO: Chief Security Officer, A company official often focused on defending an organization from both digital and physical attacks.

DDoS: An acronym that stands for distributed denial of service - a form of cyberattack. This attack aims to make a service such as a website unusable by "flooding" it with malicious traffic or data from multiple sources (often botnets).

Domain: The networking of computers and devices. A domain is a group of computers, printers, and devices that are interconnected and governed as a whole. Your computer is usually part of a domain at your workplace.

Encryption: An algorithmic technique that takes a file and changes its contents into something unreadable to those outside the chain of communication.

Exploit: A malicious application or software script that can be used to take advantage of a computer's vulnerability.

Firewall: A defensive technology focused on keeping the bad guys out. A "wall" or filter is created that judges each attempted interaction with a user's computer and internet connection to determine "should this be allowed entry or not?" Firewalls can be hardware or software-based.

Honeypot: A defensive cybersecurity technique. This technology is essentially a computer (server) that is set up to look like a legitimate and high-value target on a network. The aim is to entice hackers to focus on this computer and not on actual high-value computers or data. The bonus is that administrators can watch hackers in the act and learn to protect against their techniques.

https:// versus http:// Two online standards that allow computers to communicate.

HTTP is defined as Hypertext Transfer Protocol. Its most popular use is online to help internet browsers communicate. For example, to send you web pages from the associated computer hosting the website you're visiting.

HTTPS is similar, but it adds security, hence the "S". It encrypts all data by creating a secure tunnel between you and the website you're visiting and is commonly seen in online shopping stores where security is required.

IP Address: An internet version of a home address for your computer, which identifies it when it's connected to the internet.

Patch or Update: Most software requires thousands of lines of programming language to create, so it's difficult for a developer to ensure all possible vulnerabilities are covered. When entry points are discovered by hackers or the developer themselves, software vendors will often release new pieces of software as a fix.

Phishing or spear phishing: A technique used by hackers to obtain sensitive information, including passwords, bank accounts or credit cards.

Spear phishing is a variant of this technique, but the hacker targets a business or person specifically, instead of taking a blanket approach.

Whale phishing: A technique used by hackers to obtain sensitive information, or to conduct other malicious acts against senior executives and captains of industry.

Malware: An umbrella term that describes all forms of malicious software designed to cause havoc on a computer. Typical forms include viruses, trojans, worms, and ransomware.

Ransomware: A form of malware that deliberately prevents you from accessing files on your computer. If a computer is infected by malware designed for this purpose, it will typically encrypt files and request that a ransom be paid in order to have them decrypted.

Spoofing: A technique hackers use to hide their identity, pretend to be someone else or simply try to fool you over the internet.

Software: A set of instructions that tell a computer to perform a task. These instructions are compiled into a package that users can install and use. Software is broadly categorized into system software like Microsoft Windows and application software like Microsoft Office.

Trojan horse: A piece of malware that often allows a hacker to gain remote access to a computer. The system will be infected by a virus that sets up an entry point for the perpetrator to download files or watch the user's keystrokes.

Virtual Private Network (VPN): A tool that allows the user to remain anonymous while using the internet. It does this by masking location and encrypting traffic as it travels between the user's computer and the website they're visiting.

Virus: A type of malware for personal computers, dating back to the days of floppy disks. Viruses typically aim to corrupt, erase or modify information on a computer before spreading to others. However, in more recent years, viruses like Stuxnet, HAVEX, BlackEnergy2 have caused physical disruption or damage.

Vulnerability: A weakness in computer software. Eventually, if you do not keep your systems up to date or (Patched), you will have vulnerabilities and your system could exhibit vulnerabilities that can be attacked by a hacker due to security safeguards being out of date.

Worm: A piece of malware that can replicate itself in order to spread the infection to other connected computers. It will actively hunt out weak systems in the network to exploit and spread.

White hat hacker: A person who uses their hacking skills for an ethical purpose, as opposed to a black hat hacker, who typically has a malicious intent. Businesses will often hire these individuals to pentest their cybersecurity capabilities.

Zero Day: A particular form of software exploit, usually malware. What makes a zero-day exploit unique is that they are unknown to the public or the software vendor. In other words, because few people are aware of the vulnerability, they have "zero days" to protect themselves from its use.

Zombie: A computer system that has been infected by malware and is now part of a hacker's botnet.

Index

A

B

C

D

E

F

G

H

I

IOTSA (International Operational Technology Security Association), 7, 87, 231-32, 325

L

laws, 5, 53, 72, 116, 191, 236, 238, 241
legislation, 9, 26-27, 38, 79, 175, 177, 191, 218-19, 243, 253, 288

M

machine learning, 12, 85, 137, 182, 187, 191-93, 198, 207, 233
manufacturing, 41, 69, 73, 89, 1353, 189, 206, 209, 233, 276-79
maturity, 29, 120, 162, 166-67, 175, 177-78, 180
misinformation, 46, 130, 204, 250, 294
mistakes, 1, 19, 36, 38, 43, 103, 148-50, 158, 219, 245, 255
mobile phones, 59, 70-71, 121, 145, 279, 295
money, 21, 25, 60, 65, 67, 72, 74, 76, 85, 96-98, 101, 104-05, 107, 110, 113, 116, 123, 127, 136, 141, 145-47, 182, 185, 191, 202, 212, 215-17, 242-43, 254, 264-65, 287, 294
motivations, 28, 33-34, 38, 116, 123, 156, 278

N

nanotechnology, 198-201, 204, 206
network, 26, 63, 66, 68, 70, 74, 76, 82, 134, 153, 155, 165, 167, 185, 202, 220, 232-33, 256, 263, 267-68, 273, 296, 300-04
NHS (National Health Service), 21, 32, 37, 137, 224, 263, 293
NIS (Network and Information Security), 26, 177, 218

O

Operational Technology (OT), 87, 213-14, 217, 231-33, 263, 309

sensors, 88, 188, 233
servers, 49, 64-65, 220
shadding, 95-96, 103-04, 110
shareholders, 5, 216
Skybox Security, 258, 260
social engineering attacks, 94, 99, 101
solutions, 38, 85, 164, 166, 168-68, 178, 181-82, 184, 211, 228, 240, 258
Stamos, 46-48, 78, 249-50
strategies, 4, 25, 27, 29, 38, 166, 168-69, 251, 260
styles, 157, 159, 162-63, 228
surveillance, 34, 94, 138, 199-200, 236-38, 244, 272

T

technology, emerging, 186, 197, 204, 223
terms, 24, 33-34, 110, 112, 137, 180-81, 199, 205, 209, 213, 233-34, 248, 256, 260, 267, 299-300
threat landscape, 5, 28, 30, 33, 62-63, 78-79, 84, 116, 168, 177, 184, 186, 189, 226, 263, 286, 288, 294
tools, 2, 29, 36, 74, 84, 103-04, 108, 112, 135, 153, 163, 178, 182, 208-10, 215, 249, 270, 276, 279
Torbert, Bill, 169-71, 296
traits, 29-31, 39, 55-56, 112, 157, 159, 162, 166, 187, 293
transparency, 47-47, 78, 288
trojans, 80-82, 303

U

Ukraine, 89-90, 220-22, 227, 270

V

Printed in Great Britain
by Amazon